FINDING THE JEWISH SHAKESPEARE

Judaic Traditions in Literature, Music, and Art
Ken Frieden *and* Harold Bloom, *Series Editors*

Jacob Gordin, circa 1904.
Courtesy of the author.

FINDING *the* JEWISH SHAKESPEARE

The Life and Legacy of Jacob Gordin

BETH KAPLAN

Syracuse University Press

Syracuse University Press
Syracuse, New York 13244-5160
Copyright © 2007 by Beth Kaplan

First Edition 2007
07 08 09 10 11 12   6 5 4 3 2 1

All photographs are from the author's personal collection.

The paper used in this publication meets the minimum requirements of
American National Standard for Information Sciences—Permanence of
Paper for Printed Library Materials, ANSI Z39.48-1984.∞™

For a listing of books published and distributed by Syracuse University Press,
visit our Web site at SyracuseUniversityPress.syr.edu.

ISBN-13: 978–0–8156–0884–4
ISBN-10: 0–8156–0884–5

Library of Congress Cataloging-in-Publication Data
Kaplan, Beth, 1950–
Finding the Jewish Shakespeare : the life and legacy of Jacob Gordin / Beth Kaplan.—1st ed.
p. cm.—(Judaic traditions in literature, music, and art)
Includes bibliographical references and index.
ISBN-13: 978–0–8156–0884–4 (cloth : alk. paper)
ISBN-10: 0–8156–0884–5 (cloth : alk. paper)
1. Gordin, Jacob, 1853–1909. 2. Dramatists, Yiddish—Biography. 3. Dramatists, Ukrainian—
Biography. 4. Dramatists, American—Biography. 5. Jewish journalists—Biography. I. Title.
PJ5129.G6Z75 2007
839'.123—dc22   2006038549

Manufactured in the United States of America

Any biography or play based on the life of this remarkable character, who ventured to reform the Jewish religion and ended by reforming the Yiddish theater, turning it into a temple for the drama, would be quite as exciting as some of the productions which he created or adapted. Of more than medium height, with eyes expressive of the *weltschmerz*, set off against a patriarchal beard, all enhanced by a majestic gait—he was easily the most respected figure on the New York East Side during the early part of the century.

—A. Roback, *The Story of Yiddish Literature*

No man of genius has ever been more brutally consigned to oblivion, no writer so idolized during his lifetime so totally neglected after his death as Gordin.

—Lulla Rosenfeld, *The Yiddish Theater and Jacob P. Adler*

Theater is the greatest educational instrument in the world.

—Jacob Gordin, 1904

Beth Kaplan was born in New York City and grew up in Halifax, Nova Scotia, with a few childhood years in London and Paris. She became a professional actress while still in university, and took postgraduate training at the London Academy of Music and Dramatic Art. After a decade in the theater, she went back to earn an MFA in creative writing at the University of British Columbia and since 1996 has taught creative nonfiction writing at Ryerson University in Toronto. Scores of her personal essays have appeared in newspapers and magazines and on radio. "I spent twenty years raising two children and writing this book," she said recently, "and then they all left home together."

CONTENTS

ILLUSTRATIONS

INTRODUCTION

FOR MANY YEARS, I knew my grandmother's famous father only as a majestic bronze bust, glowering in her hall. During his lifetime, Jacob Gordin was an important and beloved playwright, his plays performed wherever Yiddish speakers lived. That I knew. But to me he was obscure and distant, a stern head on the horizon. We did not talk about him.

Every July we left our home in Halifax, Nova Scotia, and flew or sailed to broiling New York City, my father's birthplace, to visit my Kaplan grandparents. Before we even got off the elevator at their Upper West Side apartment, I could smell my grandma's welcome—borscht, kulebiaka, piroshkis. She had been cooking for days, convinced my shiksa mother was starving us to death. The apartment door flew open, and there was stumpy Nettie Gordin Kaplan in a shapeless print dress and old lady black shoes. Behind her loomed the dark glinting bust of her father, who was known in my family, sometimes with a smirk, as the Shakespeare of the Jews.

My scientist dad Jacob Gordin Kaplan never talked about his grandfather, his namesake, except with derision. His younger brother, my brilliant Uncle Edgar the champion bridge player, expressed the same disdain for his famous forebear. Why? This was a question that for years preoccupied only me, that was most relevant, of everyone in the family, to me.

All my life, words, spoken and written, have been my vocation and my joy. I began scribbling stories and letters at the age of six, and a few years later was performing on radio, television, and stage. At eleven I won a national essay-writing competition. The local newspaper came to take my picture, and the interviewer asked what I wanted to be when I grew up. "An actress," I replied serenely, "and a writer."

How did I know, so young? No one else in my family acted or wrote for a living. When I entered a London drama school at twenty-one, the director inquired what I hoped to accomplish in the theater. "To change the world," I replied. At thirty, I took leave of my acting career to get a graduate degree in creative writing. And yet it wasn't until I chose as my master's thesis to research and write the life of my great-grandfather Jacob Gordin, the writer renowned for his work in the theater, work he insisted would change the world, that I began to ponder the obvious genetic link behind both my vocations—the endless braiding of the generations, down from him to me.

I have spent almost twenty-five years unearthing my ancestor's life. When I began at the age of thirty-one, with my infant daughter sleeping beside me, I used those archaic instruments of research, the letter, the electric typewriter, the telephone, the airplane. After the MFA degree was granted, I kept on sleuthing. It is hard to grasp, now, that I didn't even own a computer until 1986, or use the Internet for research until 1997, fifteen years into the work.

Today, my daughter is ready to have children of her own, and my then unborn son is an exceptionally tall young man with a beard. And at fifty-five, I have finally said, "*Dayenu.*" Enough.

From the beginning, I worked alone except for one invaluable collaborator: early in my research I was blessed to meet Sarah Torchinsky, who became my Yiddish translator. For twenty years, Sarah translated everything in Yiddish that came my way. This book would not exist without her.

At the start, I believed with regret that all the stars of the Gordin drama were dead. How grateful I was to meet, often just before they floated out of reach, ancient relatives previously unknown to me. I journeyed three times to Queens to talk to Jacob Gordin's youngest daughter, my great-aunt Helen Gordin Zielstein, who was in her late eighties when I first met her. She died five years later in 1988, the same year as her much younger nephew, my father. I took the bus twice to Lakefield, New Jersey, to interview the Gordins' first grandchild, a cousin my father had never met: Anna Greenspoon Richmond, nearly deaf and blind at ninety-five and yet eager to tell me her tales. I managed to track down other family members lost for decades, so that once sparsely decorated branches of the Gordin family tree are now blooming with names, if not yet, for me, with faces.

I have been privileged, too, to consult through the years with knowledgeable and generous Yiddish scholars. As the Internet became a conduit, I enjoyed corresponding with experts whom I have never met, and perhaps never will.

But I worked in isolation. There was no academy, university, or granting body to steer me. Unlike other Yiddish-related books, mine contains no guide to Yiddish orthography because I did not have the slightest idea about Yiddish orthography when I began, and as a non-Yiddish speaker, I still don't. Though around me are filing cabinets stuffed with research, I am unable to make footnotes because through the busy decades I did not keep precise records. I did my work not as a scholar, but as a curious great-granddaughter.

One of my most valued critics and colleagues, the actor Jacob Adler's granddaughter and biographer Lulla Rosenfeld, complained to me once, "Details are never correct. Jews are unbelievably careless and unspecific with names and dates." She was, unfortunately, right; even encyclopedias sometimes have facts and details wrong. Undoubtedly there are many instances in this book where I am wrong too.

I have done my best to sift and sort, not only to tell the truth, but to tell a good story. Because my great-grandfather's magnificent and tragic life is a very good story.

And it is also my father's story, and his family's, and mine.

NOTE TO THE READER

GORDIN'S FIRST NAME is written several ways: Yakov, Yankev, Ya'cov, Jacob, and the nickname Yasha. I use the Russian version while he lives in Russia, the English for his years in America, and the Hebrew—Yankev—wherever it seems right.

The YIVO is often mentioned. The YIVO Institute for Jewish Research is the invaluable site in lower Manhattan where millions of Yiddish documents, including files on my great-grandfather, are lovingly stored, archived, and protected. Some relevant newspapers I found at YIVO are so ancient and tattered, however, that their mastheads are not visible, so several newspapers in the book are quoted but not named.

And a disclaimer about accountability and accuracy: there are periods of Gordin's life about which very little is known. In order to create a vivid account I have, based on research and reading, extrapolated my version of the truth.

FINDING THE JEWISH SHAKESPEARE

PROLOGUE

The Playwright's Funeral

ON FRIDAY, the lead editorial on the front page of the *Jewish Daily Forward* was banded in black. "Our friend is gone!" it exclaimed. "Keep this day holy! Meet at his grave! Gather in your halls! Bring flowers! Gordin is gone!"

The famous playwright died in the early hours of Friday, June 11. By June 13, on Sunday, the Jewish East Side of New York was submerged in mourning, and worldwide grieving had just begun.

It was 1909; the twentieth century had settled in, and New York City was in a hurry. The city's soaring parade of skyscrapers—some more than twenty stories high—astonished newcomers. In scores of storefront picture palaces, moving picture machines whirred in the darkness. Telephones, automobiles, a gleaming new subway one hundred feet below the ground—what miracle of progress next would push its way forward? A few months hence, Wilbur Wright would fly an airplane around the Statue of Liberty, and one million incandescent electric lights would burn along New York's bridges and buildings, to celebrate the anniversary of Henry Hudson's arrival three hundred years before.

But here in New York's ghetto of immigrants, a people without a country, speaking an ancient language with a brand-new dictionary, fought still for food and a decent place to sleep. One man had stood before them speaking in their own tongue, a broad-shouldered writer who had brought their old lives onto the stage, and made clear his stern views on the choices confronting them now. Jacob Gordin had tried to touch them all, and that Friday, they learned that he was dead.

Telegrams poured into the writer's Brooklyn home from mourners common and illustrious, from the Jewish Bill Posters and Ushers Union to renowned labor leader Joseph Barondess, cabling without punctuation from Montreal that he was "deeply moved at the death of our greatest playwright we wish to express our most heartfelt sorrow the terrible news has penetrated our tenderest spot and it is only with the sorrow stricken grief we realize the loss of a great dramatist a great Jew and a great enlightener of his people." Letters piled up, including one from cousin Zena Gordin in Philadelphia, who wrote, "The late Yasha was so talented—so polite—so educated." A scrawled note arrived from the Pleasant View Farm House in the Catskills: "Please send me Jacob Gordon Picture; as I would like to have it in my house all the jews in Monticello are Morning the Great lost Mr. Jacob Gordon."

The stores of the Lower East Side covered their windows in black draperies; black flags fluttered from tenement windows. On Saturday a Yiddish newspaper expressed the hope that the playwright's funeral would be even greater than the funeral of Ulysses S. Grant, Civil War general and U.S. president, because Gordin's greatness was achieved "not on the field of battle, war, ruin and blood, but on the field of culture, labor, civilization and progress."

On Sunday, crowds began to line the procession route in the early morning. A five-year-old boy, trying to leave his family's tenement apartment, found the way impassable and realized, "Oh yes, they're burying Yankev Gordin today." Eighty years after the day, my great-uncle Bill Kaplan remembered trying to push his way through. The *Encyclopedia Judaica* estimates that a quarter of a million people were packed into the city streets that morning to watch the playwright's coffin go by.

The *New York Evening Call* surveyed the scene: "Every available space on the sidewalks, the steps, fire escapes, roofs and windows were filled with mourners who gave vent to their grief in loud sobs and in an unrestrained flow of tears. East Broadway, Madison, Ridge, Grand, and Clinton streets were jammed with men and women who came to pay their last tribute to the man who for eighteen years was their teacher, essayist, lecturer and dramatist."

Vendors roamed through the crowds, selling black mourning bands and buttons stamped with Gordin's face in a choice of three poses: healthy and fierce; ill in bed with a compress on his forehead; dead. The popular poet Morris Rosenfeld, assigned by the newspaper the *Jewish Daily Forward* to write about the event, described the procession following the coffin as "a mighty people-ocean" tens of miles long—"like a great army accompanying a fallen king. . . . Thick lines of police on foot and on horse kept the crowds orderly. But who needed their presence? Those who know how to appreciate art and literature, people with modern ideas and thoughts know how to behave and to show respect and to honor one of their own."

There were no prayers, no Jewish burial rites. Early that morning, after a brief secular ceremony, the coffin was carried from Gordin's narrow Brooklyn row house. Drawn by a black horse, followed by Gordin's family and three coaches full of flowers, the hearse rolled from Brooklyn across the Williamsburg Bridge to the Thalia Theater on the Bowery below Canal Street, on the Lower East Side. A throng had gathered at the Thalia doors hours before. Although most could not enter, they continued to stand outside for hours, until the end of the tribute.

Mrs. Gordin and the Gordin children—all eleven, ranging in age from twelve to thirty-six—were ushered into the boxes. The three-thousand-seat theater was packed to its ornate ceiling. The walls were draped in black, and above the stage hung a giant portrait of the playwright. Flowers and wreaths were piled high, although Orthodox funeral custom demands austerity; flowers are for gentiles. The Thalia stage, wrote Rosenfeld, was like the Garden of Eden, the casket resembling a black leaf in an ocean of red and white roses.

At exactly 10 A.M., eight of the leading figures of American Jewish cultural and intellectual life carried in the coffin, which was left open, also contrary to Jewish funeral law. The Halevy Choral Society sang the prologue from Gordin's play *God, Man, and Devil* and the "Pilgrim's Chorus" from Wagner's *Tannhauser.* The speeches began, and the sobbing. There were some thirty speakers—a reform Rabbi, writers, theater stars, political agitators, doctors, poets. Many collapsed without finishing. Morris Winchevsky, beloved labor poet and the playwright's best friend, told the crowd that Gordin was passing from life into history. Louis Miller, editor of the *Truth* newspaper, began, "We come to bury him." The rest was drowned in tears.

Most moving was the great actor Jacob Adler. Everyone knew about the volatile relations between playwright and thespian, the recent lawsuit Gordin had won against Adler, forcing the payment of unpaid royalties. Grasping the side of Gordin's open coffin, Adler bent over with pain. "Happy is he," he groaned, turning to face the audience, "whose heart is not aching with bitter feelings of remorse!" He and Gordin had had misunderstandings, he said, because both were poor businessmen, but they had parted as friends. Gordin had sent for Adler, forgiven him, suggested he go to Russia, "the center of Jewish life," and create dramatic art there. The actor swore to uphold the honor of the drama created by Gordin, and then he began to wail like a child. The others on stage moved to stand near him. Actors Boris Thomashefsky and David Kessler spoke for all who had flourished in the roles Gordin had written for them. "The Yiddish stage was a wilderness before he came," cried Kessler, "and we were each gasping for a part."

The *New York Call* noted that "the half million men and women who came to do honor to the dead dramatist were mostly young people, showing that it was to the youth of the ghetto that Gordin appealed the strongest. . . . Some in the audience were too weak to stand the strain and became hysterical. Hundreds cried aloud, expressing in words the pain they bore in their hearts."

Gordin's youngest child, Helen, who was twelve, relived the day at the age of eighty-eight.

> The coffin was brought into the Thalia Theater onto the stage and it had a blanket of beautiful roses that some organization sent, you know—the theater was filled with flowers—and all the doctors were supposed to speak about Papa because they knew him from Russia. First the Jewish actors got up and spoke, and then the friends—and as each one got up and called him Yasha and talked about their youth and about how he worked, what a marvellous person he was, never thought of himself, everything was humanity, each and every one of them broke down with such sobs, such crying. I had never heard a man cry before. And that was the first time that my brother Leon and I cried, because we didn't know what death meant. We saw him lying there in the casket covered with flowers with a full dress suit on, but we thought he was sleeping—that's how innocent we were, naïve, we had no idea he wouldn't wake up and be our papa again.

So with these men that were always in our home and that we loved falling and covering the coffin sobbing and everybody sobbing in the theater, it was the most—it was dramatic and yet frightening and Mama . . . oh, it was a terrible experience. Everyone that loved him was there, and how they loved him.

After two and a half hours of speeches the ceremony ended; Barondess dismissed the mourners from their stiff, iron-backed chairs row by row. The procession back to the Williamsburg Bridge, toward the cemetery, was bigger than before. Marching behind the coffin was a line of 20,000 people, some from Baltimore, Boston, Philadelphia, and smaller towns, representing five hundred organizations including the Children's Jacket Maker's Union, the Philadelphia Workmen's Circle, the Capmaker's Union, the Hebrew Benevolent Aid Association, the Cloakmaker's Union, the Hebrew Kindergarten Association, the Baker's Union, the Literary Dramatic Club, the Vestmaker's Union, the Socialist Territorialists, the Eighth Assembly District Socialist Party, the Poale Zion Choral Society, the Progressive Dramatic Club.

After making a brief stop at the Educational League, the school for immigrants founded by Gordin, and another at the headquarters of the Jacob Gordin Literary Circle on Grand Street, the line broke up at the entrance to the bridge, but thousands went to the Washington Cemetery on the newly opened Brooklyn line of the subway. The Brooklyn Rapid Transit had special cars ready for the "emergency," as it was called by transit personnel.

Jewish New York had never seen a funeral quite like this, for size, for intensity. The extravagance of emotional display was uncommon even for Jews, an entire community consumed with grief, the agony of loss made worse by guilt. "People felt that a friend had died, the herald of free thought, the fighter for a better society," wrote Rosenfeld in summary. "When the speeches ended at the theater, people didn't want to leave. They wanted to shout the familiar, 'Bravo, Gordin! Bravo!' The curtain remained open, but the author failed to appear."

But Rosenfeld didn't write the truth. The audience at the Thalia had not shouted "Bravo, Gordin!" for years. For years they had turned their backs on his work, seeking simpler, merrier plays, fleeing the Jewish East Side for uptown or Brooklyn or the Bronx. The Gordin they mourned was a man they had been determined, not so long ago, to leave behind. And those actors sobbing upon the stage, Gordin's theater colleagues, had for the most part abandoned him at his worst hour.

The poet did not mention the notable absence of a key member of the local intellectual community, his boss Abraham Cahan, the editor of the *Forward*. Cahan was not there because he and Gordin, the two most powerful men among the immigrant Jews of the East Side, had hated each other. Cahan's relentless newspaper campaign against his rival, pursued only the year before, had been so vicious that many stated openly now: it was not cancer that killed Jacob Gordin. It was Abraham Cahan.

Rosenfeld did not say that Gordin's too-early death was a tragedy, but it was. Gordin died a humiliated man, bitter and broken-hearted at the age of fifty-six, convinced that his life's work—to propel Jews, and then every other citizen of the world, into social and political enlightenment with his dramatic words—had been in vain. "The day I die," he had written not long before, "is the day [the Yiddish theater] will forget me." For years after his death, despite the grandeur of his funeral, it seemed that he was right. That very Sunday, a conservative Yiddish paper published an editorial condemning Gordin's "corrupting . . . destructive . . . fanaticism." His "fallacious radicalism," said the paper, must be stopped.

The morning after the funeral, on Monday, June 14, the *Forward* printed an editorial calling for the Jewish masses to honor the playwright, and to help care for his family, by building him a monument. But the monument was never mentioned again. Though his was a hero's funeral, and his plays continued to be performed around the world, Gordin's name and reputation had been tarnished by the vendettas against him. He was disparaged even by his descendants. Most of his children, grandchildren, and great-grandchildren—my family—continued through the decades to mock or dismiss his legend. My quest, when I set out to explore his life story, was to find out why.

•   •   •

Jacob Gordin's story begins in Russia, and in some ways ends there too. Writing just after his funeral, his friend Morris Winchevsky fantasized that the playwright's spirit had gone home and was happily roaming the snowy motherland, skimming past oaks and birches in a troika. Winchevsky knew why my great-grandfather was the only Russian émigré to continue, long after arriving in America, to wear a long beard, walk with a cane, drink tea through a sugar cube clenched in his teeth, and brandish the patronymic, always, at the center of his name. Even after eighteen years in America, Gordin wanted to be known in the Russian manner as the son of his father, and of his country.

Though he was an American citizen when he died, a Jew made famous by his Yiddish plays, he was a Jew second and an American last. Always, in his ardent soul, Yakov Mikhailovich Gordin was a Russian.

RUSSIA

It is difficult to convey to the modern Westerner any idea of the sort of life which most of the Jewish families of Motol led, of their peculiar occupations, their fantastic poverty, their shifts and privations. On the spiritual side they were almost as isolated as on the physical.

—Chaim Weizmann, *Trial and Error*

IN THE MIDDLE of the nineteenth century, in the middle of the year, in the center of Ukraine, a baby was born, a sturdy boy with powerful lungs and quantities of black hair. In fact, he was so hairy that to his concerned father, at first, he looked like a monkey. When the fine down disappeared, he turned into a handsome pink infant to be proud of, always hungry, shouting for the breast.

Yakov, they called him, the only son between two girls, the prized boychild who got what he wanted. Yakov Mikhailovich Gordin, born on an auspicious day: May Day, a date turned three decades later into the international festival of the workingman, a symbol that would resonate for the rest of his life.

Many facts about the first thirty-eight years of Gordin's life, the years he spent in Russia, are in dispute and others are vague, but two are without question: May 1, 1853, his date of birth, and his birthplace, Mirgorod, an ancient and prosperous shtetl—small town—on the expansive black steppes of Ukraine. It is there still, an important spa known for cream, fruit, and mineral water. The Khorol River, cherished for the curative power of its waters, flows through its center, and a unique black pig is bred there, called the Mirgorod. The father of nineteenth-century Russian literature,

8

Gogol, was born nearby in 1808 and named one of his books after the town. The foreword tells us flatly that Mirgorod "has a rope-yard, a brick-yard, four water-mills and forty-five windmills."

"Although rolls are made of rye in Mirgorod, they are quite tasty," it also notes, although now we do not know why.

Gogol's biography, describing one of his voyages home, says, "The last stop, in the middle of the vast steppe, was the little town of Mirgorod: whitewashed cottages, unsurfaced dirt roads, haystacks, wooden fences, and puddles of water."

Encircling the little town were the Ukrainian farmers who worked the rich land that Jews were not allowed to own. The Jewish families of Mirgorod all lived near the river, in battered wooden houses that lined the village's muddy, or snow-covered, or dusty, heat-baked streets. The Gordins were one of the only fairly well-off families here, in their house with its solid enough roof and thick enough doors. They had chickens, a cow, a vegetable garden, and a local Ukrainian girl as a servant, which meant the Gordins ate regularly and lived, despite the onslaught of mud, snow, and dust, in relative cleanliness—great wealth, among their shtetl neighbors. Most Jews lived in inescapable squalor and on the edge of starvation.

My great-grandfather loved the town and the steppe, loved his mother country passionately, always. Half a century after his birth, on the other side of the world, his colleague Jacob Adler watched with astonishment as the playwright's eyes filled with tears at the mention of Mirgorod. Yet the Russia Gordin loved so desperately was archaic, black-hearted, doomed. France and the United States had long since thrown off the stranglehold of the monarchy, but Russia, one hundred and fifty years ago, was ruled like a medieval duchy. The despotic and incompetent Romanov tsars, one after another, still held absolute, unconditional power over their vast domain, with special vicious attention lavished upon their Jewish noncitizens.

By 1835, the tsars had cordoned off a chunk of western Russia annexed from Poland, an area in which lived almost all Russia's Jews, who were then prohibited from moving outside its boundaries. This was the Pale of Settlement, home to half the world's Jews, the largest Jewish community in the world. Mirgorod, midway between Kiev and Kharkov, was near the eastern border of the Pale, where Russia without Jews—beyond the Pale—began.

Ruling at the time of my great-grandfather's birth in 1853 was Tsar Nicholas I, nicknamed "The Flogger," one of the most anti-Semitic of a Jew-hating dynasty. Under his rule, Jews were subjected to an array of ever-changing laws, including one of stupefying severity: Jewish boys, some as young as twelve, were drafted into the Russian army for a period of twenty-five years, with the hope that such a devastating separation from family and religion would tear them from their Judaic roots. More often, it killed them.

Luckily, only two years after the birth of Yakov Mikhailovich, Nicholas died and was succeeded by his son Alexander II, who for a while entertained such liberal notions, not only for his Russian citizens but for Jews, that it was said during his reign "the sun rose on Jewish life." To the joy of the great Tolstoy, he freed the serfs, all sixty million of them, although most, left without land, were actually worse off than before; and to the joy of my great-great-grandparents he reduced the draft requirements for Jews to seven years, and eventually to five, like all other boys.

In the shtetl of Mirgorod, aside from the ebb and flow of repressive tsarist *ukasi* (edicts) life continued according to its own internal rhythms. Like isolated arks floating in a sea of prejudice and danger, Russia's self-reliant Jewish communities clung to time-honored ritual and law, as if the stability of their ancient faith would protect them from spiritual if not physical harm. Few questions were asked about the 613 *mitsvot* (commandments, or deeds and restrictions commanded by God) governing the day-to-day procedures of Jews. From birth through marriage and death, every moment of life was ordained and regulated by *mitsvot,* some strictly upheld and some not, but all revered. It was the job of every Jewish male to study the Talmud, be responsible for self and others, teach, establish a family, obey Jewish law, and somehow, in the face of incessant yet unpredictable hostility, survive.

But as the entire community squeezed into the rough wooden synagogue for the bris, the ritual circumcision of the black-haired baby, a few well-read members of the congregation, including the baby's father, were aware that forces of transformation were at work around them. A movement called "the Haskala," the Enlightenment or emancipation, was pushing its way east from Germany. The Haskala philosophers, known as *Maskilim* or enlighteners, encouraged secular education and acculturation to the society outside the ghetto walls. Those Russian Jewish youths and intellectuals anxious to understand and enter the wider world had begun gathering eagerly, in secret, to study works of philosophy, politics, and science, to absorb secular Western concepts considered threatening and revolutionary by the rabbinic establishment. A hundred years after the European Enlightenment in France and Germany, the Russian-Jewish Enlightenment blew change, fresh and sharp, into the tradition-bound shtetl.

Simply subscribing to a newspaper marked a shtetl Jew as a freethinking modern man, an enlightened *Maskil*. To the Orthodox, *Maskilim* were heretics who challenged rabbinical rule. Yakov's father, Mikhail Yekiel Levi, or Ha-Levi, was a *Maskil*.

Yet he was also religious, a follower of Hasidism, an eighteenth-century movement that encouraged direct communion with God, not just through rigorous study but through ecstatic prayer, movement, and music. Although the mystical Hasidim and the rational *Maskilim* approached life in opposing ways and hated each other, Mikhail Gordin had managed a compromise between his faith and his intellect. He was far from the only Russian Jew to be both devout and an enlightened iconoclast, heart rooted in Jewish ritual and mind exploring secular possibilities. And he made sure that his son was taught the new ways.

His boy Yasha did not attend the local Jewish school, the *kheyder*, with the other village youths. *Kheyder* boys spent a staggering ten hours a day, from the age of three or four, learning religious passages and Talmudic teachings under the eye, and the much used cat-o'-nine-tails, of an often harsh and hungry teacher. But Yasha was at home, tutored in the open spirit of the Haskala by his father, who brought Hebrew, Russian, and German books and magazines into the house for his son. The boy dove into the masterworks of Russian literature, meaty texts by Turgenev, Tolstoy, Dostoyevsky, and his countryman Gogol. He read the first Hebrew novel, published the year of his birth, and loved, in particular, the Bible. Later in life Gordin described himself as self-educated, saying that most of his education had come from a childhood reading and rereading his favorite books. At other times he boasted of his "rarely good, thoroughly Russian education."

By educating his son at home, Mikhail Gordin avoided the ever-shifting restrictions and quotas imposed on Jewish students. Some ambitious youths in the Pale, in order to gain an education, were forced to convert to Christianity.

My great-aunt Helen said about her father's father:

> He was a Hebrew scholar and a teacher of Hebrew, a lawyer the people always came to for help, a counselor, a marriage broker—a man of all trades, he was just everything. And gorgeous looking. And self-educated, mind you, since there were no schools for Jews to learn those things. If that man had had an education and not had to worry about the persecution of the Jews, he would have been even more famous. He was generous and loving, a genius. Everyone worshipped him, the *goyim* as well as the Jews.

Can this paean be true? Mikhail did have several professions; though Helen didn't mention it, he was also a merchant. Russian Jews, barred from most schooling and jobs, had to be jacks-of-all-trades, with no choice but to make a living in any way open to them. He was certainly a good provider. When Helen told me "there were no riches in their home except books, in every language," she was perhaps thinking of her own childhood home, not her father's. The two Gordin men enjoyed the rare luxuries of relative security, adequate nourishment, and intellectual freedom.

I wonder, did Mikhail's son enjoy his company, love him? Love was not an issue then; fathers were distant and authoritarian, not warm, not close. Fathers and sons didn't chat or play together; they worked, worshipped, and studied together. A father like Mikhail was to be feared and obeyed and perhaps, secretly, resented. It is impossible not to notice that over and over, in the plays his son began to write thirty-five years hence, the figure of the father is an irritable bully, at best blind and foolish, at worst brutal. The heroines in Gordin's stage world always love and give; his villains are often hidebound merchants crushing their offspring's dreams and freedoms. Perhaps Gordin was painting not his own father, but the typical authoritarian father of the era, or the all-powerful patriarchal figures of Jewish life in Russia. Or perhaps he was indeed casting his own father as a hard man and a tyrant.

As for his mother, we don't even know her name, although undoubtedly one of her son's five daughters—Sofia, Yelizaveta, Vera, Nadezhda, or Lyuba—was named for her. Most likely she was Yelizaveta; the name has echoed in the uncommon number of Elizabeths in the family. She was a quiet, very devout housewife whom her son adored unashamedly his whole life long and immortalized in the many glorious mother roles in his plays. A feminist long before his time, like all socialists both male and female, he repeatedly portrays his revulsion at the mistreatment of women by heartless fathers and husbands and his admiration for the rooted strength of mothers. "When you have no mother," says one of his characters, "you have no home."

"One may soon forget a wife," says another, "but a mother is never forgotten—never." From his *Wild Man:* "No power in the world is strong enough to tear from their hearts the love which children bear their mother. Not only little children, but grown-ups are unfortunate when they're motherless. There is in this world only one pure true sacred love, and that's the love of a mother for her children."

Mother Gordin chatted with her only son in Yiddish until at her husband's command she stopped. Yiddish, also known as *mama-loshen,* mother's language or mother tongue, was a language already nine hundred years old. In its richly flavored mix mostly of Middle High German, Old French, and Hebrew, it carried the legacy of centuries of Jewish wanderings through Europe. The use of Yiddish was waning in Western Europe as Jewish communities opened to new ideas and replaced Yiddish with the local language. In cosmopolitan England, France, and Germany, newly emancipated Jews judged Yiddish to be an embarrassing kitchen language, a humble jargon suitable only for young children, the uneducated, and women.

Ordinary Russian Jews, however, were so cut off from the surrounding culture that few had the opportunity or desire to converse in anything but their own familiar tongue. Rather than being demeaned by the Haskala, as it had been elsewhere, spoken Yiddish became richer and stronger in Russia and remained the tool of communication for both city and shtetl Jews. It was a rare Jewish youth who spoke not Yiddish but Russian at home. Yakov Gordin was a rare youth. To an American interviewer forty years later, he would complain about his poor Yiddish and assert, "My native language is Russian."

Exclusively in Russian now, his mother taught him to approach life with confidence, to believe utterly in himself. She was a meticulous woman, always cleaning, her fastidiousness so pronounced that her son imitated it; he was known, in later life, as a conspicuously tidy man. She cooked all day, baking, chopping, kneading. Even with the help, there was always so much to be done, and Mikhail was away often, tending to business.

Sometimes he would take the boy with him, to Elizavetgrad, a stately city to the southwest where he had associates and friends, and occasionally to St. Petersburg or to Moscow, where ordinary Jews, allowed by Alexander II to travel a bit more freely, were beginning to be tolerated. When Yasha was older, his father took him to the theater in those cities. The son had serious tastes and liked the political satires of Ostrovsky, the weighty works of the Germans Goethe, Schiller, and Lessing. Young as he was, he felt strongly about the theater, calling out praise when he was pleased and, when he wasn't, hissing or shouting disapproval. Once, after a noisy protest in a theater, he was carried off to the police station and fined. The opinionated boy was able to conduct these social and political encounters in his fluent Russian and was learning German, too, the language of poets and philosophers. For educated Jews, the greatest country in the world, intellectually, artistically, politically, was Germany.

What of his two sisters, Eva and Masha? From the sisters' clumsy, ungrammatical letters to their exiled brother in New York, it is clear that, like most girls of the time, they had not been well schooled. I assume that Eva, also called Hava, was older, because her tone is insistently nagging, though respectful. Masha, whose name is the Russian short form for Maria, that most Christian of female names, was likely much younger; her infrequent correspondence radiates shy formality and reticence. She remained so unconnected to her brother that later, more than a decade went by between letters. When a child of hers died, it was years before her brother in New York heard about her loss.

Young Yakov was isolated, with only two sisters and without friends from the *kheyder*; he befriended the servant girls and their brothers and learned to speak Ukrainian, which was unusual. But he played very little. For him, as for all Jewish children, play was a frivolous waste of time with so much to be learned, so much work to be done. Good Jewish boys dreamed not of fame or wealth, and certainly not of girls, but of becoming the most scholarly and learned, the most philanthropic.

One of Gordin's New York essays is an ode to the joys of a Russian boyhood, comparing the cynical, wisecracking American Maxie with innocent Yossel who lived in a shtetl world of "fantasy and wonder," running in the open fields, watching the clouds, listening to "the trees whispering their secrets." But Gordin was idealizing, as he always did about his early days. His childhood was not spent frolicking in the open fields and gazing at the sky. Even as a boy, Yakov was hardworking, stern, and resolute, as he remained for the rest of his life.

• • •

By the time of his bar mitzvah in 1866, the precocious youth was spouting socialist slogans. All around him, society was in ferment. Revolutionary groups, social movements, idealistic cultlike societies were springing up throughout the western world, as secularity challenged the dominance of religious thought and discontented citizens sought alternatives to the stagnant status quo. Young Jews had begun to align themselves with the political aspirations of their Russian brethren; young Gordin, too, identified himself less as a Jew than as a Russian, or even, shockingly, as a Ukrainian. At the age of seventeen, in 1870, he joined his Ukrainian friends in their fight for independence from Russia, later translating the first chapter of Karl Marx's exhilarating new *Das Kapital* from German into Ukrainian for a magazine of the Ukrainian underground revolutionary circle.

Growing more confident and outspoken, he began to write for the Russian-Jewish magazines and the liberal Russian and Hebrew newspapers that he had read most of his life. He wrote sarcastic stories, fables, and satirical articles mocking superstition and ignorance, all signed, of course, with a pseudonym because government censors were virulent. He called himself "Ivan der Beissende," Ivan the Biting, or "Ivan Kolyuchii," the Prickly—Ivan, again, a most Russian and gentile name.

Certain books were required reading for young Jewish-Russian radicals like Gordin and his later colleagues Winchevsky and Cahan, who absorbed into their very pores the Haskala literature urging Jews to turn to humanism, to break free from the narrowness of Jewish life and join the world. They took in the work of the Russian populist and nihilist writers Belinsky, Dobroliubov, Pisarev, and especially Chernyshevsky, whose *What Is to Be Done?* was a bible to young would-be revolutionaries. Russian radicals preached the bliss of socialism in a natural communal setting.

They believed that art should lead to social action, that the artist's job was to transform the future, that women should be liberated from the chains of monogamy and marriage. Thirty years later these directives would inform every one of my great-grandfather's plays.

Many restless intellectual Jews, convinced that modern Western thought was the enlightened way of the future, needed to conclude that the Jewish life of their parents was the opposite: irrational, backward, a dead end. Unable to explore new ways without annihilating the old, they broke with the shtetl and everything it represented. In choosing as their life's work the struggle to prepare the peasants for the revolution, in seeking to make the whole world, not just the Jewish world, a good and just place, they were more traditional than they knew: Jewish literature, Jewish life itself had always focused on moral betterment and the general good. And so, too, as he absorbed the credos flaring into life around him, did Jacob Gordin.

The compulsory draft was not a problem for him: he was exempt as an only son, or else his father simply paid for a substitute to go in his stead. Yakov was lucky. A young Jew with his fiercely contrary nature might not have survived even five years in the tsar's anti-Semitic army.

Jewish males were required to consecrate their lives to Torah, marriage, and good deeds. The third of these would be a lifetime preoccupation for this youth; the first was of no interest at all. By his nineteenth birthday, in May 1872, the time had come for him to marry. He was a prime candidate for a girl whose parents did not insist on religious and political orthodoxy. Although hot-headed and outspoken, he was also liberally endowed with the blessings of *yikhes*, which means he had high status, a pedigree formed from good breeding, virtue, intelligence, and especially learning. (Writer Daphne Merkin defines *yikhes* as "the Jewish version of lineage, like having a blood relative on the Mayflower.")

Until this time of social upheaval, Jewish marriages had always been arranged between parents and marriage brokers. Gordin's generation, making its own rules, was the first to propose marrying for love. Love? Mikhail Gordin, the sometime marriage broker, had no interest in sentiment; marriages were practical business and family arrangements, too important to be left to the risks of romance. Although the young people had at least met and consented, Gordin's parents still held sway in a matter as vital as this. Yakov was betrothed to Anna Lazarevna Itskewitz, whose father Lazar, a business associate of Mikhail's from Elizavetgrad, was a wealthy businessman primarily in the grain business. Anna, who bore the affectionate diminutive Aneuta, was one of Lazar's many daughters.

In the fall of 1872, Yakov and Anna were married with pomp in the Great Synagogue of Elizavetgrad, an ornate striped edifice with imposing windows that, completed in 1853, was exactly as old as the bridegroom. The bride, born in 1859 and six years younger than her intended, had just turned thirteen. No one gave her age a second thought; marriage of very young girls, and boys too, was the norm. Life expectancy at birth, after all, was under fifty. No one worried about the success of a union between a fiery, sophisticated nineteen-year-old man already sporting a beard, and a shy, barely teenaged girl who, though educated enough to speak Russian as well as Yiddish, had spent most of her childhood looking after younger siblings and doing housework with her mother. Anna was short, solid, and round-faced with melancholy dark eyes and a heavy jaw and brows; later, after many children, she became rotund and doughy, like all the other mothers. By temperament sweet-natured, loyal, and selfless, she adored her virile young husband, as she would adore him her whole life long; and he loved her, although not, it is sure, to the same degree.

Her love was tested just after the wedding. Aneuta's husband delighted in her black hair that fell in curls to her waist, and which as a married woman she was obligated to cut off. Standard Orthodox law decreed, and still decrees, that a married woman must cover her head when out in public or at home when guests are present because her hair is a sexual enticement reserved for her husband. Most Orthodox women cut off their hair and wore the *shaytl*, the marriage wig. Helen told me that her Papa said, "I want that beautiful head of hair. Don't cut it." Mama cried, "But I have to! My parents will die if I don't!" "No," said Papa. "Your parents won't die."

She felt like a criminal, her mother wept, but she rebelled. She kept her hair. Wearing the *shaytl*, or a head covering of some sort, was an inviolable law for a married orthodox woman in the Pale. Anna's was not a small rebellion.

The couple settled first, as tradition warranted, in the home of the bride's parents in Elizavetgrad, halfway between Mirgorod and Odessa in

Ukraine. Later renamed Kirovograd, the town was a sophisticated center of commerce and industry, a metropolis for a young man from the shtetl. In his memoirs, Jewish revolutionary Lev Davidovich Bronstein told of his first visit there when he was a young farm boy. "Not a single capital in the world, neither Paris nor New York," he wrote, "made such an impression on me as Yelizavetgrad with its sidewalks, green roofs, balconies, shops, policemen and red balloons. For several hours, with my eyes wide open, I gaped at the face of civilization." Bronstein was later better known by the name Leon Trotsky.

Gordin received a generous sum of money as a dowry with his bride, a sign of his appeal, his *yikhes* as a son-in-law. He invested the money in a series of hopeless business ventures that all went bankrupt, and lost everything. "Papa wasn't a businessman; he was never good with money," Helen told me, with pride. Though continuing to write stories, he now embarked on an odd series of jobs. Leaving his young bride with her parents, he followed his Tolstoyan bent and labored for a time as a farm worker and then as a stevedore in Odessa, fashionable employment for a young revolutionary-in-training. Several histories report that he became for a time an actor in a traveling Russian troupe, but his youngest daughter doubted this, and so do I; could someone so domineering and proud endure the mortifications of acting and, even worse, touring? What's sure is that he took time to be a young man, free and alone.

But not much time. Jewish couples are enjoined to "be fruitful and multiply," and in this, if in few other Talmudic laws, the Gordins complied. Though he may have been exploring the world far from his family responsibilities, Yakov was making conjugal visits: Sofia Yakovlevna Gordin was born July 20, 1873, her father just twenty and her mother fourteen. The baby, known as Sonia, had health problems and was found to be epileptic. The young couple's second child was conceived when the first was not yet seven months old; another daughter, Yelizaveta, nicknamed Liza, was born on November 8, 1874. Aneuta was now the fifteen-year-old mother of two infant girls, one of whom was in precarious health. It was time for her roving husband to settle down.

He chose a profession that came as naturally to him as arguing, and that was now open to him as a married man. In 1873 he became a teacher at Elizavetgrad's "Russified" Talmud-Torah, a Jewish school for practical boys anxious to fit into the country around them, where some secular subjects were taught in Russian, not Hebrew. The young autodidact was an impatient teacher. He didn't beat children, as teachers often did, but his expectations were rigorous and his judgment severe, with little understanding or memory of what it was to be a child. Yet a few of his students became followers in his next venture and remained his disciples always. A Russian letter at YIVO, sent to America, is from a former student who writes with fond reminiscence, "In spite of my young age, you left an indelible impression on my memory. I have not seen you since I visited you in Elizavetgrad, my dear teacher."

My great-grandfather, born to teach and to preach, never stopped doing both. Even as the most successful Yiddish playwright in the world, he still gave lessons and lectures directly from the stage, in the school he had founded, and through his writing. But his main concern in 1873 was less in the classroom than in the disaffected young people who had begun to gather around him in the evening, a group conscious of innovative currents in the world and eager to find a new way to live.

Gordin was interested in the German Stundists, who considered the Bible their only source of religion and extolled the joys of communal farming. A greater inspiration was Count Leo Tolstoy, who convinced followers worldwide that salvation lay in living among the peasants, the real people, as much as possible by the labor of one's own hands. Gordin so admired Leo Nicholayevitch that he later named one of his sons Leo, unaware that Tolstoy's theories, like those of many visionaries, applied not so well to the great man's own life. While the aristocrat cobbled his own shoes and agonized about living simply, his long-suffering wife Sonya ran their vast estate and literary enterprise and raised an army of children.

In 1880, inspired by Tolstoy and the Stundists, Gordin took over and made his own a loose-knit group formerly led by the Ukrainian Dr. Mikhailovich. Many Russian-Jewish socialists had come to believe that one of the main reasons for the virulence of Russian anti-Semitism had to do with the despised middleman positions held by Jews, as dealers and traders, merchants, peddlers, moneylenders. If Jews would only work at simple menial labor, they felt, toiling on the land like their peasant neighbors, they would be embraced by the good-hearted Russian people. Jewish Stundists ignored the fact that mercenary Jews, like Gordin's father, dealt in money or liquor or other peoples' crops and timber because they were forbidden to do much else. They were also forbidden to own land.

Gordin named his group the Dukhovno-Bibleyskoye Bratstvo (Spiritual Biblical Brotherhood) and developed the principles by which they would all live: they would not keep Jewish holidays, would reject the Talmud and Jewish rituals of circumcision and marriage, and would follow the ethical teachings of the Bible. Refusing to participate in tawdry commerce, they would support themselves with the physical labor of farming—as soon as they could find some land to farm. The "Biblical" name was chosen to convince the authorities that the group was a dissident religious sect, not political as it really was; at least, that is what Gordin later claimed about the quasi-Christian name. He defined the Brotherhood as "a socialist collective, whose aim was to teach members the communal ideals of friendship and brotherhood, to preach love and respect for each other, and to fight and work for these ideals."

As his commune took shape, the idealistic young leader was still teaching and writing, his stories and essays published as far away as St. Petersburg. He was made the editor of a local Russian newspaper *Yuzhnii Krai (Southern Frontier)*. And Aneuta at last gave birth to a son: Semyon, or Sema, was born December 10, 1877. What triumph: their two daughters had been welcomed, but at last, a boy!

I wonder if it dawned gradually, or all at once, that the infant had a damaged mind. Cleverness is the most important attribute of a Jewish male; this boy child was mentally impaired. Did Gordin feel pity, or guilt? Outwardly, then and always, he showed mostly irritation with the mental handicap afflicting his firstborn son. And yet several of his plays feature wise "half-witted" characters who, like seers, always intuit and speak the truth.

Despite this misfortune and Sonia's epilepsy, the Gordins were nonetheless lucky and rare in the relative health of their family. Tolstoy's mother-in-law, a wealthy woman married to a doctor, lost five of her thirteen offspring in childhood. Sturdy Anna suffered not a single mortality in twenty-four years of childbearing.

Nearly three years later, the couple celebrated the birth of a healthy son: Alexander, known as Sasha, was born on September 1, 1880. Named like the tsar, he was coddled as if he were royalty. His privileged position as the anointed firstborn son, his father's favorite, would trouble him and his siblings until the end of their days.

• • •

In the western reaches of Eastern Europe, a surprising but healthy theatrical birth was taking place. A former rabbinical student called Abraham Goldfaden, living in Jassy, Rumania, in 1876, noticed the enthusiastic response to folksingers in the local cafés and began to write and produce scripts for the café stages. Goldfaden drew in performers—young men only at first—singers, musicians, even cantors like the talented youth Sigmund Mogulescu. Before long young women did the unthinkable and ran away from home to work on the stage. In only a couple of years, Goldfaden's troupe, through feuds and necessity, split into two and then three different groups traveling throughout the Pale, performing in Yiddish.

Until then, Jews were almost unique among the peoples of the world in having no indigenous theater. Costumed performance had been discouraged by Talmudic law for three thousand years. Not only was theater considered pagan and vulgar, but neither men nor women could perform female roles; respectable women were forbidden to act, and Jewish men, unlike the Shakespearean boys and men who played female roles, obeyed Deuteronomy 22:5: "A man shall not put on a woman's garments." Jews enjoyed playacting only on the joyful holiday of Purim when, like medieval mummers, men and boys would act out elaborate, costumed renditions of the story of the evil Haman and the heroine Esther.

At other times, with neither time nor money to spare, the Jews of Russia had little interest in frivolous entertainment and in any case were forbidden by tsarist law from gathering in large groups. Plays had been written in Hebrew and even Yiddish, and sometimes read aloud, but never performed. Goldfaden's first attempts at theater, as exuberant as Purim plays, came at exactly the right time in modern Jewish history, as age-old interdicts crumbled. He was known, ever after, as "The Father of the Yiddish Stage."

In order to survive, the barely established theater troupes stayed on the road, touring throughout the Pale. In 1879 one band of actors played in Odessa, where Jacob Adler, a debonair youth working as an official in the Department of Weights and Measures, fell in love with them all, especially the leading lady who later became his wife. Awakened to his true calling as an actor, Adler jumped aboard. His troupe spent some weeks in Gordin's prosperous Elizavetgrad, where perhaps a quarter of the 45,000 inhabitants were Jewish. Many of those Elizavetgrad Jews flocked to see the sensational new Yiddish theater, but Jacob Gordin was not among them. The very words "Yiddish theater" were a contradiction in terms for Jewish intellectuals, who recognized as the only languages of the intellect and the arts their much-admired German and Russian and Hebrew, the sacred language of the synagogue. The Jewish-Russian newspapers for which Gordin wrote targeted the Yiddish theater, ridiculing its actors and scripts.

But at the same time, the status of Yiddish as a written language was improving. The grandfather of modern Yiddish literature, Sholem Abromovitsh, who took the pen name Mendele Mokher Sforim (Mendele the bookseller) had realized in the 1860s that because 90 percent of his countrymen spoke mostly *mama-loshen,* they were unreachable in any other language. He, and later his renowned colleagues I. L. Peretz and Sholem Aleichem, chose to write in Yiddish rather than Hebrew. In 1883 Sholem Aleichem, who would become the most famous Yiddish writer in the world, was spurred on by a series of horrifying pogroms—murderous anti-Semitic riots often fomented by the tsar's agents—to submit his first story to a Yiddish newspaper.

Jewish life in Russia was changed forever on March 1, 1881, when a group of nihilists, including a pregnant young Jewess, blew up the carriage of the relatively moderate Tsar Alexander II. His son and successor, Tsar Alexander III, revealed himself immediately as a reactionary anti-Semite determined to reverse the liberal reforms of his father. In the weeks of unrest following the assassination, authorities deflected discontent away from St. Petersburg and onto those ever-convenient scapegoats, the Jews. A string of pogroms boiled up during Easter week in Elizavetgrad, triggered when a Jewish innkeeper challenged a gentile, probably an instigator, who had refused to pay his bill. This skirmish flamed into an inferno of robbery, vandalism, and bloodshed throughout the Pale.

For centuries Jews lived beside their Christian neighbors in Russia knowing that murderous violence could flare up at any time, that once friendly or neutral faces might suddenly convulse with hatred, particularly during the holiest week of the Christian calendar, Easter. The pogrom in Elizavetgrad lasted more than two days. A synagogue and many homes and shops were completely destroyed, one hundred houses were pillaged, one Jew was killed and two hundred were wounded; the number of rapes went uncounted. Jewish houses were not burned down only because, in this unusual town, Jews lived intermingled with gentiles. "Neither women nor children were spared," said a newspaper of the time, "and had not many Jews been armed a wholesale massacre would have taken place."

The Gordins, sheltered in the cellar of a sympathetic gentile neighbor, tried to block out the din as they hushed and consoled the infant Alexander, three-year-old Sema who could not understand, six-year-old Liza, and fragile Sonia, aged seven. The riots were extinguished at last in Elizavetgrad but subsequently erupted in over two hundred towns and cities, in Smela, Kiev, Berditchev, Odessa, even Warsaw.

A hundred years later, my great-aunt Helen offered a sanguine view of events. "Papa was so loved by Jew and gentile alike that someone always warned them about the pogroms," she told me. "The Gordins were never hurt."

In all the histories of Jewish life in Russia, the year 1881 is listed as a watershed. Until then Jews had been willing to band with their Russian brethren to fight not just for the betterment of the Jewish minority but for all the inhabitants of Russia. But when their Russian comrades supported the bloodthirsty peasants during the pogrom, insisting that the anti-Semitic attacks would spark the countrywide revolution that was their goal, even Jewish dissidents were forced to see the truth: in Russia, Jews would always be outcasts.

As if to reinforce their despair, the new tsar pushed through the infamous "May Laws Concerning the Jews," a series of hostile government policies forcing far greater restrictions on the inhabitants of the Pale. Chaim Weizmann, the first president of Israel, wrote wryly about his shtetl childhood: "As one read, year after year, the complicated *ukasi* which poured from St. Petersburg, one obtained the impression that the whole cumbersome machinery of the vast Russian Empire was created for the sole purpose of . . . hedging in the existence of its Jewish subjects until it became something that was neither life nor death." The tsars were more specific in their purpose. Their stated aim was to force a third of the Jews in Russia to emigrate, a third to convert to Christianity, and the final third to die of persecution or hunger.

Jacob Gordin's intemperate response to the Elizavetgrad pogrom

came in the form of a pseudo-letter to his paper *Southern Frontier,* criticizing not the destructive mob but his fellow Jews who, he felt, had provoked
the attacks.

> Brothers, Jews, why does all Russian society hate you and no one pity
> you? Is it only because of our religion? Our love for money, our meanness
> and desire for profit, our arrogance and disputatiousness, our foolish,
> slavish aping of the dissolute Russian nobility, our usury, inn-keeping and
> all the other dishonest deeds turn the Russian people against us. Yes of
> course, there are honest people among us, but they are lost in the mass of
> moral traitors who think only about a ruble and have no other interest in
> their lives. . . .
>
> The events of the last days give me the right to remind you that now
> is the time to extract the rotting teeth with which you bite others, and
> which time and time again have caused you suffering and loss. Become
> honest and industrious, and live lives without exploitation. Brothers,
> awaken, begin a new life!

Gordin read the letter to the members of his brotherhood, who begged him
not to publish it and were outraged when it appeared, under the pseudonym "Brother Biblist," in early June.

What could have possessed my great-grandfather to write this savage,
self-righteous treatise just after an attack on his people? In his tactless way,
he was trying to help. Gordin was an assimilationist, one of many who believed that Jews would be accepted in Russia if they were less determinedly different, apart, in the way they lived, worked, and worshipped.
A Russian newspaper report agreed with Gordin, citing as cause of the
pogrom "the anomalous position of the Jews, whose disabilities prevent
their absorption by the rest of the population and compel them to have re-
course to usury and huckstering in order to gain a livelihood."

Socialist Abraham Cahan, who like Gordin believed in taking the
larger worldview, wrote later that he simply ignored the pogroms, which
evoked no sympathy in him and his comrades. "We considered ourselves
human beings, not Jews. Jewish matters had no special interest for us," he
said.

But I see in Gordin's missive, too, the poisonous undertone of Jewish
self-loathing. All his life, my great-grandfather had confronted the anti-
Semitism growing like a foul weed around him; his world was rife with

overt, omnipresent hatred of Jews. His Mirgorod neighbor, the venerated Gogol, laces his famous novella *Taras Bulba* with horrifying anti-Jewish sentiments presented as the natural state of the world: a street in Warsaw called "Dirty or Jew Street," the main Jewish character a cringing and greedy caricature, a cheery pogrom in which Cossacks throw weakling Jews into the river for sport. Now as then, perhaps because they are constantly absorbing the negative images projected upon them, Jews are known for adroitness at self-criticism. As Sholem Aleichem put it, "No outsider can find more withering things to say of us than we ourselves."

I believe that Gordin was not a self-hating Jew, as he was accused of being, but that he was, in this instance as in others to come, heavy-handed, sanctimonious, bullheaded, and a poor judge of timing. A rebuttal by the writer M. L. Lilienblum was published in the newspaper *Rassvet (Dawn)* attacking "such ignorant, hypocritical and foolish little brothers" as the anonymous writer of the letter "who have just now found the opportune moment to castigate the Jews." My great-grandfather never admitted that his diatribe was a mistake, but Lilienblum, who became a foe of Gordin's in Russia and criticized him in the press, wrote in a Russian newspaper after Gordin's death that he believed the Brotherhood leader had come to regret his ill-advised letter.

After the terrifying pogroms and the imposition of the May Laws, some Jewish radicals changed their names to become invisible as Jews, though not long thereafter that, too, would be forbidden. A few even converted. Many more, like Cahan, left the country forever. That year, 40,000 Eastern European Jews arrived at Castle Garden in New York, a dramatic increase from the year before. In 1881 there were more than 3 million Jews in Russia and a tenth that number, about 300,000, in the United States; those proportions were about to change dramatically. The shtetls buzzed with talk of America; letters from over the sea were passed from hand to hand, smudged pages from relatives and neighbors who had gone on ahead, sending back word of dollars and soft white bread.

Jacob Gordin hunkered down. To keep his damaged brotherhood together, he applied for a grant to establish an agricultural colony. The government, not surprisingly, refused to allow a ragtag group of Jews to buy land, and the St. Petersburg fund of the wealthy Jew Poliakov, also not surprisingly, refused the controversial brotherhood a subsidy.

Instead, Gordin packed up his wife and four small children and moved to a village, where he spent a year and a half as a farmer. How did he survive? A law in May 1882 forbade new Jewish settlement outside cities or shtetlach; Jews were not permitted to own or manage land or farms, and yet Gordin was in a village, farming. He must have had friends in high places or a friendly contact on the land. Helen said about her father's agricultural ambitions: "Listen, Mama always said that he would have been a wonderful farmer, and he loved farming. That part I can believe, that he was a farmer, because he loved the soil, and he wanted his people to be farmers. He thought they'd be better as farmers than as business people because he didn't like what the Jews did with money."

While Gordin farmed, or attempted to do so, and the tsar's henchman Count Ignatieff thought up new laws to stifle Jewish life, men who would soon become Gordin's peers and colleagues moved far afield on their chosen paths. Goldfaden's troupe toured as far as Moscow with a play that would add a classic word to the Yiddish vocabulary: the eponymous *Shmendrik,* which came to mean an ineffectual small man or an inexperienced boy, a role written specifically for the brilliant comic Mogulescu.

Pretty young Boris Thomashefsky, future star of the Yiddish theater, sailed in 1881 from Antwerp to New York City. The slightly cross-eyed young revolutionary Abraham Cahan, future newspaper editor, also landed that year at Castle Garden, determined to be part of an agricultural colony, although he soon changed his mind and plunged into socialist politics and the newspaper business.

In Germany, the dour Norwegian genius Henrik Ibsen wrote two scandalous dramas at this time: *A Doll's House,* in which a young woman walks out of her marriage, famously slamming the door behind her, and *Ghosts,* a daring dramatization of the problems caused by family untruths and venereal disease. These tragedies about the day-to-day lives of middle-class people, speaking in their own voices, heralded the perfecting of the theater of realism. Realists rejected the contrived melodramas of the time; they wanted natural acting and plays with lifelike plots and dialogue. Sir Paul Harvey, editor of *The Oxford Companion to Literature,* has defined realism as "a movement devoted to the facts of life, especially if they're gloomy."

The first Yiddish realist playwright loved gloomy. My great-grandfather would also, and more fittingly, be known, at the time of his fame twenty years hence, as "The Ibsen of the Jews."

• • •

Impossible as it is to imagine, after the chaos and bloodshed of 1881 the situation for Russian Jews deteriorated further. Half a million Jewish citizens, not including Gordin who was still struggling in the village, were forced by Russian authorities to abandon their homes in rural areas for towns within the Pale. Jewish schools and some newspapers and societies were shut down. The ragged troupes of Yiddish actors, already barely surviving, came to the surly attention of the tsar, and in 1883 a decree was passed banning all Yiddish theater. The law was pushed along, some suspected, by the rabbis, who were as happy as the tsar to see the end of the godless thespians. Others were sure that jealous Russian actors had had a hand in forcing out their lively new competitors.

The troupes tried to survive by pretending they were performing in German, but it was clear they would have to emigrate. Jacob Adler sailed for London and many others for New York, at the beginning of the mass Jewish exodus out of Russia. Snobbish London, then the center of the world economy, was a harsh landing for Jewish immigrants. America was more welcoming.

In New York in 1883, sixteen-year-old Boris Thomashefsky helped mount the Goldfaden operetta *The Sorceress* at Turn Hall on East Fourth Street. This fairy tale about a little girl, her evil stepmother, a bad witch, and a good peddler, presented by one Israel Barsky, was the first American production of a Yiddish play. A committee of established German Jews, determined to prevent the play from taking place, was suspected of bribing the leading lady to succumb to a mysterious sore throat on opening night. The company would not be permitted, the committee said, to perform in a despicable jargon that would make Jews look like fools. They offered to pay the actors' expenses until alternative "decent and useful occupations" could be found. Their offer was ignored.

Gordin believed that Jews should remain in Russia rather than emigrating, but he was ready to abandon village life. By the end of 1882, as the bitter Ukrainian winter blew in, the imminent birth of their fifth child prompted the Gordins to return to the relative comforts of town; the baby was born January 2, 1883, in Elizavetgrad. Vera, whose name means *faith*, was the only child to inherit her mother Anna's placid generosity. The first-born Gordin children were not endowed with pleasant qualities; as adults,

Sonia, Liza, and Alexander were estranged from the rest of the family. But Vera, a family favorite, shone with obliging goodness her whole life long.

After the Gordins' move back to town, the Brotherhood followers reassembled around their leader, and for the next eight years, Gordin supported his ever-growing family as a writer and editor and as the leader of his sect. The dissident group was growing too, not only in membership but in unpopularity. On June 16, 1884, a group of Jews attacked the Brotherhood meeting place; like parents today facing cults with suspicion and hostility, some of the vigilantes were parents of members. The attack consolidated rather than dispersed the group, and on September 30 Gordin applied to the police for the legalization of his Spiritual Biblical Brotherhood. The application listed thirty-four names, mostly from Elizavetgrad but with small groups from Odessa and the villages Nikolayev and Uman, and others. The following year, the Brotherhood was officially legalized by the governor of Kherson province, an aristocrat who had become, somehow, my great-grandfather's admirer and friend.

The Elizavetgrad branch met on Wednesdays and Saturdays. That day's leader, most often Gordin, would read from the Bible and then lecture or sermonize from a wide range of intellectual sources: Darwin, Kant, the Greeks, even Shakespeare and Lord Byron, and, of course, Tolstoy. The group, which practiced self-criticism and liked to analyze the place of Jews in Russian society, was considered too cerebral to relate to ordinary people. "Sermons without God had no hope of success," said a Russian article about the "brothers." Their leader was described as "a well-built man with large dreamy eyes, a big cane and a beautiful black beard" who argued that Jews weren't living as they should because they were unproductive. "When Gordin spoke he would stroke his beard," says the writer, "as if all his cleverness came from his beard."

Though the group declared circumcision to be barbaric, Gordin's own sons were circumcised. (When I took the liberty of asking George Gordin Jr. about his father George, one of Jacob Gordin's youngest sons, my first cousin once removed thought the question not intrusive but absurd.)

At the branch of the Brotherhood in the shtetl of Uman, traditional wedding ceremonies were given up, replaced by a ceremony called "Registration." Like a "happening" in the counterculture Sixties, the bride carried red flowers and the groom had a red flower in his buttonhole; walking into the hall arm in arm made them man and wife. A pioneering few of these marriages took place between gentiles and Jews.

These cult followers of Gordin's were an assortment of misfits: Tolstoyans, dispossessed youth seeking an "alternative lifestyle," students, teachers, artisans, even a few doctors and merchants and a lawyer, some highly intelligent and well educated, and others, especially the women, barely literate. Their leader's forceful, magnetic personality held them together along with the crusading belief that fulfilling their task—to love and to improve the lives of the ordinary folk of Russia—would save them all.

Tolstoy had decreed that men and women should strive continually not only for simplicity but for cheerfulness; one of the Brotherhood tenets was to "speak softly with goodness and loving kindness." Even so, a female disciple indicated later that Gordin could be sharp and "despotical" with anyone who criticized him, once telling her angrily, "It is not your business to teach me!"

The bacteriologist and future Nobel Prize winner Ilya Mechnikov was fascinated by the Brotherhood and became a good friend of Gordin's. He later wrote that he had "the best memories of Jacob Gordin and his activities of that time." I wish he had specified what those activities were.

In 1886, the thirty-three-year-old group leader accepted a job as the editor and drama critic of the Russian newspaper *Odesskie Novosti (Odessa News)*. Cosmopolitan Odessa, with an opulent new opera and theater building just nearing completion, was a European, open-minded city— "The Paris of Russia." Among its more than 300,000 citizens were a disproportionate number of foreigners, artists, dissidents, scientists, poets—and Jews. By the end of the nineteenth century, almost one third of Odessa's population were Jews, who enjoyed greater freedom here than anywhere in the Pale; they were allowed to reside in all districts of the Black Sea port and to compete in business. When a Jew lives "like God in Odessa," in the well-known Yiddish expression, he is enjoying a holiday from righteous responsibility. Appeals to God were rare in the city of heretics.

Though their leader had now moved some 150 miles southwest, the Brotherhood groups continued to meet as before. Aneuta, meanwhile, was producing a brotherhood of her own: son Yakov, named in defiance of the Ashkenazi tradition that a newborn child be called after a dead relative, not a living one, was born on November 4, 1885. Though known as Yasha, like his father, this son in later years did not resemble his father in any way. Two years after his birth, on December 3, 1887, came Mikhail, or Misha. Upright, demanding Mikhail Gordin was dead, and his son's seventh child was named in his honor. Gordin's older sister, now known by her married name Eva Liaznova, also produced a Mikhail at this time. Mikhail Gordin turned into Mike in America. Unlike some of his brothers, Mike was a good-natured man, unambitious, unassuming, and tall.

In 1887 a large tract of land—at last!—was offered to the Brotherhood by the Russian millionaire Sibiriakoff. Jubilant, Gordin traveled to St. Petersburg to claim 6,000 acres in the province of Stavropol in northern Caucausus, but, without explanation, he was turned away. About the disappointments of that trip, he wrote only that he was "ordered by the Government of St. Petersburg to leave the capital." There would be no land for the Biblical Brothers.

Two years later instead, a group led not by Gordin but by his acolyte Isaac Feinerman, a Tolstoyan intellectual turned "cabinet-maker," did move to the country. According to a follower, the group "rented in the village of Glados a piece of land and three cottages. They dressed themselves up like peasants and left proudly and happily to live the life of peasants . . . and when the group returned three months later empty-handed Gordin said smilingly that it was a very good experiment."

Feinerman, who later converted to Christianity, appears in Henri Troyat's biography of Tolstoy as one of Tolstoy's "unattractive" hangers-on. "Then there was Feinerman," writes Troyat, "a Jew converted to Tolstoy, who had left his pregnant wife and child to receive the master's light and, even more, his hospitality." In 1905 Feinerman wrote to Gordin in New York, telling his former leader that he was "involved in a big project, *Reminiscences of Tolstoy.*" "I am sending you my play, *Decay,*" he added hopefully. "I would be very happy if you would produce it at your theater."

In Odessa, on August 21, 1889, Aneuta produced an eighth child, a dark-eyed girl called Nadezhda, which means *hope.* Nicknamed Nadia, she would turn into a devoted if plaintive daughter who played the piano and painted in oils, an unloving status-conscious wife and a good cook, a nagging, humorless mother to my father and his brother, and an affectionate if uncomprehending grandma to me. But not for many years, and not in Russia.

By the end of the 1880s, Gordin's ally the sympathetic governor had been replaced; the new man had no patience with the band of Jewish malcontents propagandizing among the peasants. Others of whom the government disapproved had been sentenced to years of hard labor, to banishment in Siberia, or even, like Dostoyevsky, to death. The Brotherhood leader was in increasing danger of arrest. "Don't write this in your book," said Helen, "but it was a person very high up who warned Papa that it was time to get out. It was a cousin of the tsar. Don't write that down!" The warning must have come from her father's friend the former governor of Kherson province, whose descendants will surely be spared retribution if this fact is revealed. But Gordin refused to leave Russia. "He, like all [of us]," wrote a follower, "was attached to the land where he was born and where he developed and imbibed in his soul the best, the most beautiful, the most refined and the highest Russia had to offer."

As he delayed, the noose of anti-Semitism was pulled ever tighter. The number of Jews allowed to attend high schools and universities was cut to a quota of only 10 percent inside the Pale, and 3 to 5 percent outside. It is surprising that the father of eight wasn't eager to emigrate for that reason alone. This year a new *ukase* was passed, summarily expelling those who had taken advantage of the previous regime's tolerance and were living outside of the prescribed boundaries. Twenty thousand privileged Jews from Moscow, St. Petersburg, and Kiev, some in chains, were dragged from their homes on the first day of Passover and pushed onto trains for the Pale.

And still, my stubborn great-grandfather did not leave Russia of his own volition but was forced to flee. In June 1891, according to family myth, he escaped hidden under bales of hay in a farmer's cart just as the tsar's soldiers were coming for him. His scanty baggage consisted mostly of books, including a Russian-English dictionary bought for him by his disciples, who were planning to follow as soon as possible. Anna, with eight children clustered around her very pregnant belly, was left behind, full of absolute faith in the abilities and devotion of her vanished husband. He would make money in America and send for them or, even better, return, as soon as he could.

When little Nadia kissed her papa goodbye, she was not quite two. She didn't see him again until she was nearly five.

On August 31, exactly a month after Gordin landed in New York City, his ninth child, a fair-haired boy Grigoriy—Grisha—was born. A month after that, the Spiritual Biblical Brotherhood was permanently disbanded by the Russian police.

Helen told me about those days, and about the journey.

> Don't forget, living in Russia . . . there were pogroms, they had to hide—the tsar didn't let them go very far. Papa was not working only for himself and his family, but for humanity, to make a better life for people. Rise up, don't stand for these outrages! Be somebody, fight for your rights! Do you know what a risk that was with the tsar? He was risking his life every minute—every breath he took!
>
> He missed Russia terribly. He loved his music and the language and the Russian people. He used to say the Russian people are so sweet and so simple and so hospitable, and the Russian music is so beautiful. He used to sing Russian songs all the time. But he had to leave. He didn't want to be shot—sent to Siberia. What would his wife have then? At least he had a chance to survive this way. They covered him, I'm telling you, his gentile friends—not Jews.
>
> When Papa came it was in the wintertime and it was a terrible crossing, it took months and he didn't have the proper clothes. Friends packed a little something for him, it was freezing cold on the boat—but he told them to bring him a Russian-English dictionary.

My great-aunt had one detail wrong: her father came not in wintertime, but in July. It must have been freezing cold, though, on the boat.

In his flight from Russia, Gordin joined an exodus, a stream of emigrants swelling into a flood. American immigration statistics are astonishing: between 1850 and 1914, 30 million Europeans emigrated to the United States, six times the population of the entire country in 1800. Between 1880 and 1920, 2 million of those emigrants were Jews. Not until the twenties did the U.S. government begin to restrict entry; until then, America admitted almost everyone who knocked. Unlike other newcomers, very few of those Jewish travelers returned to the old country. They had no old country to return to.

Golda Meir, the future prime minister of Israel who landed fifteen years after Gordin, said that going to America in those days was almost like going to the moon. The difficulties of the journey into a vast unknown have been recounted many times. Those who wanted to leave their homelands with legal documents were delayed for months or even years by endless bureaucracy, knowing that departing without the right papers would prevent them from returning, should they ever wish to. Most, like Gordin, did not or could not wait. They bribed Austro-Hungarian border guards into letting them cross, they were smuggled through woods at night, or, as in the case of one Shmuel Gelbfisz, they swam across border rivers and walked northwest. Gelbfisz later made his considerable mark in America under the name Samuel Goldwyn.

My great-grandfather made his way from Brody, a besieged border town overrun by would-be emigrants, to Berlin. He traveled thence to the northern port city of Hamburg, where again the overcrowding and desperation were epidemic as travelers battled for place on the huge human cargo carriers, the steamers. Gordin eventually found passage on the rusty S.S. *Devonian* of the Anchor Line. Its picture postcard is there with hundreds of others just like it that cover one whole wall of the Ellis Island Museum of Immigration.

For their $37 steerage fare ($47 third class, $87 first class), hapless passengers endured eight to fourteen days of filthy, cramped quarters below deck, poor quality, sometimes rotting food that Orthodox Jews could not eat anyway, bad water, devastating sea sickness, homesickness, feverish anticipation, terror. Gordin left no comment on any of this, though living enmired in dirt and unable to escape the stench must have been hellish for a fastidious man. One traveler reported that, because "neighborliness, obedience, respect and status were valueless among the masses struggling for space," steerage prepared passengers for the reality of America.

All we know about Gordin's journey is that he was cold and used his time on board to sit with his dictionary and teach himself, and some fellow passengers, bits of English. Abraham Cahan, crossing almost ten years earlier, spent his evenings on deck communing with the others. "Our hearts would reach out with longing," he writes. "We would gather together and sing Russian folk songs—the plaintive and colorful airs of the villages of Ukraine." Though Gordin loved those songs, he couldn't bear to hear them as Russia vanished behind him. Unlike his fellow emigrants, he had no desire to start again in the "golden land" of America. He didn't weep with joy, as they did, to see the five-year-old Statue of Liberty looming on the horizon, holding high her torch beside "the golden door."

Jacob Gordin wanted Russia, and he continued to look homeward, with longing, for almost all of his years in America.

A RUSSIAN JEW IN AMERICA

We cannot devote ourselves to theater reviews because most Jewish readers, regrettably, do not understand what theater criticism is. Also it would not help to improve the theater. Most of the plays on the stage do not deserve serious reviews. The fault lies in the low taste of the Jewish public.

—Abraham Cahan, *Worker's Newspaper*, April 11, 1890

MY GREAT-GRANDFATHER surveyed the vast approaching city with mistrust. Here, he was sure, greed and selfishness were rampant, scholarship and philanthropy worth nothing. How would he find the strength and moral force to do battle?

And yet, even for a reluctant traveler, the journey on the smaller boat ferrying passengers from steamer to shore was awe inspiring. The skyline of New York City was unlike anything else on earth, a thicket of towering buildings anchored in the bedrock of the island, spiking as high as sixteen stories into the air. In 1891, 111,284 Jewish immigrants gawked at the view, nearly double the number who had come only two years before, and nearly three times the number in 1881.

Entry into America was more chaotic for Yakov Gordin and his fellow passengers than for those in previous years. The old immigrant processing center, Castle Garden, which stank "as if a thousand cats were living there" according to Abe Cahan, had been closed down, and the new one on Ellis Island would not be ready to receive the huddled masses until the following year. On July 31, Gordin and hundreds with him were processed at an interim facility, the Lower Manhattan Barge Office.

There, my dignified ancestor received the customary treatment: hour after hour of humiliating lineups for inspection of eyes, lungs, and mental, physical, and financial health. Those found infectious, indigent, or insane were sent home. Yakov Mikhailovich Gordin had to prove he was of sound body and mind and had some money before the letter of admittance was chalked on his back. In the last lineup, he cleaned his pockets of rubles and stashed away around eight green dollar bills, the amount possessed on entry by the average Jewish immigrant. Then he stepped out into his new life—as Jacob.

His arrival had been anticipated in the local Jewish-Russian community, which was well informed about his activities. His friend, fellow socialist newspaperman Philip Krantz, and others from the old country were undoubtedly there to greet him, to steer him the mile and a half east through the sweltering midsummer heat, through the overwhelming speed and noise of the city to the crush of the Lower East Side. How evocative to this day, the ring of those names—Canal Street, Hester, Grand, Broome, Delancey, Rivington, Chrystie, Orchard—teeming thoroughfares shoving at the newcomer their bewildering smells, their trolleys and horsecars, raucous crowds and saloons.

Sweating as he walked in his dark wool suit carrying his belongings, heavy with books, my great-grandfather heard for the first time the cacophony of unintelligible Chinese, Italian, and Irish shouts and curses; he saw the faces of free black men and women. And then, like a lunatic version of home, like market day in an overblown shtetl, he saw hundreds of pushcarts lining the streets, manned by shrieking vendors. "Shoelaces! Pickles! Fish! Bread! Bananas!" Yes, edible yellow fingers called bananas. How would he adapt to this madhouse?

He went to stay on Ludlow Street near Houston, with a family of *landslayt*—fellow Jews from Elizavetgrad. His new home, typical for a boarder in a tenement flat, was a mattress and chair in the corner of a crowded room, made private only by a sheet hung from the ceiling. The building was steps from Katz's Delicatessen, which had opened under another name in 1888, and is still in business today.

Developed New York then stretched as far north as Seventy-second and Central Park West; beyond Columbus and Seventy-eighth, shanties and subsistence farms still scratched at the land. To the south of the farms glittered a prosperous and cultivated swath of New York. More than half of

America's millionaires, 1,800 in all, lived in or on the edges of the metropolis, many in ornate mansions stretching for more than two miles along Fifth Avenue. The glamorous event of that year's social calendar, for the inhabitants of those uptown palaces, was the inaugural concert of Carnegie Hall with the much-lauded Tchaikovsky as guest conductor.

The Russian musician wrote in a breathless letter home that all of the sixty-two boxes "were filled with lovely women in beautiful gowns glistening with jewels that vied with the thousands of electric lights." He was dazzled by the energy and comfort, the hospitality, vastness, and originality of America. A few months later his countryman Gordin would be subjected to the other side of the American dream, the side Tchaikovsky did not see: the fetid slums of immigrant life downtown.

It is an oft-repeated fact that the Lower East Side of New York at the turn of the last century was more crowded than Bombay. Nearly a quarter of New York's entire population lived in dismal poverty on this tiny wedge of Manhattan, ruled by the corrupt politicians of Tammany Hall. New arrivals, landing penniless and disoriented, went immediately to live in dank overcrowded tenements and to slave in factories and sweatshops, at home doing piecework or in the markets as pushcart peddlers.

As lost as any other greenhorn in this bewilderingly freewheeling, fast-paced, multiracial society, my great-grandfather immediately got down to work. He had farmland to find.

His timing was good. The Baron de Hirsch foundation, which paid for Jewish agricultural colonies in Europe and South America, had just been set up in New York with an endowment of more than $2 million. The influx of hopeful neophyte farmers from Eastern Europe, a movement called Am Olam (Eternal People), hadn't abated, though few Am Olam colonies would experience success. The Hebrew Emigrant Aid Society in New York complained of a rumor spreading through Russia "that every emigrant coming over would receive land under cultivation, and the result has been that many persons who never planted a seed in their lives have, on their arrival here, styled themselves farmers in the hope of acquiring land."

Jacob Gordin was among them. On August 1, after only a few hours in New York, he sent a long letter to the Baron's fund. In awkward, misspelled English translated from his Russian by an only slightly more adept English-speaking acquaintance, the writer describes his Brotherhood as a "group of more or less intelligent people living in Elizavetgrad [who] decided to give up their professions and trades and engage themselves exclusively to productive labor, especially to agriculture." Their goal, he wrote, was to combat Russian anti-Semitism by moving Jews out of cities and towns, thus lessening the competitiveness and isolation that were a problem for Jewish city laborers. "The soil . . . makes them good citizens," wrote Gordin, "while city life demoralizes the masses. Agricultural labor only can strengthen their phisical forces which factory work could thouroughly ruin."

He tells of the offer of "2000 desiatins" of land by the "Millioner Mr. Sibiriakoff (a Christian)" which the group was not allowed to accept, and continues:

> Having been unable to realize their desire to become farmers, the members of the group decided to learn different trades for the time being. They gave up their business as clerks, school teachers, store keepers etc. and learned thouroughly different branches of manual labor, only a few found chances to settle illigally in a small hamlet Glados near Elizavetgrad as farmers. At present the group consists of 8 locksmiths, 6 cabinetmakers, 4 wheelers, 3 tailors, 2 shoe makers, 3 druggists (one woman druggist), 4 stocking-knitters, 4 underwearmakers, 5 dressmakers, 1 midwife, 1 milliner, 4 farmers etc., alltogether about 60 persons (15 families,) young strong, mentally and morally developed.

"The group does not mean to ask charity," he meekly concludes.

> But as your committee has the object of colonization near at heart, we ask you to help us in the form of loan the sum of money enough to purchase land for 15 families and to start us farming on it.
>
> Asking your committee kindly to consider this application I can add that the members of this group have all chances to become good workers and once becoming farmers, they will be able to set a sample worth to be imitated.
>
> Most respectfully
> Yours Jacob Gordin

The Baron de Hirsch fund, unmoved by the prospective "sample" of all those wheelers, stocking-knitters, and underwear-makers, turned him down. If eager, unattached young people were making a hash of things, what chance was there for a thirty-eight-year-old ex-newspaperman and his motley fifteen families? Gordin, who had counted on the grant, was dismayed. Some members of his Brotherhood had already set out to join him on their farm. He had to support himself, send money to Anna and now not eight but nine children in Russia, save for ten steamship fares, and find a way for his followers to live. How?

He later wrote lightheartedly about his situation:

> On the 31 of July, in the year 1891, the boat Devonia [*sic*] docked rather early, opposite the Statue of Liberty. On the deck of the boat, among other greenhorns, was a Russian Jew with a long black beard and big plans to establish a new agricultural commune in the United States . . . The Baron de Hirsh managers told him to throw his plans away. And so I, Reb Yankl, the son of Mikl the Levite . . . became a Yiddish literat instead.

Unlike his brethren, he did not become a tailor, peddler, or cigar maker; he picked up his pen. His fellow immigrants were desperate for news both of their old home and of the new, for information, especially, on how to understand and survive this bewildering foreign place. Social activists and religious conservatives had come to the same conclusion in America as in Russia: in order to reach their audience, they had to speak and write in Yiddish, the only language common to all the Eastern European Jews now living here, the Galitzianers, Poles, Ukrainians, Byelorussians, Rumanians, Litvaks (Lithuanians). Newspapers in *mama-loshen* were being founded on kitchen tables and in basement offices to satisfy the hunger of transplanted Yiddish speakers. In Russia there was no Jewish daily press, and the weeklies were severely limited by censorship. Here in America, nothing better symbolized a greenhorn's mind-boggling newfound freedom than reading a daily paper in Yiddish.

One of the first, *Di Arbayter Tsaytung (The Worker's Newspaper)* had been founded four years before by Abraham Cahan and Louis Miller, a socialist lawyer and editor. Its first issue trumpeted, "Our Program: . . . the building of a social order on the principles of true freedom, equality and brotherhood, in place of the present capitalist order, which is founded upon oppression of the people, mass poverty, and internecine strife." The paper, which fostered plenty of internecine strife between the social democrats and the anarchists of the quarter, was now edited by Gordin's friend Philip

Krantz, a prominent journalist recently brought over from London. It was clear what Jacob Gordin should do until he found his land: he should write for newspapers, as he had from the age of seventeen. But here in New York he would have to write, for the first time in his life, in Yiddish.

He still had no use for the language, unlike his colleague Sholem Aleichem who had been promoting Yiddish literature in Russia for almost ten years (although, like most of the Russian-Jewish intelligentsia, in his own home only Russian was spoken). Gordin wasn't ashamed that his Yiddish was rusty. Many of his fellow immigrant intellectuals, like Krantz, had had to refresh their vocabularies or even learn the language for the first time; one transplanted writer described Yiddish as the "language I had to extract from the memory of my mother's tongue." Despite fond memories of his mother, Yakov Mikhailovich would have preferred to write in Russian, or even German, or, later, in English.

But write in Yiddish he did, an article in early September for the *Worker's Newspaper* entitled "The Pogrom in Elizavetgrad." Unlike his controversial "letter" of 1881, he no longer condemned Jews for provoking violence. The pogrom, he charged, was an eruption of gentile greed, perpetrated by "Elizavetgrad Christians and peasants who [came] to rob the Jews. Many peasants came specially from the villages with large wagons to take Jewish goods." He signed this first piece in the new world with a pseudonym, Yankev ben Mikhl (Jacob, son of Michael). It wasn't yet clear to him that in this democracy ruled not by a tsar but by an elected president, President Benjamin Harrison, he was free to write critically and satirically under his own name.

Krantz wanted more. For his next story, "Pantole Polge," Gordin invented a winning character, a poor dead tailor in Heaven speaking to God, with humility and without rancor, about his starving scrap of a life. This time the work flowed easily because the characters were conversing with each other. Yiddish, he found, was easier to write in dialogue because it was a spoken, not a written, language. When he handed "Pantole Polge" to Krantz, little did either of them know that this small tale of a chatty tailor would transform the life not only of its author but of Jews worldwide.

Philip Krantz showed Gordin's tailor story, before it was even published, to the actor Mogulescu, who recognized its potential and immediately had it adapted for the stage. He performed it as a monologue three days later in a benefit at the Union Theater, where it was seen by the actor destined to be linked to Gordin until the end of both their lives and beyond. Jacob Adler had heard of the Russian *literat,* "whose stories of life under the Tsarist terror," he later wrote, "were making a stir in our literary circles." But "Pantole Polge" revealed another talent, for theatricality and dialogue. Adler, by far the most cultured of the Jewish actors, was an inspired tragedian with a limited gift for singing and dancing, essential skills for the operettas and historical musicals then the mainstay of the Yiddish stage. Desperate for weightier material to perform, he asked Krantz to set up a rendezvous with the newly arrived writer.

Though Gordin was aware that there were Yiddish theaters in New York, they interested him as little here as they had in Ukraine. To him, theater meant the great problem plays of realism, like those by the master play builder Ibsen that he had applauded in Odessa. He loathed the very notion of farcical melodramas in Yiddish. But despite the disapproval of religious conservatives, and of the opposition socialists who disapproved for different reasons, the Yiddish theater had flourished in New York. After a few painfully lean years in London, Jacob Adler was now enjoying acclaim at the Union Theater on Eighth Street. Boris Thomashefsky, his new wife Bessie, and the diminutive singing comic Mogulescu, the first Yiddish acting stars in New York, were thriving in the Rumanian Opera House, a former beer hall on the Bowery, just below Grand Street. Gifted actors like David Kessler and Keni Lipzin worked with one company or the other.

The plays, by Goldfaden or by two lesser though prolific lights Hurwitz and Lateiner, were glories of amateur excess; the melodramas of poorer quality were even called *"shund"* (trash) by both fans and critics. This very year, Goldfaden had written a six-act play that charged from one improbable coincidence to the next, the characters burdened with his favorite authorial devices: tics, speech defects, and physical deformities. Thomashefsky had starred in a piece of *shund* by Joseph Lateiner, described by the bemused drama critic of the *Philadelphia Record* as "a tragical musical melodrama or an operatic-realistic drama with a terrific climax in which 3 of the characters die violent deaths [followed directly by] a comic topic duet . . . The end comes with a parade of New York's foreign citizens, all in red, white and blue regalia and red flannel yachting caps, headed by a brass band playing 'The Star Spangled Banner.' "

Jacob Gordin did not attend.

Before his meeting with Adler, my great-grandfather suspected that as soon as he expressed interest in writing a play, the actor would "start to emote: wipe his nose on his sleeve, jump on a chair, and recite one of the popular rhymes of the day." Gordin was not alone in his condescension; it would be many years before thespians were considered even marginally respectable in Jewish society. A Lower East Side memoirist wrote that his old-fashioned father might begrudgingly accept a musician or a writer, but "an actor, never an actor!"

Instead of an illiterate bumpkin, however, Gordin met a well-spoken, intelligent gentleman with a silk hat and handkerchief. "I noticed eyes sparkling with talent," he wrote. "Really, I thought, if the Jewish actor is a gentleman like other actors on the world stage, why should the Yiddish theater not be like all world theaters?"

More than an intelligent gentleman, Adler was a magnificent specimen of a man, very tall, with a thick head of shining white hair though only in his mid-thirties, and the noble carriage and flamboyance of a star. Irresistible to women—at least one of his illegitimate children appeared unexpectedly on his doorstep, to the chagrin of his third wife Sara—he was also much admired by men. The two artists and Krantz (and maybe, according to some accounts but not others, Mogulescu) met in a wine cellar on Essex Street, a favorite watering hole for the Jewish intelligentsia. With his actor's panache, Adler swirled in wearing a cape, a cravat. Gordin, with his socialist writer's rejection of material things, wore his only threadbare suit, although he brandished his proudest possession, a silver-headed cane.

The two men, greeting each other in fluent Russian, were overjoyed to discover that they shared a love for the language of their motherland. They admired each other's proficiency; only educated, distinguished Jews spoke such good Russian. As they drank glasses of hot tea, dissolving the lumps of sugar they held in their mouths, and as Gordin smoked cigarette after cigarette, they discussed life in Russia, life in America, and, of course, the Yiddish theater, the bad plays and good actors. Adler handed the writer a German play he had in his pocket, saying, "Here—a ready-made subject. Perhaps you can make a play from it."

The writer handed it back.

"If I write a play for you," he said, "it will be a Yiddish play, not a German play with Yiddish names."

Gordin pulled out the *Worker's Newspaper* and scanned it until he came upon a dramatic news story: a Russian Jew, wrongly convicted of a crime, escaped on his way to Siberia and managed to rejoin his family, with whom he led a peaceful life in disguise for many years. When a jealous rival discovered his secret and betrayed him to the police, he was torn from his loved ones and sent away again. Here was the subject of Gordin's first drama.

Writer and actor came to a financial understanding, and Gordin promised to have the first act ready in three weeks. Adler invited him to the Union Theater to see his first Yiddish play. The writer went, and was appalled. "I saw an old Jewish miller, blind, dancing around the stage, speaking kitchen German and singing an aria from an Italian opera. And along with the miller a village crowd, singing like a choir in a Russian temple. Two Jews fought a duel, the audience whistled. The theater smelled of rotten fruit . . . children shrieked and boys ran around yelling 'soda water, apples!' Everything I saw was far from Jewish life: cheap, false and ugly."

A more forgiving viewer might have said "exuberant, unsophisticated, unconstrained." Yiddish theater had been a success on the Lower East Side from its inception. After grueling days in the sweatshops or behind a pushcart, exhausted workers carrying babies and food flooded in to see the stars they idolized, to hear the voices of their distant homeland. This faithful audience of workingmen and women, known satirically to those on the other side of the curtain as "Moishe," an uneducated simpleton, resembled less the politely restrained rows of today than the impatient brawling groundlings in the pit of Shakespeare's theater. Paying from twenty-five cents to a dollar, fifteen cents for matinees, Moishes squeezed into the theaters, eating bagels, cheese, fruit, leaning far over the balconies to listen avidly, afraid to miss a single word, weeping or laughing with gusto. Sometimes audience members shouted out directly to the actors, who loved to ad-lib back. The actors posed and orated center stage, with embellished phrases, flamboyant gestures, and lavish costumes no matter what the role. Peddlers selling soda water, candy, fruit, and halvah clamored about their wares to the crowds between the acts as the audience members greeted old friends and *landslayt* (countrymen), so eager to converse that the play was forgotten until the music heralding the next act began.

An early letter to the Yiddish press complained that "audiences applaud at the wrong places, whereupon someone cries out Order! and then a second person yells, Order! to the first one, and a third, Order! to the second. You don't find this in any other theater in the world." Everyone except the most orthodox went; like food for the displaced soul, the Yiddish stage gave its Moishes *broyt mit teyater* (bread with theater). These Jews had lost country, language, ritual, family, even the bedrock of the synagogue, which many no longer attended. (So far only a handful of rabbis had immigrated to the new world, so there were few synagogues in any case.) The Yiddish theater, for a few hours, replaced all those losses.

Other immigrant populations nearby, the Irish and the Italians, had almost no theaters. They still had their churches, however; live costumed performance held no special magic for nationalities still enjoying the timeless rituals of meeting and mass. Jews were elated to discover something daring and unique that brought them together, gave them music, laughter, and tears, and sounded like home.

Although he had no knowledge of the histrionic world he was about to enter or of the technical requirements of playwriting, Gordin was determined that his play be of a far higher caliber and more attuned to realism than any Yiddish play yet seen in New York. Inspired by Ibsen, he also must have known of the German Meininger Company that had played in Moscow in 1885 and again in 1890, pioneering ensemble acting, historically accurate costumes and scenery, and realistic crowd scenes. Gordin wanted to incorporate all these theatrical innovations. In a humorous article entitled "How I Became a Playwright," he states that when, with endless cigarettes and glasses of tea, he sat down to work on his play, "I wrote with my blood charging through my veins, with all my brain power. Oh, the holy fire of a poet when the strength of a prophet speaks through him! Oh, the holy fire of a greenhorn who comes to a foreign land and wants to educate the natives!"

Rather than bringing the first act in three weeks, as arranged, Gordin walked into the Union Theater one week after meeting Adler, carrying all four acts and prologue of his play *Siberia*—titled in Yiddish *Sibiria, lebensbild in 4 akten un prolog*. He was accompanied by three *landslayt* from Elizavetgrad as bodyguards because he had been told that all Jewish actors were "thieves and robbers" who might grab his work and run away with it. But only after rehearsals began did the actors steal his play. At this point he was greeted respectfully, and he sat down to read to the assembled group: the stars Adler and his actress wife Sara who would play the man and his wife, Mogulescu as the faithful servant Shpendik, Kessler as the villainous Russian district attorney, and actors for the smaller roles including Sigmund Feinman, his wife Dinah, and Leon Blank. Following Adler's instructions, Gordin had tried to write something special for each of them.

As the writer read his play, the actors, with the exception of Adler, were horrified. It was turgid! It was relentlessly serious! No singing and dancing, no grand speeches, no magnificent costumes and settings, no gloriously uplifting happy ending. The characters were ordinary people who spoke in ordinary speech instead of *Daytshmerish*, the pretentiously embellished, Germanized Yiddish that the actors loved to spout. On top of that, the play was only four acts long, not five or six like other plays. Adler would be ruined, they were sure.

Unaware of their discontent, Gordin turned his words over to the troupe and, gratified, led his protectors out. Adler was left with the job of transforming a band of peevish actors and a difficult script into an evening of theater.

On Friday, when Gordin came to the general rehearsal to see how his play was taking shape, he was galled to find some of his dialogue rewritten. Instead of his line "Reb Beryl, why do you want to make me unhappy?" one actor declaimed, in finest *Daytshmerish*, "My great Herr Beryl, when the tiger leaps and springs, when the leopards rear and bite, then truth will reign in heaven, and the true Jewish patriotic feelings will sing 'Live, O Israel!' "

Then Gordin discovered that a section of the opera *Hernani* had been inserted into the first act. Why? What harm if Kessler's character the district attorney sang a fine song, which happened to be the same song the actor was performing soon in a concert and needed to rehearse? The writer let this pass, ignoring the complaints of the cast that even more songs were needed. But when in the third act Shpendik the heartbroken servant suddenly began to sing and dance, Gordin lost his temper. That the audience would want Mogulescu to sing and dance, whether in a fairy-tale operetta or an Ibsenesque tragedy of realism, didn't stop the playwright from jumping to his feet and roaring, "What kind of nonsense is this!"

Mogulescu, who had been furious from the first reading that his part wasn't funny or musical enough, cried back, "A comic has to sing and dance, no?"

"I won't allow it. You're a scoundrel," snapped Gordin.

Mogulescu protested that Gordin the black-bearded Jew must be an anti-Semite. He had written the most pious Jew in his play as a villainous informer, whereas the lax Jews were good and the most honorable citizen was gentile; what loyal Jew would write such a thing? Kessler and Feinman jumped in, siding with Mogulescu, while Adler desperately defended the play. At last Mogulescu cried out his ultimatum: Gordin must leave the theater immediately, or else he, Mogulescu, would, and he would not return. And that would be the end of the production.

Gordin turned on his heels and stormed out, hearing, as he left, the actor call out that he was not to return, even on opening night.

Gordin did not return. "I didn't attend the first . . . performance of my first play because I was sick, nervous, insulted, displeased," he wrote. Just as well; a nerve-wracking premiere lay ahead. Adler could force his actors to embark upon a new theatrical experience, but it was much harder to force Moishe to do so. As the first two acts unrolled, the audience grew restless. Like the actors, they wanted what they were used to: music, colorful costumes, a panoply of emotions. They came to the theater to get away from real life, not to be pummelled with it; why pay hard-won money to see downtrodden, plain-speaking Jews just like themselves? They began to whisper and giggle, even to laugh and then hiss their disapproval.

Adler made a decision. After the disastrous second act, he pushed his way onstage. Standing in front of the curtain, he signaled the squirming house for silence, and with tears in his expressive actor's eyes, he drew himself up to his great height. "*Gospoda,* citizens," he cried, "I stand before you humiliated and humbled, my head bowed in shame, that you, *gospoda,* cannot understand this masterpiece from the pen of the famous Russian writer Yakov Mikhailovich Gordin." Tears rolled down his cheeks. "If you would open your hearts, if you would open your minds and listen, and attempt to understand, you wouldn't laugh. You would give the play your full attention!"

His audience, shamed into silence, obeyed; what the great Yankev Adler asked of them, they would do. When the third act curtain rose, instead of waiting grudgingly for songs and jokes, the audience settled into listening to the speeches, watching the actors' faces. They heard unfolding a story of injustice and persecution like their own; the wronged man on the stage could be an uncle or a grandfather still trapped in Russia. The story pulled them in, the tension growing, the time of crisis drawing close.

The actors, too, were swept into the drama. Actor Leon Blank remembers, "The scene where Adler begged Kessler not to betray him made a powerful impression. When Mogulescu as Shpendik came to the line, 'Master, we are parting,' he burst into real tears and could not go on. And the great artist played the scene in such a way that the whole audience wept with him."

That night the far-sighted Adler was proven right: this difficult, modern play brought forth a new depth and intensity of involvement, from both audience and actors. In his own actor's soul, a huge tragedic talent began to flower.

After the performance, Adler, Mogulescu, Kessler, and Feinman wrote a letter of apology to Gordin and searched him out in an East Side wine cellar. He was mollified and embraced, and at the theater the following night, "I became acquainted with my first-born dramatic child," as the father of nine put it.

"He came to the second performance," says Adler, "and was given a warm ovation from a house filled with his friends." Gordin, never guilty of playing down his own successes, said of his first attempt, "However bad *Siberia* might have been, I can say that for a beginning it was very good. And my first play was the dove that brought the news that the flood was over."

Unfortunately, the audience couldn't read the dove's message, not yet. The play ran only two weekends because of poor houses. "The press supported it," wrote Adler, "but the public did not come."

The press, however, was almost more important than the public at this juncture. And particularly one man of the press: the prickly, gimlet-eyed Abraham Cahan. The night *Siberia* opened was the night Cahan turned into a theater critic.

In his Russian youth, Cahan, trained as a teacher, was swept into the anarchist movement. Fearing arrest, he had fled to New York. The fiery young writer and editor immediately made his presence felt with a string of articles popularizing science, explaining socialist concepts, and exhorting generally. He also made a mark as a socialist rabble-rouser. At a meeting of strikers in Philadelphia, Cahan gave support to those on strike by attacking the strikebreakers. "Such girls should be laid down and flogged," he had seethed, "their flesh should be torn from them piece by piece . . . to remember forever not to scab for your bloodsuckers!"

Now it was time to share his thoughts about the performing arts. Drama criticism was second in importance only to editorials in New York's Yiddish newspapers, which contained, incidentally, no sports news at all. Cahan liked and praised *Siberia*, with reservations. "However great its shortcomings may be," he wrote, "it is still a talented and truly literary work. It stands alone among all the plays written specially for the Yiddish stage."

Instead of "second-hand Bowery melodrama," the actors had a play that "belongs to real literature." The critic was especially happy with the opportunity for artistic excellence that the play had granted the actors, praising Adler as "an exceptional artist" and "Madame . . . as well." The actor Feinman acted his small role better than previous roles in which he had starred, and Mogulescu, "also in a small role, almost without a joke or *shtik*, showed a God-given talent." The play, he wrote, would bring about a complete revolution on the Jewish stage.

The critic continued the next day on a less laudatory note, pointing out structural weaknesses, complaining that "in a few spots Adler starts to declaim like Othello," and criticizing the title *Siberia*, which he found overly sensational because nothing in the play actually takes place in that desolate locale. In his memoirs he reiterates, "If it were put on now, [*Siberia*] would be thought a melodrama, and a weak one, though very dramatic." But he wrapped up his second review with more words of praise and, as usual, exhortation. "Just present real life, speak like ordinary people, portray real problems," he urged, "and the plot alone will touch the finest strings of the Jewish soul. The uneducated Jew will understand. It will speak to his heart."

Gordin and Cahan together, Russian realist radicals in America, still intent on enlightening the peasant soul.

The Yiddish actors were intrigued by Adler's theatrical experiment, in which actors conversed naturally, as though they weren't onstage but at home. "Everyone was curious about the play," wrote Bessie Thomashefsky, "and even more curious about the new writer. There were different opinions about the play itself, but everyone agreed that Gordin was a man of intellect, a real judge of theater. Because of this some of the actors were frightened of him."

On November 22, some of Gordin's Spiritual Biblical brothers and sisters landed in New York City. To their shock, they found their leader working not on a farm but in a theater. Four days after their arrival, they were able to attend a benefit for the *Worker's Newspaper,* at which Mogulescu again performed "Pantole Polge," the monologue that had launched Gordin's new career.

In the meantime, the new playwright had written in one weekend a second play entitled *Tsvey velten, oder der groyser sotsyalist (Two Worlds, or The Great Socialist)* which Adler produced in early December. Though its success was even more limited than his first drama, Gordin brought forth a third. That is, only five months after stepping off the boat from Europe, a man who had never before written for the theater, or in Yiddish, had already had two groundbreaking plays produced in the Yiddish theater and had written the next.

Deciding not to take the new work, Adler mounted instead a piece of popular *shund,* to give both actors and audience a rest. There was no rest for the playwright.

Gordin took his third play to the Thomashefskys at the Rumanian Opera House at 104-106 Bowery. Silky-voiced, jovial Boris Thomashefsky was now the most popular actor on the East Side, adored as a matinee idol. One writer of the time, not as besotted as the shop girls, described Boris as "a listless barnstormer . . . a large fat man, with expressionless features and curly black hair, which he arranges in leonine form." Bessie Thomashefsky also excelled at comedy and music, though she, like her husband, had an as-yet unexploited talent for more profound and challenging work.

Script under his arm, Gordin stood waiting, ignored, at the Rumanian while the Thomashefskys rehearsed until an actor recognized him and cried, "That's no *yold,* that's Jacob Gordin!" *Yold,* Yiddish for "fool," was the insider's nickname for an inexperienced playwright. Bessie writes, "A moment later Gordin walks in, a tall, thin broad-shouldered man with a handsome face, deep eyes, a beautifully combed head of thick curly dark hair, a dark flowing beard, a neat, shabby dark suit, a wide-brimmed black hat, a walking stick. He wants to sell us a play."

Jacob Gordin in 1895.

He was carrying only a child's small notebook, and Moishe Finkel, who was directing the Thomashefskys, scoffed, "Is that all?" Gordin looked him up and down. "It's enough" was his retort. He read them the play. The Thomashefskys listened, whispered, and decided to buy it. Penniless Gordin was offered a generous sum as payment—$60. He replied, "If you play it just as I wrote it, yes."

A problem, immediately: the small but important role of the *pristav*, the Russian policeman, obviously required an actor who would speak the lines as written, in Russian. Thomashefsky had to admit that there wasn't a single Russian-speaking actor in his troupe, and he proposed that they cast a Pole. Or failing that, a talented young actor who—one minor detail—spoke only Yiddish. "Imagine," snapped Gordin, "a Russian policeman who opens his mouth and speaks Yiddish. How realistic!" He wouldn't hear of it.

Thomashefsky offered the part to Gordin himself, for five dollars a week. Joking that a man with eleven pairs of shoes to buy couldn't turn anything down, the writer accepted the job. In fact, he wanted to be at rehearsals anyway. The productions of his first two plays had taught the new playwright that Yiddish actors thought of writers merely as springboards for their own imaginative turns of phrase and flights of fancy. The primacy of the playwright's work was a concept unknown thus far in the brief history of the Yiddish theater. He wanted to safeguard his words.

He also wanted this production to be truly realistic, with no fantasy or melodrama or self-indulgent, absurd bits of shtik added in. Jacob Gordin made trouble at each rehearsal of *Der pogrom (The Pogrom in Russia)*. He was involved in every decision, insisting on authenticity of detail. The actors playing peasants were made to wear realistic rags instead of charming tatters. They wanted a song? The author added a folk song that might actually have been sung at the time. When the director tried to insert a comic song and dance in the first act, Gordin picked up his script and stalked out of the theater, until he was brought back with promises that the troupe would obey his orders. Most of all, he insisted his lines be spoken as written and forbade impromptu asides and ad-libs to the audience, already one of the most beloved traditions of the Yiddish performer.

On opening night, the audience was unlike any the Thomashefskys had yet welcomed to their Opera House. Tonight had brought in force the Russian intellectuals who had always despised the lightweight capers and *kuplets*—rhyming songs—on the Yiddish stage. Sitting beside the cloakmakers and the peddlers were august socialist minds like Philip Krantz, Louis Miller, and Abraham Cahan. They had come to see the Thomashefskys attempt realism, and they had come to enjoy the stage debut of their friend the Russian *literat*.

The play went well until midway through the second act, when it was time for Gordin to make his entrance. The man was not an actor, and the pressure of opening night was torment; he was pale and rigid in his handsome Russian uniform. He heard his cue; the Jewish housewife, played by matronly Bina Abramowitz, said the lines about hearing that *pristav* skulking about. Gordin lifted his fist and knocked on the set; the door opened. He had dreaded this moment; the lights were dizzying, there was such a crowd . . . and suddenly, as he stepped onto the stage, he heard a deafening noise. The audience was applauding him, calling his name! He stood frozen at the door, with Bina's false smile of welcome fading from her face as she watched him struggle to remember his lines. From behind the flats, he heard Thomashefsky's concerned whisper: "Gordin! Friend Gordin!"

His memory flew back; he stepped into the bright room with its terrifying fourth wall of faces and spoke his own words in rolling Russian. Bina's smile returned. In the scene, she had to placate the feared and hated policeman by offering him food and wine. Duly she said, "Good day, Herr Pristav; perhaps a little something to eat and drink?"

"I could eat a wolf, Olga Borisovna," growled Gordin.

"No wolves today, I have only schnapps and herring!" trilled Bina, laying out the prop food and drink. And now the actress couldn't resist. Such an opportunity—how could she turn it down? Besides, Gordin was pretending to drink; he wouldn't notice. She stole close to the footlights and, winking to the house, she ad-libbed behind her hand, "May he choke on it!" There was a huge laugh.

Suddenly, a noise behind her. She whirled around. The Russian policeman had leapt to his feet, knocking over his schnapps. His face was beet red, he was pounding his fist on the table, and he was glaring right at her. "Stop it right now!" shouted the *pristav,* still pounding. "That is not in the script! STICK TO THE SCRIPT!"

After his first acting experience, which was also his last, Gordin went back to writing. And the Thomashefskys, for the time being, returned to *shund.* "It was a pleasure to do a fine play with artistic dialogue," Bessie writes, "but the real supporters of theater, the great, almighty public, did not come."

Five months later, on June 28, 1892, Jacob Adler and Jacob Gordin signed a contract binding them together indefinitely. Adler had founded a troupe, the Union Theatrical Company, with "the aim of driving from the Yiddish stage all that is crude, unclean and immoral" and presenting to the public "only beautiful musical operas and dramas giving truthful and serious portrayals of life." What theater in the world could sustain this exalted credo?

The core company consisted of the Adlers, the actress Keni Lipzin, and Gordin. Adler was to be lead actor, "stage manager and régisseur," his wife Sara the "first leading Prima Donna," and Lipzin the "first leading lady (dramatic parts)." Mogulescu, Kessler, and others, convinced that Adler was condemning them all to bankruptcy, had fled to join the *shund* playwright Hurwitz at the National Theater. Jacob Gordin was contracted to be the Union Company playwright, "to write a suitable play at the rate of one per month." That is, an original four- or five-act play giving truthful and serious portrayals of life, and tailored to specific actors with specific dramatic requirements, every four weeks.

Presumably my great-grandfather was doing nothing but write, a solitary life for a family man who had lived nearly twenty years with an accommodating spouse and a passel of children. Lonely dislocation was the fate of married men who emigrated before their families, their solitude more acute than that of the unwed. It happened not infrequently that by the time a man's wife got off the boat she found her husband transformed, uncomfortable with her old-country naïveté and involved with an Americanized woman who had kept him company through the days and nights.

But it was unthinkable that my great-grandfather had permitted himself that kind of impropriety. He was a man noted for sexual self-control; Great-Aunt Helen brought the subject up one day, unbidden. "There was an actor who hated Papa and wanted to smear his name in revenge," she told me. "He looked and looked for some scandal to throw at him, and couldn't find any. You think, such a fine handsome man, surrounded by actresses, beautiful young women willing to lie down for him in a minute. But he never touched one."

In *Portraits of Eleven,* writer Melech Epstein confirms Helen's story: "The actors respected and feared him. Their respect was heightened by Gordin's aloofness from the opposite sex in the theater. A man of undeniable passion, the playwright, dedicated to his new calling, steered clear of becoming involved in affairs with the young attractive actresses whom he helped to stardom."

Sara Adler, used to trembling adulation from admirers, found Gordin "different from any man I've ever known." Though she thought him the handsomest man she had ever seen, she noted that he looked at her without desire, making her feel like a ten-year-old. "The man is all brain," she concluded, "and in his mighty breast flickers not a spark of romance and love."

She was wrong. Early in my research, my "Author's Query" about Gordin was printed in the *New York Times Book Review,* and I received a reply that painted a different picture. "In response to your note about Jacob

Gordin I can offer the following—my grandmother Jennie had a very intense affair with him," I read, incredulous.

> She was part of a group of followers of Tolstoy and that may have been
> how they met. She left her husband and took her young child to be with
> him. The story told to me by her and my mother (her daughter) was: He
> got her a box seat at the opening of one of his plays that he said was writ-
> ten for her. The message in the play was clear. He was urging her to return
> to her husband. This she did. I think his wife was coming over here at that
> time.

My correspondent, an elderly teacher, told me that her grandmother
never got over this romance, although it was not her only one. "I may still
have a photograph of Gordin in his coffin," she wrote, though it transpired
that she did not. "Sadly in her later years when she probably had
Alzheimer's, the only way my grandfather could keep her calm was by listening to her talk about Gordin."

"A very intense affair"? The Tolstoy group sounded right, but the rest
did not. I wrote back in a cautious yet encouraging tone, asking her for
specifics, and finishing, "Is it sure that their affair was sexual, and not the
love of teacher and student, or leader and follower?"

The letter writer blasted me with her reply. I wanted him to be "pure
and God-like," she chided, when he had "cheated on his wife and then
chickened out." Her grandmother had had numerous affairs, though
Gordin was probably her first lover. "She made it clear that she was with
him three years until his wife came. I want you to know, Beth, that my
grandmother never spoke of Gordin except in the most glowing loving
terms. She justified his every act in a most romantic way. She loved him
and I think he was the only man she ever loved. Life, she felt, forced him
into what many of us saw as 'wrong behaviour.' She saw his return to his
wife and children as an act of honorable duty."

This was the truth, obviously; still I found it hard to believe. My stern
great-grandfather, nearly forty and the father of nine, living with a married
twenty-year-old woman and her young child Minnie, with no report of the
affair anywhere—was it possible? Jennie's little Minnie was the exact age
of Gordin's daughter Nadia, my grandmother, far away in Russia. The
teacher told me that when Minnie later married the Yiddish poet and nov-

elist David Ignatoff, a dark-eyed young man of literary talent and sultry good looks, Jennie was jealous that her daughter had been able to claim a writer, as she had not.

David Ignatoff wrote a book called *Af vayte vegn (Pathways Far Away)* based on the Tolstoy circle of which Jennie was leader and Gordin an important member. My correspondent told me that her grandmother found the book so uncompromisingly true to life, she wanted to sue the author, her son-in-law.

In the very long book, Jennie and her husband become the Feinmans, part of a circle of Russians who want to live communally and mend their own shoes in the Tolstoy way. They also drink and party wildly, and practice free love. "Men and women would mix in every way. There were no rules. They were poor and lonely, with nothing to hold onto other than their own bodies or the one nearest them. To them the body was everything. After these revels they'd wake the next day, or two days later, on the floor amid the empty bottles, or on the table, or under the table."

"Fania Feinman's respect for a Russian revolutionary was without bounds," Ignatoff writes about his mother-in-law as a young woman. "It was a gift to give herself to a true revolutionary." When I read this passage, I appreciated Jennie's urge to sue.

Gordin appears as Frankl, for whom the circle arranged an evening of welcome on his arrival in New York. The newcomer was touched to find such an idealistic gathering, like "a breath of his beloved Russia," living an almost communist life in capitalist America. "Frankl was an enthusiast, but also a bit pedantic," wrote Ignatoff. "Everything had to have a name and a logical explanation. He gave the circle a name—Torn Leaves." (During a trip to Europe toward the end of his life, Gordin told his audience, "Anyone who arrives [in America] without a good friend will be lost like a leaf in a forest.")

> When Frankl came to Feinman's the women begged him to tell his story, which he did to hushed silence and attention. All the questions and talk were in Russian, because that was the language closest to their hearts. Gabriel [a Russian revolutionary and Mme. Feinman's lover] soon cried out, "Frankl . . . these beautiful women are giving you their attention and you're just giving them a lot of talk!"
>
> Frankl blushed and realized he'd carried on too long . . . After some discussion and a few drinks, all . . . carried on kissing and drinking.

Madame Feinman threw her arms around Frankl and kissed him. The group carried him on their shoulders, shouting, singing and dancing, "Look what Russia and the sea has sent us—a Frankl who gave us a name!" More beer, more wine. Then they sang sad Russian songs and became more and more homesick. Later Shaliapnikov recited a long poem by Pushkin.

There, a vivid portrait of transplanted Russians, including my great-grandfather about to begin an affair with a married woman almost half his age. Interestingly, the couple had the tacit approval of her husband, who was involved in affairs of his own. This was an era of revolutionary change; these young people were socialists or anarchists, nihilists or populists, secularists, freethinkers, rationalists. They were atheists who believed with Nietzsche that God was dead; they were agnostics who didn't know what to believe any more, except in free love and the equal rights of women, and in discarding the 613 commandments that had bound them since birth.

In my correspondent's long letters and in the book, Jennie emerges as an astonishingly modern woman, forthright and open-minded. The young mother was a voracious reader who spoke fluent English and knew her way around New York. Later she taught herself to play the piano, then wrote a play and tried to have it produced; her attractiveness to a creative man alone in a strange land is understandable. The story about Gordin's message to her through a new play is also possible. His play *The Brothers Luria*, in which Romeo-and-Juliet-like young lovers are thwarted and kept apart by a family feud, opened in 1894, around the time Anna and the children arrived from Russia.

Even so, I wasn't convinced about the affair until some handwritten letters from the YIVO files were translated from Russian. One of them, headed "Highly esteemed Yakov Mikhailovich," turned out to be from a woman desperately, almost pathetically in love with Gordin. After beginning, "Your play is wonderful," she continues coolly for a line or two, discussing *The Brothers Luria*, which she adored except for "one thing that bothers me, the Luria brothers in your play speak in a Middle German dialect," though in reality "ordinary Russian Jews don't know this German jargon and the intelligentsia prefer to speak Russian."

After this bit of criticism, she writes that she has seen the play many times, and each time her admiration of the daughter's character grows, because the daughter loves so powerfully.

> When women love strongly and sincerely, nothing can stop them, they fear nothing. I know every woman has a time in her life when she would give her blood, drop by drop, to her beloved. Not expecting anything, aware of the fact that she is not loved and will never be loved.
>
> Take me, for example. It is painful for me to realize that not only do you not love me, but that you are avoiding me, you don't want to see me. Nevertheless I continue to love you passionately, slavishly. I want to be near you, to breathe the same air as you. When I saw you in the publishing office, I envied the pencil you were holding in your hand. I envied your desk. I want to do everything for you. I want you to think about me.
>
> I can bear anything, even hate from you, but not indifference. Oh Yasha, Yasha! Is it always going to be this way? Don't I even have a little bit of hope? I'm ready to wait weeks, months, even years. Why are you avoiding me? I'm not asking you to sacrifice anything. I don't want to become your wife. Am I despicable to you? I'm young, healthy, not ugly. You're so kind and generous to others. Yasha, Yashinka! You are my eagle! Please stop your coldness toward me. Love me, love me! At least a tiny bit. You can do anything you want with me, but don't push me away. Yasha, Yasha, pity me!

A second letter is so faded it is hard to decipher, but again, she expresses an almost incoherent love.

> I want so much to stand behind your chair and watch you write. I want to read your thoughts and live through your ideas. Don't judge me too harshly. You yourself told me that I am too young and romantic . . . Yakov Mikhailovich, what is the purpose of it all, why me? Why have I been cheated by destiny? Yakov Mikhailovich, my dear, my kind one, my blood. Come to me. Do not refuse my request. I promise, I give my word, that I will not cross the boundary of friendship, but that I will be a good, good girl. Just to look into those black, wonderful, sunny, bright, smiling, sparkling eyes! Let me! Give me just one more time. Tell me yes!

I almost blushed upon first reading of these missives, so heated, intimate, and revealing. Then I noticed that the ardent writer signed herself not "Jennie" but "Marussia." Could the man have had more than one young lover? Surely not. Perhaps Marussia—literally, "my Russia"—was Jennie's Russian name, or nickname, although her granddaughter had never heard it.

I wonder, did my great-grandfather use this woman to keep him company at a lonely time and cold-heartedly abandon her when she became redundant? I do not think so. The fact of his familial responsibilities cannot have been a surprise to her; he could and would not have concealed the wife and huge number of children he was saving to import. It's more likely that he loved her but knew that when his family sailed into the harbor he would have to push her away. In most of his plays, marital love leads to wretchedness if not to murder; true love is found outside of any legal bond. His heroines are often vehement, freethinking intellectuals and fighters, who are certainly not fashioned after his wife.

But why did he, or someone, carefully preserve these tormented notes for a great-granddaughter to read a hundred years later?

• • •

Mistress or no, Gordin had deadlines, one opening night after another. It is not surprising that this is the point at which he took up his lifelong habit of adapting the work of other playwrights for the Yiddish stage, including two plays by Goldfaden, though it is hard to imagine how or why he adapted plays that were already in Yiddish. In any case, they were not successful. Next, in one of the bravest leaps of his career, he set out to write a play based on what some feel is William Shakespeare's greatest work. Gordin's version was called, simply, *Der yidisher kenig lir (The Jewish King Lear)*.

Scene by scene, Gordin transposes Shakespeare's tragedy to a middle-class Russian-Jewish setting. An aging merchant, David Moisheles, decides to entrust his wealth to one of his sons-in-law in order to follow his dream of retiring to the Holy Land. His two older daughters, groveling housewives pretending to be pious, profess great love for him; the youngest, a Russian radical who wants to go to medical school, is disinherited for her honesty. Her rationalist lover warns the old man of his folly by telling him the story of King Lear.

In the second act, the greedy custodian of the estate denies his relatives money, and by the third the Yiddish Lear has had to return from Jerusalem because his son-in-law has not sent the promised funds. In a towering rage, he demands the return of his keys, but, remembering that he has given the two faithless daughters his word as well as his fortune, he hurls the great keys back to them with a curse. Before long he is not only a beggar but blind. His youngest tries to care for him, but, unable to bear the truth about his folly, he gives way to madness, and accompanied by his faithful servant he gropes his way offstage, crying, "Alms, alms for the Yiddish King Lear!"

Unlike the seminal work and most of Gordin's other plays, there is a happy resolution. In act 4, he finds shelter in the home of his loving daughter, and as the curtain descends he is assured of the return both of his eyesight and his estate.

In his autobiography, the fledgling actor Boaz Young, who was just starting work with Adler's company, describes the first reading of the play in Poole's beer hall next to the Union Theater, formerly called Poole's Theater. The troupe sat around a table while Adler read the play aloud. (Today at a first reading, thanks to copy machines, all the actors read their roles from their own script. In Gordin's day there was only one script, read by the star or playwright.)

> When Adler finished reading, and the troupe was leaving the saloon, I heard Bernstein joke, "What will I do in that play? Catch flies? Ha!"
>
> Tobachnikoff was beside himself.
>
> "Is this what Adler brought me to America for? I haven't even a spot to sing a number. And what kind of part is that for Adler? Some ordinary old Jew in a long coat and a *yarmulke* ..."
>
> "It'll be on the boards from Friday to Saturday," another joked.
>
> All complained to Vilenski, the director. Vilenski, who had already had a few years of experience with plays, was the only one of the troupe who saw that Adler would perform wonderfully in the role.
>
> "I tell you that it will play many weeks; we just have to change the name. But unfortunately the Jew with the black beard won't allow us to change the name."
>
> He meant Jacob Gordin.

Sara Adler picks up the tale. "The complaints of the cast soon died away. It was clear from the first rehearsal that Adler was going to do something extraordinary with this part. Everyone caught the spirit. And if any of us clung to the old bad way, striving for cheap laughter, cheap effects, it only reminded us how great was the change taking place before our eyes."

She doesn't mention that the play nearly closed before it opened. Just before the premiere, she and her husband fought about suspected mutual infidelities. When Sara, playing the youngest daughter, decided to quit the production, Adler became ill to the point of breakdown. Gordin, desperate, intervened, speaking so eloquently to Sara that he convinced her to come with him to talk to her husband. Peace was made, and Sara agreed to stay.

On opening night, just after the curtain rose, the audience took in a breathtaking image: the merchant David Moisheles, wearing a traditional long coat and Hasidic hat trimmed with fur on the festival of Purim, sitting at the head of a long table surrounded by a large entourage of friends, retainers, and daughters. Sara writes that when the audience saw her husband as Gordin's king, "From the orchestra to the gallery, the theater crashed! . . . His part had 'taken' before he spoke a word. He was not an actor that night, he was a force. All of us played with inspiration, but the great figure that night Gordin had given to Adler, and the triumph was his own. It was equaled only by the thunder that filled the house at the end of the third act, when Gordin took his bow."

Gordin's play had a profound impact on the Lower East Side. In one much told story, a distraught playgoer was so swept into the drama that after a tragic scene he ran down the aisle toward the stage, shouting that Adler should leave his heartless daughters and come home with him. Young people, witnessing the degradation of the elderly man, were stricken with remorse about their own parents. It is another famous legend that local bankers knew which nights the play was being performed because early the next morning, youths afflicted with guilt were lined up at the banks, waiting to send money home.

Gordin had hit an exposed nerve: in immigrant families, conflict between the generations was the most painful and insoluble of problems. Children who had behaved with proper deference in the old country became alarmingly irreverent and rebellious in the new; they tried to acclimatize to a vastly freer capitalist culture while their parents tried to enforce the old ways. Like King Canute ordering back the tides, Gordin was to thunder at this theme again and again, insisting on respect for the wisdom and experience of the elders. Boaz Young describes the effect of his message on the audience: the play "was on the lips of all classes of Jews in New York. Fathers brought their children, so that they would learn the moral lessons. Hundreds of thank you notes were sent to Adler by Jewish mothers; their Sammys and Morrises had become better children since seeing the play."

A few years later, *Harper's Weekly*, one of the first English-language magazines to take note of the Yiddish theater, reviewed a production with almost the same cast. The favorable notice praises the Adlers and the smaller parts as well, singling out Mogulescu as the Fool: "His grotesque nonsense affords a comic underplot to the saddest scene, precisely as in Shakspere's [*sic*] 'Lear' . . . I have much consolation in Shakspere *à la Yid.*" The writer continues:

> It lacks the colossal grandeur of the true Shaksperean play, the splendor of Shakspere's diction, and the infinite wisdom of Shakspere's characterization. Yet this primitive "Lear" of the Ghetto has a certain Shaksperean quality that no one would dare to hope for in a Broadway theater. Its costume and scenery are as simple and unobtrusive as were those of the original play as presented at the Globe; and the audience of Jewish tailors and shopkeepers is as whole-hearted, and no doubt quite as keen and imaginative, as an audience in the little world of Elizabethan London. If anyone wants to know what our best plays seemed like to the people for whom they were written, he will find much satisfaction. . . .

Jacob Adler's granddaughter Lulla Rosenfeld, in childhood, saw her grandfather play the role, and she remembered "anger like crashes of thunder, scenes mounting in epic strokes . . . That cry of pain, that *'Shenkt a neduve der Yidisher Kenig Lir'*—'Alms—alms for the Yiddish King Lear!'— echoes still across the gulf of fifty years or more."

Adler owned the exclusive rights and continued to play the role for almost thirty years, until the very end of his career. Even after suffering a debilitating stroke, he made appearances at benefits to perform the first act, in which he could remain seated throughout. In his memoirs, he asserts that the play "was then and still remains the greatest success of the Yiddish theater."

Despite this first popular triumph, Gordin didn't think of himself as an American playwright, but still as a Russian group leader, farmer, and newspaperman-to-be. In March 1893, in an office at 204 East Broadway, he and his friends Alexander Evalenko and Dr. George M. Price founded *Russkii Novosty (Russian News)*, its banner: "The only Russian weekly newspaper in the country." Dedicated to "the interests of truth, humanity and freedom," the periodical gave Russian immigrants news of the local Russian colony and of home. Evalenko was the publisher, and Gordin was paid $10 a week "to be and act as an Editor"; for that amount he wrote nearly the whole newspaper by himself until he couldn't afford to any longer. He still had not accepted the fact that few Russian Jews were, as he was, nostalgic for the Russian language, or even fluent in it. Most immigrants from the Pale spoke Yiddish in the streets, were learning English as fast as possible, and didn't want to hear Russian ever again. *Russian News* was the first of several Gordin ventures into the world of newspapers, all of them ultimately unsuccessful.

He did not succeed, either, in his ongoing attempt to find farmland. Also early in 1893, he and his followers were set to join the thriving five-thousand-acre Baron de Hirsch agricultural colony in Woodbine, New Jersey. Gordin and the head of the settlement, Professor Sabsovich, had an amicable meeting about the allocation of land for the Biblical Brothers. When Sabsovich took the group on a tour of the farm, however, Gordin discovered that all the Brotherhood members were expected to live in central dormitories and go to shul with the other settlers. But his group must live apart from the others, Gordin insisted, and would not attend the synagogue. Sabsovich rescinded his offer, Gordin returned to the city, and his flock, some of whom had already started work at Woodbine, were thrown once again on their own resources. That is the last we hear of moving back to the land—although a subsequent letter to Gordin from a friend in Russia asked hopefully, "Have your agricultural projects taken off, and the livestock raising?"

On May 1, 1893, my great-grandfather confronted his fortieth birthday with his two intended careers in disarray: the Russian newspaper was failing and, without a farm, he had no pastoral flock to lead. But as well as his prolific play and short-story writing—Gordin wrote scores of short stories in America—another career had opened up: he was now working steadily as a lecturer. Throughout his life, he often spoke publicly about the history of the Yiddish theater, the lives of writers and playwrights, or about his own work. On December 21 he gave a talk entitled "About Shakespeare and My 'Yiddish King Lear,' " in which he told of a conversation with an elderly audience member after one performance.

"It was a good play, just like life," said the old man, who didn't recognize his companion.

"Thank you," replied Gordin.

"Why are you thanking me?" said the man.

"Because I'm the author. I wrote it," said Gordin.

"Why did you have to *write* it?" queried the man, puzzled; to him, the actors were simply living their lives upon the stage. Gordin fast became a popular and much-followed lecturer, although he was not a great speaker, and on occasion the scholars and intellectuals in his audience knew more about the subject than he. They listened in respectful silence, a friend of his wrote, "because it was Gordin."

Adler had moved from the Union Theater to the National Theater on the Bowery, also known as the Rumanian Opera House, where the Thomashefskys had reigned. (Bessie and Boris had moved to the 2,500-seat People's Theater, on the Bowery between Rivington and Delancey.) Though Gordin could not continue to provide a play a month, his work was still appearing quickly and steadily. Exactly as he had done the year before, after a string of failures including a potboiler named *Der mord in medison evenyu (Murder on Madison Avenue)*, Gordin produced a hit in November, a play one writer called his "first original masterpiece." *Der vilder mentsh (The Wild Man)* was another triumph for both writer and star, and this time for Mogulescu as well, not as an actor but as a composer. By now Gordin understood the need for music in the plays and always incorporated musical occasions like weddings and holiday parties into his scripts.

The story is gothic, filled with horror: the wild man is Lemach, an epileptic boy born with a damaged mind, a combination of the writer's own children Sonia and Semyon. Lemach, a sensitive innocent, has been brutalized throughout his life because of his disjointed, erratic behavior and truthtelling. In a speech very like Shylock's, he cries to his tormentors, "You think if you strike me it doesn't hurt? You think if you laugh at me I don't feel it? Look—when I cry, I shed tears just like yours."

His mother is dead and his loutish father has recently remarried, the young wife a "loose woman" who brings her pimp lover into the house. The good daughter, played by Sara Adler, is turned out into the street, although she has no skills with which to earn a living. As the family disintegrates, the wild man goes mad; no one understands that he has fallen in love with his dissolute stepmother. He confesses his love to her, and, crying "Father! Father, I have married!" he stabs her to death.

I wonder if this fraught play wasn't, at a subliminal level, Gordin's conscience torturing him for the affair in which he was then embroiled. He presents an irresponsible, lascivious boor carrying on with a woman half his age and thereby forever harming his children, including an unloved son with a damaged mind just like Sema far away in Russia. Was my great-grandfather putting a hidden, perhaps unconscious judgment of himself on the stage?

Adler was brilliant as the brain-damaged boy. Of his work in *The Wild Man*, American critic and Yiddish theater fan Hutchins Hapgood wrote, "Adler's portraiture of the idiot is a great bit of technical acting. The poor fellow is filled with the mysterious wonderings of an incapable mind. His shadow terrifies and interests him." Like *Lear*, *The Wild Man* remained Adler's exclusive property until his death (although this legality was meaningless to actors and theater managers; the play was pirated and performed around the world, as were many of Gordin's works.) According to Adler, "After the success of *The Wild Man* every star followed the new trend. Kessler, Lipzin, the new idol Bertha Kalish—everyone clamored for Gordin. He was the man of the hour, the voice of a new Yiddish theater."

Cahan gave the play a relatively good review. "The scenes are well put together . . . one sits absorbed and impressed," he wrote warmly, though his jab that "three-quarters of the play smacks of Lateiner" would have drawn Gordin's blood. His rivals Hurwitz and especially Lateiner, though popular, were writers without subtlety or integrity who "baked" plays like buns in a bakery. When actors who had appeared in past Lateiner plays were cast in a new one, they didn't have to memorize lines; they just learned the general outline of the plot and winged it because the lines were always the same. Gordin despised Lateiner, who despised right back.

In 1894 Adler was still at the National and Gordin's plays were still flying from his pen, including *The Children Are Leaving*, a comedy in four acts; its subjects are listed on a drama Web site as "melodrama, Russia-Bessarabia, anti-Semitism, interfaith marriage, Jewish folk beliefs, Jewish-Gentile relations." In May Gordin's one-act play *Yokel der opern makher (Yokl the Opera Maker)*, satirizing contemporary playwrights, was produced as a benefit for him. From Monday to Thursday night, benefits were big business in the Yiddish theater; benevolent associations, unions, *landsmanshaft* organizations would buy the whole house, play included, for $175 to $225 and sell tickets for an inflated amount to raise money. Occasionally the event was organized by and for a worthy actor or even writer; in May it was Gordin. What was the occasion? I think the Lower East Side was helping him prepare for the arrival of his wife and children.

Anna and seven of the Gordin children arrived on Ellis Island by the end of June 1894, almost three years after the hurried departure of their patriarch. Twenty-year-old Liza was left in Europe with Sema, seventeen, to come later on their own, probably due to concern that Sema would be barred from America because of his mental handicap. Being rejected and turned back was the greatest nightmare for immigrants. Later the list of reasons for exclusion was extensive, but in 1894 a new arrival could be denied entry only for cholera, trachoma, scalp fungus, insanity, and—the source of the Gordins' anxiety—mental impairments. Liza and Sema subsequently made it through, possibly by traveling in luxurious cabin class and thereby avoiding the scrutiny of immigration officers.

Immigration files for certain early years were lost in a fire on Ellis Island; I know the approximate date of my great-grandmother's journey not through steamship receipts or official records but because the tenth Gordin child, Leo or Leon Benjamin, was born in New York City on March 31, 1895. He grew up to be the jolliest of the tribe, a humorous if vulgar *luftmentsh*, a man with no visible means of support, living on air. And I, the nosy great-granddaughter, ponder why Leon is the only one of eleven Gordin offspring to be conceived in the five warm months between May and September. My guess is that the Gordins spent part of their Russian summers in a dacha, a summerhouse that consisted often of one big room with no privacy; or else Anna and the children were in the country while Gordin labored in town. But in June 1894 Yakov and Aneuta were reunited in America, and privacy did not matter.

Quiet, *zaftik*—pleasantly rotund—underrated Aneuta, now thirty-five, had kept the family going in Russia by returning to her parents. What can it have been like, after nearly two decades of marriage, to move back home with eight children and a newborn baby, and to stay there for three years? Then Anna shepherded her brood, ranging in age from two to twenty-two, from central Ukraine to a port in northern Europe. In *The Promised Land*, author Mary Antin, who made the journey at the same time, describes the turmoil and desperation in transit, the terror of women at the mercy of a succession of immigration and shipping-line officials. At least Jewish immigrant-aid societies were now functioning effectively in the ports to help ease the passage. Was it they who persuaded Aneuta to leave two of her brood behind and sail with only seven?

I picture my shy, bewildered great-grandmother on Ellis Island, loaded down with bulky parcels of feather bedding and the old family samovar, staring at the promising statue, dealing mutely with barking officials, exhausted children, and the tedious, petrifying lineups—her desperate anticipation and fear. Many wives coming off the boat didn't recognize their husbands, who had shaved off their beards and put on natty American suits and hats. An acclimatized husband and a greenhorn wife looked at each other from different centuries.

But there he was, the man she had loved since girlhood, not waiting with the crowd beyond the gates but allowed inside to claim his family— her Yasha, tall, austere, still bearded and dark-suited. He looked just the same, but now he was a playwright, a success in the Yiddish theater, what to make of that! The younger children didn't remember him; Grisha the youngest had never even met his father.

Did Gordin have mixed feelings as he watched his multifold tribe approaching, or was he simply glad to be a family man again? My guess is that gladness or regret did not enter his mind. Here came his wife and children, the responsibilities he would shoulder to the best of his abilities, as men did.

In anticipation of this arrival, he had moved far north, from his last room on the Lower East Side—20 Jefferson Street—to a tenement on East 109th in the former Dutch enclave of Harlem. Obviously he needed a much larger place to house his children. Perhaps, too, there was someone he needed to leave far behind. Because at this time came the opening of his Romeo and Juliet play, *Der litvishe brider luria (The Brothers Luria)*, which was called in one review "a memorial to old-fashioned Jewish life," and which provoked a certain young woman to a tempestuous and despairing letter.

The Brothers Luria, which starred Thomashefsky and Keni Lipzin, may have been based on facts about an actual wealthy Russian-Jewish industrialist family called the Lurias, or the name may have been another of

Gordin's provocative titles guaranteed to catch his audience's eye. The two Luria brothers, one rich and one poor, continue for decades to fight viciously over an inheritance while behind their backs the son of one and the daughter of the other fall in love. When the girl falls deathly ill because of the family tension, her father and uncle make peace, and the children are united.

Again, the play features an insensitive, overbearing father, a bully to his wife and to his daughter, whom he tries to force into marriage with a feckless youth whom she hates. The theme of the play is one of Gordin's most constant: he is in favor of the simple life and against wealth. As the wise rebbe says in the play, "If we can eliminate the superfluous and have just enough to satisfy our frugal needs, with a little extra to contribute to charity—that's supreme happiness." Gordin's and Tolstoy's supreme happiness, at any rate.

Frugal Jacob Gordin the union sympathizer and tight-fisted Jacob Adler the actor-manager were now locked in struggle. Most Yiddish actors were paid not at a flat rate but by share; when the company fared badly, the actors suffered the consequences, and presumably they enjoyed the good times along with management. But when Gordin's hits produced sizeable crowds night after night and still the actors' pay did not improve, they went out on strike against Adler. Gordin went with them, though the play that was shut down was his own. An ad in the *Worker's Newspaper* read, "FRIENDS!! DON'T GO TO THE ADLER THEATER! THE WHOLE COMPANY IS ON STRIKE! Read the newspapers! Soon there will be an announcement of a play from the author JACOB GORDIN which we'll present, and also the location. Don't Go to a Scab Theater! The committee."

There cannot be many playwrights who have gone on strike against their own play. Gordin organized a benefit for the actors at the Thalia Theater and asked for public support. But this time the battle was lost, and actors and playwright returned to work. In the spring of 1895, Gordin wrote a new play for Adler, *Der Rusisher yid in Amerike (A Russian Jew in America)*, his most openly political play to date, and the first about Jewish political life in America.

At this time of depression, unemployment, and labor troubles, all leftist activists were involved not only in the creation of political parties— Daniel De Leon's Socialist Labor Party and Eugene V. Debs's Social

Democratic Party—but also in the push to create and legalize unions. A movement organizing solidarity of employees against bosses was desperately needed on the Lower East Side, where ruthless abuse of workers in sweatshops and factories—and theaters—was endemic. But Gordin, a full supporter of the union struggle, had become increasingly concerned about the one aspect of the movement no one else wanted to address: he felt that some organizers were greedy hypocrites, pretending to care for the workingman while working to enrich only themselves. In his scathing new play, he created among other corrupt types the character of an opportunistic union official called Huzdak. This by a writer whose audience was filled with fellow unionists, guaranteed to be offended by the portrayal of a union crook.

Many were indeed offended, none more so than Abraham Cahan. Seated in the Windsor Theater on opening night, Cahan couldn't control himself when he heard Huzdak's smug and damning line, "What do I need brains for, when I've got a [union] constitution?" The critic jumped to his feet in fury, and shouting in Russian, *"Eto lozh!"* ("It is a lie!") he pushed his way out of the theater.

Cahan and Gordin tackled each other promptly on the pages of the *Worker's Newspaper.* Cahan actually praised *A Russian Jew:* "a true slice-of-life," he wrote, "that can hold its own among the best plays presented for the most intellectual section of the American public." He liked some of the characters, "so lifelike, so artistically drawn that their every word fosters in the playgoer deep, ethical pleasure." These realistic portraits prove the real excellence of Gordin's work, he wrote. He admired the simple honesty of Adler as the Russian Jew, and of Sara Adler as the daughter, saying, "This is the best role in which she has ever appeared."

The trouble was Huzdak. Gordin was describing only "the wormy apple, only the callousness of union members," presenting the negative side of unions "without a ray of hope for the listeners." At same time, Cahan complained, in order to celebrate the good life in the United States the writer showed a most unlikely thing—a humane judge and jury.

"A real artist," concluded Cahan sternly, "has no right to be a friend or enemy of his subject. He may only be a friend of the truth, and an enemy of one-sidedness."

Gordin replied in a similarly restrained tone to Cahan's "useful and learned remarks." With Huzdak, he explained, he is demonstrating to his audience the critical intelligence with which they should approach membership in unions; real union men with ideals and principles understand the purpose of the union movement. He disagreed vehemently with Cahan's assertion that an artist must remain aloof from the subject of his plays. As a writer with beliefs, compassion, and "a heart to hate suffering," he must write the truth as he understands it, "to awaken feelings of contempt for that which I hate, and sympathy and respect for that which pleases me."

He finished with a jab of his own: "When I read Cahan's decree—an artist has no right to see only the dark side but must also see the light—I said to myself that my friend Mr. Cahan must be a bit of a despot."

In a reply complaining of Gordin's sensitivity to criticism, Cahan swore that he would no longer review Gordin's plays. He later wrote, "We made up, but for a long time I did not write about his dramas. On a personal level we remained on good terms."

The altercation after *The Russian Jew in America* was the first in a series of flare-ups between friends who, though of the same political stripe, increasingly approached the world from opposite vantage points. Gordin and his colleague Adler fought often only to forgive and fight again, both of them mercurial and emphatic, with explosive Russian temperaments and generous Russian hearts. Gordin, says historian Ronald Sanders in *The Downtown Jews*, was "completely the dashing, sentimental Russian life force that Cahan felt himself to be in his heart and was never able to be in his person." Abraham Cahan was a Litvak, a Lithuanian Jew, a breed purported to be cold and analytical. Cahan was both—Sanders paints him as "dry, reserved, cerebral"—and he was also willing, as he was to prove many times, to bear a grudge forever.

On the other hand, a gentle Litvak called Morris Winchevsky, the opposite of the stereotype, had just become my great-grandfather's dearest friend. Winchevsky was born Lippe Ben-Zion Novakhovich; he changed his name first to Leopold Benedict, which was his moniker in the Gordin house—Great-Aunt Helen called him Mr. Benedict—and then to Winchevsky. He was not the only Russian intellectual with a choice of names. Nearly every political immigrant on the Lower East Side had switched at least once—Phillip Krantz was formerly Jacob Rombro, Louis

Miller's last name was actually Bandes—to the point that a reference book about the time has an index of pseudonyms at the back. I thought that Gordin too, on occasion, used a pseudonym—"Professor Jacoby from London"—but I learned that many Yiddish playwrights, when a substandard work of theirs was produced, disguised themselves with that generic name.

In 1878 the humanitarian later named Morris Winchevsky spent nearly five months in a German prison as punishment for his work with the socialist press. He was then deported to London where he lived for fifteen years, writing essays, stories, poetry, and translations for the radical press, and frequenting British socialist circles that included William Morris and Eleanor Marx. Though the two had never met, Winchevsky admired Gordin's work from afar, and wrote a defense of Gordin's use of Shakespeare as a source.

Unable to make a living in England, like many of his compatriots, Morris Winchevsky left for New York in October 1894. He was already called *der zeyde*, grandfather of the Jewish worker's movement, though he was only thirty-eight. Gordin was the same age when he emigrated; the fact that both men had arrived in America well into adulthood was an important link between them. Most immigrants were much younger; Cahan, more typically, was only twenty-one when he disembarked.

A respected editor as well as a "worker's poet," now Winchevsky was about to become entangled in the Yiddish theater. The evening after his arrival found him in Adler's theater watching one of Gordin's plays, which he had been asked to review. He had previously written about and translated Ibsen's seminal play *A Doll's House*, and in January 1895, only three months after landing in America, he collaborated with Gordin on a Yiddish adaptation. *Nora, oder Nes bitokh nes (Nora, or a Miracle Within a Miracle)* was not a success, but the friendship was. Through all the troubles that befell them both over the years, the two never wavered in their allegiance to each other. Leopold Benedict was even executor of Gordin's estate, continuing to watch over Aneuta and the children long after his best friend's death.

On my desk nearby is Helen's framed photograph of Yankev Gordin and Mr. Benedict, seated at a table. The playwright gazes at his friend and contributes his noble left profile, as he always did in photos. The poet, his beautiful hands in his lap, gazes limpidly at us. I had always thought this a moment in which Gordin deferred to his friend, until I saw another photograph, taken at exactly the same time, in which Winchevsky looks at Gordin and Gordin looks at the camera. In formal portraits, as in everything, the two men were rigorously equal.

Gordin's output had not slowed. His colleague Jacob Adler had decided to join forces with the talented though irascible actor David Kessler, and Adler's favorite playwright dutifully prepared new plays for two male stars, none of which was a success. But once again, after repeated failures, a hit: in 1896 Gordin wrote *Shloymele sharlatan (Shloymke the Charlatan)*, a play apparently adapted from Ostrovsky, although he had surely heard of a successful 1893 American play, *Shore Acres* by James Herne, about a lovable ne'er-do-well with a malicious brother. *Shloymke* is described by Lulla Rosenfeld as "a piece of theatrical bravura with a leading role to make any actor's mouth water."

As in *The Brothers Luria*, two brothers are at loggerheads over an inheritance; Shloymke, who has been cheated of his, is a reckless free spirit with nothing left but his joie de vivre. Both Adler and Kessler were anxious to play the part; when they drew lots, the right to play the lead role on opening night went to Adler. The next night they switched. At the turning point of his career and indeed of his life, David Kessler played Shloymke with such brilliance and depth that Adler never touched the role again. "From that time on," writes Adler's generous granddaughter Rosenfeld, Kessler "was considered as equal to Adler. And there are critics who feel that in the Yiddish theater Kessler's was the greatest talent of all."

High-reaching Adler now made a grand announcement: he and Kessler would perform in *Othello*, alternating the roles of Othello and Iago. Across the street at the Thalia, their competitor Thomashefsky had just enjoyed a huge triumph in a "historical" drama by Lateiner: *Alexander, Crown Prince of Jerusalem* ran for an entire season. The matinee idol appeared bare-chested in golden tights on a horse and played the romantic love scenes with such flair that women packed the theater, swooning and even screaming.

When he heard about *Othello*, however, Thomashefsky immediately decided to produce *Hamlet*, with Keni Lipzin as Ophelia. Warmed to Shakespeare by Gordin's *Lear*, the public cheered both renditions, enjoying *Hamlet* so much that cries of "Author! Author!" regularly filled the theater

Morris Winchevsky (left) and Jacob Gordin circa 1905.

after the final curtain; a member of the troupe would appear to explain that because the author lived far away in England, he had been unable to attend. From this translation came one of the most famous lines of the Yiddish theater: *"Zayn oder nit tsuzayn—dos iz di frage"* ("To be, or not . . .").

Adler asked to meet with his rival from the theater across the street and proposed a merger: the three stars working together, an unbeatable constellation at the largest of the East Side theaters, the thirty-five-hundred-seat Windsor. When Thomashefsky accepted, Gordin adapted a Victor Hugo play entitled—what else?—*Di dray printsen (The Three Princes).* The Lower East Side responded with a frenzy of anticipation, but the collaboration was short-lived; a stage is a small platform for three titanic egos. It must have been during the run of this play that a famous epic battle occurred onstage. One night Kessler mimicked Thomashefsky, who was supposed to break a plate during the scene. Furious, Thomashefsky broke two plates, at which point Kessler broke a few plates himself, and Adler joined in with some plate smashing of his own. Luckily for the props department, Kessler, the most antagonistic of the stars, lasted only three weeks before decamping to Chicago.

As for Gordin and Adler, the long-time associates had begun veering in and out of professional connection with each other. In May 1896 a newspaper ad appeared in Newark, New Jersey:

Gordin's Dramatic Company
An Evening of Great Pleasure
Friday evening May 8 1896
Come to the opening of the masterpiece which has
had the greatest success in
New York.
For the first time in Newark, from the one and only famous author,
Jacob Gordin
"THE TWO WORLDS"
A slice-of-life drama in 4 Acts with a Prologue

Extra news:
Madame K. Lipzin as Deborah
Herr Myerson in the role of Shrolik Shuster
Herr Max Rosenthal in the role of Boris
Mr. Max Abramavich will present his famous song-cycle of 88 songs.

Mr. Jacob Gordin will lecture, between the acts, on the state of the Yiddish theater. The new people's stage troupe under the name "Gordin's Dramatic Company" brings you the best and most loved actresses including Lipzin, Vilensky, Manne, Fredenburg and others.

Actors: Meyerson, Rosenthal, Abramavitch, Moscovitz, Kalish.

There has never been in New York such a great concert and lecture presentation. There has never been such a troupe, with the goal of transforming the Yiddish theater into a free people's theater. The audience has not yet heard of a Yiddish theater such as Jacob Gordin will describe in his lecture. No one has heard such a song-cycle as Mr. Abramavich will sing for you Friday evening, May 8.

Prices: 25, 35, 50, 75 cents and $1.00.

With this tour Gordin now attempted, briefly, to set out on his own. If the list I've compiled primarily from Zylbersweig's exhaustive *Encyclopaedia* is accurate, then in 1896 Gordin founded a company to tour his early work *The Two Worlds* and wrote up to nine full-length plays, adaptations, and translations including *Medea,* adapted from Grillpartzer for Keni Lipzin, and his successful *Shloymke Sharlatan.* He also found the time to write a highly controversial playlet, once again showing his unfailing ability to place himself at the heart of the Jewish immigrant's difficulties in America.

"The Russian-American Association for Broad Aims" was Gordin's first poke at a sore spot in New York Jewish life: the gulf of mistrust, dislike, and mutual incomprehension between uptown German Jews and downtown Eastern European Jews. The cream of the assimilated uptown crowd, the *Yahudim,* led by wealthy and genteel American citizens such as Jacob Schiff, Louis Marshall, and Isidor Straus, had emigrated from Germany decades earlier, worked very hard, and done very well. In their grand Fifth Avenue mansions, they were as well integrated into American life as Jews could then be.

Still, they were not at ease or fully accepted, and now feared their hard-earned respectability would be jeopardized by the mass influx of poor uneducated Jews, foisted upon them as brethren. They worried that the presence of wild-eyed radicals and socialists downtown would bring about a rise in anti-Semitism. In 1891, the year Gordin landed, Schiff, the wealthiest and most philanthropic of all the German Jews, headed a committee urging the president to ask the tsar not to force out Russian Jews, in order to slow the inundation of America.

Despite their concerns, Schiff, Straus, and their uptown kinsmen generously established and endowed many much-needed charities on the Lower East Side, most importantly the Educational Alliance. The Alliance, housed in a high-rise building at East Broadway and Jefferson, served as a free school, library, bathhouse, and meeting-place. It operates still, doing its work now in Spanish and Chinese rather than in Yiddish—though ironically, in its earliest days, spoken Yiddish was forbidden within its walls. A recent book celebrating the centennial of the Alliance tells us that at the end of the nineteenth century, many of the uptown crowd thought of the greenhorn Jews as "a mongrel race of Asiatic peasants with whom the established American Jews could have nothing in common," their language merely "a degraded form of German." In 1889 a rabbi who served the *Yahudim* called for "a vigorous program of Americanization to help them shed their awkward differences and thus reduce the friction with American society."

This shedding of "awkward differences" was exactly what the classes at the Educational Alliance were intended to do. Many Russian Jews felt with resentment that their haughty assimilated cousins were trying to turn the newly arrived hordes into Jews just like themselves: bland, barely Jewish, capitalist Americans. Gordin's one-act play, performed in Russian, was a satirical attack on rich Jewish philanthropists. In a newspaper article that year, 1896, he accused the *Yahudim* of fearing that the originality and independence of the Russian Jews would offend "John and Peter, their Christian fellow citizens." He charged that by attempting to control the lives of "hundreds of thousands of Jews, their education, their religion, their press, their politics," the wealthy few were only taking care of their own interests.

The uptown Jews took little notice of the complaints of Gordin and his friends. Community-minded Jacob Schiff was pleased to escort his family down to the Lower East Side to see *The Jewish King Lear*. The enmity between these two Jewish colonies continued to simmer, however, only to erupt again a few years later, fanned by another playlet from the sometimes-vitriolic pen of Jacob Gordin.

In 1897, between plays and playlets, Gordin wrote a reminiscence entitled "How I Became a Playwright" in which he bemoans his situation. "It is hard to walk alone in a new direction," he writes. "In Russia if an author came forward with a program of improvement like mine, he wouldn't stand alone; the pillars of Yiddish literature would come to his aid. Here, if I stopped writing today, no one would notice. Only I would notice what was missing—a few dollars. Oh the dollar! Is there no love of literature among the Jews in America? The theater exists only for business." In his idealization of Russia, his touch of self-pity, and his frustration with Jewish acquiescence to capitalism, my great-grandfather set down some of the tones and themes he would play until the end of his life.

Gordin continued to produce a stream of didactic short stories for the Lower East Side newspapers, which were in constant ebb and flow; to paraphrase Bob Dylan, those not busy being born were busy dying. The oldest Yiddish paper, *Tageblat (The Daily Page)* founded in 1885, was Orthodox and politically conservative, an enemy to Gordin and his friends. *Di Zukunft (The Future)* was a left-wing monthly about art and politics, founded in 1892 by the same group of intellectuals who had started the *Worker's Newspaper* two years before. It was again edited, at first, by Krantz. (Three times—at the *Worker's*, at the *Future*, and in their next venture—Krantz would be forced out of his editorship to be replaced by Abraham Cahan.) Leading with the manifesto "We can express our program in three words: we are social-democrats," the *Future* survived several extended periods of inactivity and is still in print.

Another great newspaper founded in those days publishes still. In 1897, Winchevsky, Miller, and Cahan labored together to create a brand new socialist paper, an alternative to the *Worker's Newspaper* and the others of the left. At a series of meetings to raise money for a new left-wing paper to be called the *Forverts (Jewish Daily Forward)* the faithful threw their gold wedding rings and watches into a hat.

After the paper's launch on April 22, Gordin immediately penned editorials, columns, sketches, and other features, joining the founders Winchevsky, Cahan, and Miller, who wrote almost everything else. The paper was run, for a time, by Cahan. The editor was now not only a leading political figure in the community but a literary light after the recent publication of his well-regarded English-language novella, *Yekl*. So far, Cahan alone among East Side immigrants had enough command of the English language to be able to write fluidly in his new tongue.

Cahan's Yekl is a handsome, vigorous immigrant from the Pale whose wife sails over years after him, as most wives did. Stubbornly old-fashioned, she adapts reluctantly to America; he hates her greenhorn ways, and the two divorce. Written at the suggestion of the esteemed American editor and writer William Dean Howells, who liked Cahan's short stories, the book was well received by the English press. Cahan was compared to Stephen Crane, whose *Red Badge of Courage* had been brought out earlier by the same publisher. Howells wrote a long article in the *New York World* about a new realist literary star, the sensational Abraham Cahan. Sales of the book, however, were not good. (Decades after the writer's death, the bittersweet movie *Hester Street*, directed by Joan Micklin Silver, was based on the plot of *Yekl*.)

When Cahan translated his novel from English to Yiddish, it was serialized in the *Worker's Newspaper*, and for some reason it fell to Jacob Gordin, who was writing for the *Forward*, to review it. Was the review a chore he reluctantly undertook? Or more likely did he, with his unerring instinct for turmoil, volunteer for this duty? I wasn't surprised to learn that my great-grandfather didn't like the book and wrote a review to say so. In the English version, Cahan's authorial device, the transliteration of the speech of the Jewish characters into Yiddish-accented English, is at first amusing but becomes tedious and condescending. "I ain't get ekshitet at ull; but vot'sh de used a makin monkey beesnesh?" is a typical bit of dialogue. A great deal must have been lost in the translation Gordin read; how to render a coarse Yiddish accent back into Yiddish? Possibly Cahan was imitating Mark Twain, who a decade before, in *Huckleberry Finn,* had become the first American author to grant black characters their actual speech patterns. But without Twain's warmly inclusive tone, Cahan's book, though clever and insightful, sounds patronizing.

This Gordin noted. "Cahan writes his 'Tale of the Ghetto' not as a former child of that ghetto, not as one of its own, writing about his own people," was his judgment. "He describes them as a stranger writing about strangers. He remains cold and distant from his own heroes. He mocks them and tries to be humorous, even when their situation is tragic." He also found fault with Cahan's style, the long passages of dialogue, the "gratuitous and irrelevant witticisms. Too much attention to trivialities," he wrote, "and too little to human beings!"

When Gordin arrived at the *Forward* offices to deliver his piece, Cahan had just resigned after another altercation. He had heard that Gordin liked *Yekl,* but seeing that the review was negative, he asked Gordin to hold it back until he, the book's author, had left the paper. The playwright replied stiffly, "Jacob Gordin is not in the habit of making deals about publication." At least, that is how Cahan's memoir quotes him. The review ran. Cahan left the *Forward* to take a job writing about the Lower East Side, in English, for *The Commercial Advertiser,* a literary American newspaper. But Gordin's review of *Yekl* was a sharp little pebble lodged forever in his shoe.

It is my guess that the deadly current of mutual jealousy and disdain, which would eventually overwhelm these men, began its course here. The circumstances are ironic. Gordin, who had worked constantly in Russia as a newspaper writer and editor and even as a drama critic, would try several times to establish himself in the New York newspaper world, to no avail. Cahan always had newspaper work in New York; he would spend most of his very long life as writer, editor, and drama critic for the most successful Jewish paper in America. Yet he was drawn to the life of the theater. He had even written a play once, in 1887, but, disgusted by the necessity for jokes and songs, he had become a critic instead. "The stage is a key which opens doors," he wrote in his memoirs about Gordin, surely with a touch of envy, "and he was the center of the Jewish stage. He became popular and important. Everyone wanted to know him."

Gordin had the theater, but Cahan, who had learned his perfect English by attending high school with the youngsters, had just made a great success of writing for American readers. He was now the only East Side immigrant to have entry to prestigious English-language literary circles. The playwright knew that the future of Yiddish in America was limited and, like his immigrant colleagues, was casting an eye on the English-language market. Although English did not come easily to him, he was doing his best to learn; I found a scrap of paper in the Gordin files at the YIVO on which he had carefully practiced, in his elegant scrawl, "brought, thought, sought, naught, caught, fraught."

My great-grandfather could not live flexibly, as Cahan did. The newspaperman could afford to be flexible; compared to Gordin he was a free man, able to take risks and move around. Unhappily married, childless, he didn't even have a home; he and his intellectual wife, also named Anna, lived in a series of hotels. Cahan was small and testy, with a limited and diminishing inner circle; the writer Baranov, one of Cahan's few friends, ended the acquaintanceship after a political disagreement. Cahan's adversary, as we know, was magisterial and admired, and lived surrounded by wife and family, a growing number of friends and acolytes, and the thick enveloping social life of the theater.

Each man wanted something of the life of the other, the lack of which was a constant goad. But their battle was so visceral that I think it went deeper. Cahan once wrote, "My mother was more forceful and more practical than my father. Her soul was not agonized by the idealism and vague longings that disturbed [his] peace." Perhaps, in the overpowering and critical Cahan, Gordin was subliminally fighting the shadow of his father, and in the idealistic Gordin with his vague longings, Cahan was fighting his.

Cahan describes his clever mother as "stubborn and unforgiving and prone to make a mountain out of a molehill." Clever like her, he too was stubborn and unforgiving, and a veritable manufacturer of mountains.

•   •   •

In these last years of the nineteenth century, besides writing himself further into war with a former friend, Gordin was tending to his non-theater duties: lecturing, corresponding, turning out reams of short stories and articles. His plays had started to tour, usually in unauthorized versions; in 1897 *The Jewish King Lear* was the first Yiddish play ever performed for the large Jewish community of Montreal. He was playwriting now with a difference, providing material not just for the male stars and their wives, but for an actress who was considered by many on the East Side to be the greatest of her generation: Keni Lipzin.

Lipzin's career began mythically, like a Hollywood story. At eighteen, a barely educated seamstress in the Ukrainian village of Smila, she sat sewing one day by an open window, and as she worked she sang. Yiddish theater founder Goldfaden and his star Adler, who happened to be performing not far away, passed by, heard the pretty voice, found its owner and pleaded with her to join them. She ran away from her Orthodox parents to join the troupe, and eventually followed Adler to London. There, on the death of his first wife and costar, she became his leading lady and, if the gossip is true, his mistress.

After enduring the starving years in London, Lipzin became increasingly dissatisfied with the poor literary quality of the troupe's plays in New York. She retired, in protest, after her marriage to Michael Mintz, wealthy owner of the *Yiddish Herald* newspaper, but her interest in Jacob Gordin's works enticed her back to the stage. When my great-grandfather heard that the illiterate actress had to learn her lines by having them read to her, he taught her—with his children's alphabet books?—to read.

The petite, vivacious redhead was to become, in Ronald Sander's words, a "symbol of artistic and spiritual aristocracy through her performance of Gordin's plays." American theater personality Harold Clurman remembered her as "all fire—a genius." Her fans called her the "Yiddish Duse," after the Italian star noted for naturalness, as opposed to the flamboyant theatricality of Sarah Bernhardt. Now, after appearing in several Gordin plays, Lipzin asked the playwright to write something specifically for her. Capitalizing on their success the year before with his version of *Medea*, Gordin wrote *Di vilde printsesin oder medeas yugend (The Wild Princess, or Medea's Youth)*, a historical drama in four acts, for her. This venture, though a failure, launched one of the most fruitful of his artistic and personal friendships.

Keni Lipzin showed her reverence for the man she called "Master" by paying him $85 per play, more than double the $35 he now received from the other actor-managers. Despite his successes, Gordin's financial situation was still precarious. His "better" dramas had not yet caught on with a mass audience, and most producers then as now hated to risk their profits with serious works. "Making money was never associated with such a play," wrote a contemporary. Gordin kept the family going by writing for the *Forward*—news, articles, feuilletons, sketches, and stories—for ten or twelve dollars a week.

And yet, this same year, he accomplished for Boris Thomashefsky what he had done for Adler with *Lear* and for Kessler with *Shloymke:* he wrote the role that lifted the actor to an elevated artistic plane. After his success in Gordin's next play, *Dvoyrele*, which was adapted from Ostrovsky, Thomashefsky was honored for the first time as a great artist. Bessie exults in her memoirs, "In 1897 we presented Gordin's *Dvoyrele* with great success. Boris was acclaimed by the public as well as the press and the intelligentsia. This gave my husband a name as a classical actor. I was overcome with happiness that my husband had made his name in one of Gordin's plays. At this time a race was being run among the stars over Gordin's plays. It was the Gordin period. Every star wanted to excel in a Gordin play." The actors may have been racing to acquire Gordin's plays, but with his family living on the edge of hunger, the man himself was churning out stories to keep bread on the table.

In a pattern repeated again and again, my great-grandfather followed a playwriting success by launching into an idealistic enterprise with no remuneration whatsoever. Gordin was lecturing to the Russian Social Democrats about the best world playwrights, Shakespeare, Molière, and Ibsen, when a non-Jewish Russian stood up to scold the gathering. Here they were learning about European drama, he pointed out, when they should be working together to improve their own. "Have you forgotten your responsibility to your own [Jewish] people?" he asked. His speech made an impact, "especially because it came from a Gentile," according to playwright Leon Kobrin.

On the spot, the group founded and organized the Free Yiddish People's Theater, a reading and discussion club that would work to produce a higher-quality Yiddish theater, abolish foolish melodrama and operetta, and organize playwriting competitions and productions. Gordin was elected to head the group and became its driving force. Many of the local intelligentsia were members, Jewish doctors from East Broadway as well as musicians and artists, some of whom had never before shown an interest in Yiddish literature or drama. "There were even a few real Russians—the well-known Socialist Stalishnikov, the architect of Carnegie Hall," Kobrin says with pride, and continues, about one of their meetings, "Gordin is speaking. All are watching the imposing figure of the speaker, who with a straight face tells an anecdote that makes everybody laugh. The speaker strokes his beautiful black beard, surveys the audience with his piercing black eyes, and doesn't crack a smile. When the audience is finally quiet, he sticks his thumbs in each side of his vest, pushes out his chest— and only then, smiles at his joke. The crowd laughs again." Perhaps there was more actor in the playwright than he liked to admit.

•   •   •

As the century counted down its last years, all manner of events and discoveries were reordering my great-grandfather's world. In 1897 a young Jewish immigrant, Adolph Zukor, saw his first moving picture, one minute long, and a grand ambition took root in his mind. On January 13, 1898, as Captain Alfred Dreyfus, an army officer sabotaged by anti-Semitism and framed for treason, languished in a French prison, the great novelist Emile Zola published his open letter "J'Accuse," charging the government and the military judges with conspiracy and fraud. Gordin's one-act play about Dreyfus was produced in October of that year. The officer was not acquitted until 1906.

In Stanislavsky's newly founded Moscow Art Theater, Chekhov's *The Seagull* was revived in 1898 and given a worthy production. During its first run two years before, the actors undermined the play's naturalism by delivering their lines in the usual grandiloquent style; no Adler appeared before the curtain to beg the audience to listen, and *The Seagull* failed. "Never again will I write plays or have them produced!" Chekhov had declared.

Sigmund Freud, an atheist Jew three years younger than my great-grandfather, published *The Interpretation of Dreams* in 1899, beginning to delve into the analytic theories that would matter so much to subsequent generations. In 1900, Queen Victoria died, Seurat painted "La Grande Jatte," the first modern painting, and Mrs. Pankhurst and her suffragettes brought the vote for women to the forefront of political debate. During the 1900–1901 New York theater season, ten works by the playwright Clyde Fitch were produced in the city or on tour. It was said of Fitch (as it would later be said of a playwright in my family) that he "failed to achieve true depth because of the haste with which he wrote."

In 1900, factory girls sewing at the Triangle Shirtwaist Company were making less than $1.50 a week. Eleven years hence, 146 of them would be burned or leap to their deaths from the windows of the blazing non-union factory, where the fire escape doors were kept locked to discourage union organizers and theft. The fire, one of the most terrible tragedies New York had ever witnessed, would as its only positive outcome provide a boost for the union movement.

By 1901, the electric streetlights installed on Broadway caused it to be known as "The Great White Way." That year Theodore Roosevelt was elected president, and Marconi sent the first radio signal across the Atlantic. Free public schools were open in many but not all U.S. cities. The giant retail emporia Macy's, Bloomingdale's, and Lord and Taylor were in full operation in New York, and a few years hence, the first Model T would roll off the line, affirming America as the world's richest industrial nation. The country also housed the world's greatest concentration of urban poverty.

And the Lower East Side was as crowded as it would ever be; as crowded as anywhere on earth. In 1900, the *New York Times* reported that the block bounded by Delancey, Broome, Allen, and Orchard was the densest in the city, with 2,223 residents or 1,089 persons per acre, four times the densest block per acre now. Two years before, five boroughs around New York City had merged to create the second largest city in the world, the world's largest Jewish city. The annexation helped relieve the congestion downtown. Soon the Gordins would follow the immigrant crowd across the East River, to the respectable borough of Brooklyn.

In the meantime, the Gordin family lived at 102 East 120th Street, where nine Russian-born children were doing their best to learn English and a new way of life. They had insisted on Americanizing their names, whether their parents approved or not. The young Russians Sonia and Liza Yakovlevna, and Sema, Sasha, Yasha, Misha, and Grisha Yakovlevitch GorDEEN, had turned into Sophie, Lizzie, Sam, Alex, Jim, Mike, and George GorDIN. In an even more extreme conversion, my eight-year-old grandmother demanded that instead of Nadia, she be called Jeanette, a coquettish name she kept for the next ten years. Vera, fifteen in 1898, was the only one to keep her Russian name.

Sophie, the eldest, had married Ben-Zion Greenspoon, a heavy-eyed druggist with a flourishing moustache. At Christmas 1896, the Gordins received a welcome present from the couple: their first grandchild, born December 25, a girl named Anna after her much-loved grandmother—once more defying the injunction against naming a newborn for a living relative.

A few months before, on August 13, 1896, Yakov and Aneuta had produced a present of their own: Helen, their fifth daughter and last child. Anna, who hadn't yet learned much English, delivered at home on 120th Street, attended by Dr. Sergei Ingerman, founder of the Russian Social Democratic Society and one of the Gordins' closest friends. On the baby's birth certificate, the father's occupation has been left blank. Perhaps it was considered self-evident.

Helen Gordin and her niece Anna Greenspoon, four months younger, grew up like sisters. Helen's Russian name was Lyuba; the three youngest Gordin girls were Nadezhda, Vera, and Lyuba—Hope, Faith, and Love. My sarcastic Uncle Edgar told me that Lyuba's name became Anglicized to Helen as a cruel family joke, because she was not a pleasing child, the opposite of a beauty who could launch a thousand ships. Though Helen was no beauty, I do not believe the story. In the year of her birth, "Helen" was the third most popular woman's name in America, after "Mary," perhaps the least acceptable name for a Jewish girl, and "Anna." I think that a more plausible explanation for her name.

The family—Yankev, Aneuta, and ten children, from Lizzie, twenty-four, to newborn Helen—were described by writer Leon Kobrin, who worked with Gordin there, as living in a place of "large rooms, a large household full of black-eyed children, and an even larger poverty. In those years Gordin was a very poor man." Gordin brought the young playwright to his study and closed the door, so the noise of all the children playing wouldn't disturb them. In the kitchen, cleaning, nursing, cooking, sewing, and attempting to comprehend this new country, language, and life, was Aneuta. There were times when she had no money to buy food or kerosene for the lamps.

My grandmother Nettie, whom I never saw outdoors, even in Florida, without her sturdy black shoes, formless dress and jacket, and absurd little hat, was playing in the middle of that gang of black-eyed children, a Russian princess with a thick dark braid down her back and a big white bow as her crown, bearing the exotic name of Jeanette. She had looked forward to living in America, where she would reclaim the adored father who had vanished from home one day in Russia. But he was so busy she rarely saw him here.

And sometimes, Jeanette was hungry, and the rooms in which she lived were dark. She never talked, in old age, about the difficult times of her childhood. All she told me, again and again, was that her father was a great man, a god, to his people.

THE GOLDEN AGE

I still see him walking along the streets, straight as a palm, his princely
beard covering his broad chest, his eyes like two bits of fire, sharp as dag-
gers. In his right hand he carries a cane; in his left, one of his plays. He is
going to the theater to read it to the actors. Those who know him say,
"That is Jacob Gordin." Those who do not know him stop and remark,
"What a fine man!"

—Leon Kobrin, *Erinerungen fun a Yiddishn dramaturg*
(Reminiscences of a Jewish Playwright)

ONE DAY IN 1897, an anxious Keni Lipzin sought out the Gordin family.
As Jacob Gordin's most eager and financially secure disciple, she had commissioned another play tailored to her talents for which she would pay the
astronomical sum of $200. When the playwright disappeared, not to be
seen at the theater or even in the cafés where he loved to spend hours
drinking tea and talking, she became concerned. Finally she went to his
house, where she found him unkempt, his hair uncut, so caught up in his
new work that he hadn't left the house for six weeks. "What a play—what
a role he wrote for me!" she later gloated.

The play, opening in August 1898, was *Mirele Efros*, subtitled "The Jewish Queen Lear, a real life drama in four acts" (*Mirele efros, die idishe kenigin
lier, lebensbild in fir aktn*), with music by Elyohu-Zalmen Yarikhovski. With
this drama, which fast became one of the best-known and most-performed
plays of the entire Yiddish repertoire, the Yiddish theater itself came of age.
Only two Jewish theatrical works have rivaled *Mirele Efros* for popularity
and frequency of production: S. Anski's *The Dybbuk* and the adaptations of

Sholem Aleichem's novel *Tevye the Dairyman*, which metamorphosed into *Fiddler on the Roof.*

Mirele Efros has never stopped being performed around the world, in Polish, Italian, Hebrew, Ukrainian, English, Hungarian, Russian, German, and other languages. Its central role has been a dependable warhorse for legions of actresses, most notably the indomitable Esther Kaminska, "The Mother of the Yiddish Stage." It has been made into two movies, one in 1912 in Russia with Kaminska; the other in 1939 in the United States with Bertha Gersten. And the play continues to be performed in our own times. In New York in the 1980s, *Mirele Efros* was transformed by writer Nathan Gross into an English-language musical called *Pearls;* in Yiddish it is regularly in production somewhere in the world, in New York or in Montreal, in Eastern Europe or in Israel.

What has guaranteed the longevity of *Mirele Efros* when so many other Gordin plays vanished instantly? The writer takes the bones of Shakespeare's *Lear*—a loving but misguided and egotistical parent hands the family resources to two ungrateful offspring, and pays dearly for the mistake—but sets it solidly in the Russian-Jewish merchant class of his own background. Like Chekhov in *The Cherry Orchard,* Gordin demonstrates the end of an old-fashioned, cultured, privileged way of life, and the beginning, for better or worse, of a new way.

Mirele Efros is a rich widow from Grodno near Poland, a respected and feared businesswoman who, in the eyes of the community, took over her husband's profitable business after his death and built on its success. She has two sons, the older of whom, Yossele, she wants to marry off not to a sophisticated city girl but to a simple child of the land. She hears tell of such a girl, but after meeting Sheyndele and her parents, sees that instead of the honest village folk of her fantasy, they are embarrassingly vulgar and grasping. Yossele, however, has fallen in love, and against her better judgment, Mirele allows the match to go through.

In the following acts, she suffers for her indulgence. Sheyndele devastates Efros family life, insulting and even beating a faithful servant who is like a family member. She needles both young men into bad behavior, helps herself to Mirele's jewels, and insists that Yossele take over the family business as his due. The matriarch, goaded beyond endurance, tells the young people the truth: her husband died with his business in ruins, leav-

ing nothing but debts, which she has secretly paid off through years of as-
tute management and hard work. The family wealth belongs not to the
sons of her bankrupt husband, but to her.

Even so, in a moving scene Mirele leaves the house in which she can no
longer live. Penniless, she goes to the home of her former financial manager, who is honored to take her in and give her work. All is not lost; Yossele and even Sheyndele feel remorse at her exile, and the occasion of their
son's bar mitzvah becomes a time of reconciliation. Mirele's son, daughter-
in-law, and then her grandson Shloymele beg her to come home. For the
boy's sake, she does.

Like *The Jewish King Lear*, this play's homilies resonated throughout the
Lower East Side: cherish your mother who gives everything, her very life,
for you; treat your elders and betters with respect, or your home and heart
will be irrevocably damaged. Beware the new values of brash selfishness
and greed; uphold the old values of deference and courtesy, family close-
ness, cleanliness, order, respect. This is one of Gordin's only works in
which the author's urgent message is not delivered directly by his characters but is revealed through the action of the play. The writer's heart is
clearly on stage, beating in the upstanding, pig-headed, generous, belea-
guered person of Madame Efros. As if to emphasize the similarities between creation and creator, Mirele carries a cane that she pounds on the
floor to make her point, just as Jacob Gordin did.

This was the greatest role of Lipzin's career; before her death she was
reputed to have played Mirele Efros more than fifteen hundred times. The
elder son Yossele, in the script a youth of twenty, was played in this first
production by David Kessler, who was nearly twice that age and only four
years younger than Lipzin as his mother. Jacob Adler's former wife Dinah,
now Mrs. Feinman, played Sheyndele; her daughter with Adler, Celia,
played the grandson. Celia was nine when she was cast in the play and
taken to the Thalia to hear Gordin read it for the first time. "I remember the
concentration of the cast members and the respect they showed Gordin,"
she wrote six decades later.

> I noticed the wonderfully imposing head of Gordin, his beautiful black
> beard interwoven with steel grey, and felt a bit afraid. I'd heard a lot about
> his tough attitude toward actors during rehearsals and performances of

his plays. I'd noticed the nervousness of the actors—you'd hear, "Watch your lines—Gordin's in the theater!" At the reading all the actors listened attentively. There was none of the light-hearted joking around at the expense of the author and his work usual at these readings.

At the end of my first scene, when I left the stage, I saw Gordin standing with my mother. He kissed me on the forehead and said, "That was very well played, Celia. You gave my Shloymele a very fine soul. You've made me very happy."

The role of Shloymele would become a famous family tradition. Many a lengthy career was launched with the child role in *Mirele Efros*, including that of Ida Kaminska, who played Shloymele to her mother Esther's Mirele. In the 1950s and 1960s, when a middle-aged Ida toured the world playing *Mirele Efros* with her own Yiddish troupe, she had taken over the starring role and her own daughter Ruth played the boy. Gordin's critics have pointed out, as a major flaw in this play, that the pivotal scene in which Shloymele persuades his grandmother to come back home takes place offstage. Why would Gordin miss the opportunity for such high drama? Perhaps, thinking of the very young actors who would be playing the role, he decided not to burden them with a long emotional scene.

In her memoirs, Ida Kaminska writes that once on tour in Israel, when she was again asked to play *Mirele Efros*, she remembered her mother's words to her: "My daughter, you'll have performed a lifetime and you'll have presented more than a hundred different plays, but you'll still have to endlessly repeat 'Mirele.' " A photograph in the memoir shows her backstage after a performance in Israel in 1968, still in her black act 4 Mirele costume, clasping the hand of Golda Meir.

I have my own bond with the play. In November 1994, almost a hundred years after the play's opening night, the long-lived Yiddish theater company Folksbiene presented *Mirele Efros* at their theater in Manhattan. I flew to New York to see it, and after much arm-twisting persuaded my reluctant Uncle Edgar to come with me. This was his first time, extraordinarily, watching one of his grandfather's works on stage. We listened to a simultaneous translation through headphones, along with most younger audience members. The production starred a fine actress called Zypora Spaisman, and had been cleverly adapted so that there was only one set, instead of the several called for in Gordin's script. Though the old-fashioned well-made play is not my favorite kind of theater, I enjoyed this one enormously, proud of my genetic and emotional ties to the play and its author. I relished the obvious enjoyment of the audience members around me. The playwright's grandson remained scornful. "The best I can say," he commented as we left, "is that it wasn't as bad as I'd feared."

Audiences in 1898 were not so critical. The play was a huge hit from the outset and ran for eighteen consecutive weeks, an unprecedented run on the Lower East Side, where impatient fans usually demanded a new play after a few weekends. Even Abraham Cahan, writing about the play years later, was almost full of praise. "In its written form it had the impact of something between *shund* and literature," he wrote dismissively, but did conclude that, "with all its flaws, *Mirele Efros* is a play which has earned the brilliant success it has had for so many years."

According to another contemporary, the young playwright David Pinski, "It was as though 'Mirele Efros' made [Gordin] a new person. Thereafter he grew, he found himself." He was also able to charge a great deal more after *Mirele*. His price tripled—for Lipzin, at least—to $1,800 for three plays in one season. Thanks to this long-awaited box-office success, there was now no lack of food and light on 120th Street.

•   •   •

The Golden Age of the Yiddish Theater is also called the Gordin Age, and is generally defined to span Gordin's life in America, more or less—1891 to 1910. But now begin its richest years, building to a peak in the first years of the twentieth century. The excitement generated by the Yiddish stage flowed through the Lower East Side like an elixir. Each week found the troupes—the writers, producers, managers, actors and actresses, the musicians, prompters, front of house and technical staff—engaged in the work of luring and mesmerizing audiences. The plays ranged still from sentimental costume dramas and operettas to the latest shocking real-life drama from the pen not of Henrik Ibsen, but of Jacob Gordin.

Or of one of his protégés, for his followers were growing in number: younger men like David Pinski, Z. Libin, and Leon Kobrin admired and imitated him, some of them joining, temporarily, his circle of intimates. It was a time when to an entire population, theater mattered nearly as much as work or family or food. Those of us who have played on the modern stage can only imagine what it was like, to command the boards at a time when the playhouse was the heart of a worshipful community.

Every well-known writer and actor had a fanatical assortment of fans known as *patriyotn,* who followed every movement of their chosen artist's career, every footstep and breath. And each group of *patriyotn* had a café where their proclivities were known and encouraged. The fans who supported the artists of the Windsor Theater gathered at the Campus Café on Delancey Street, under the leadership of a Rumanian theater fanatic nicknamed Yussel Mameliga *(mameliga* is a Rumanian dish made from cornmeal), while those who most appreciated the People's Theater went to the Café Essex, ruled by a head *patriyot* fondly known as Mr. Izzelle Tzailemkop. Supporters of the Thalia Theater, under the Hungarian Moishe Goulash, met at Schwartz's Hungarian Café on Rivington Street, near Forsythe. Moishe was famous among theater patrons because once, during an altercation at the Thalia, he toppled over the gallery handrails into the orchestra pit and walked ever after with a limp.

These hundreds of obsessives scrutinizing their favorite's work, the arguments and hysteria, the fistfights even, are reminiscent today in their extremes of sports fanatics, or teenagers in a frenzy about a new band. But in an age before electronic entertainment, the theater had always inflamed its followers. Nearly fifty years before, New York was the scene of such provocative rivalry between William Charles Macready and Edwin Forrest, two actors opening simultaneously in *Macbeth,* that hundreds of warring fans had rioted, resulting in twenty-two deaths.

At the theaters of the Lower East Side, however, *patriyotn* were not simply admiring, and fighting over, the artistry of great actors. A tightly packed group of citizens all going through the same arduous process—the shedding of the skin of one culture, and the growing of another—sat as an audience for the first time in their lives, to hear the comforting language of childhood and to watch skilled and talented men and women speak eloquent words about monumental emotions. Heady, thrilling, glorious days of the theater.

When word of this novel theatrical intensity reached out beyond the latticed fire escapes of the ghetto, English-speaking journalists and audiences began to venture downtown. They were keen to see a new kind of theater done in a new way in a language that sounded like German but wasn't. John H. James, one of the first American newspapermen to explore the downtown East Side theaters, takes pages to describe the *Jewish King Lear*—"an uninviting story of greed and turbulence"—and all the locale's stars and writers. He was particularly amused by a custom unique to Yiddish theater: if actors wore beards and wigs during the play, their "hirsute appendages" were quickly removed for the curtain call. (Even when Adler later appeared in *Merchant of Venice* on Broadway, he removed his beard before receiving the audience's accolades.)

"Owing to the unusual number of parts a Hebrew actor is compelled to learn during a season, letter perfection is out of the question," James wrote in an article published on July 4, 1900, in his paper *The New York Dramatic Mirror.* He noted the importance downstage center of the prompter, who not only read every word to the actors, but snapped his fingers to show them their moves. (Actors who had forgotten lines would invent business or gaze thoughtfully into the distance until the prompter came through; Sara Adler called this kind of stalling "pecking corn.") James also commented on "a great deal of walking to and fro during a scene by those not immediately concerned in the dialogue." He continued admiringly, "Crowds swarm at the doors a full hour before opening time to such an extent that one is impressed with the idea that it is the height of bad form in Yiddish society to come late to the theater. The Jews are often accused of being penurious but when one remembers that a majority of the patrons of these houses come from the sweat shops and stores of the small tradesmen of the East Side, one can understand that a considerable part of their earnings are spent this way." The plays often don't start till 9 P.M., he said, and "the record for late closing is 1.45 A.M." for an especially elaborate production. And most importantly, he had discovered this: "Jacob Gordin, an exceedingly talented writer, easily stands at the head as a writer of original plays, and as an adaptor."

Another admiring English language article written in 1900, naming Gordin "The Shakespeare of the Jewish theater," went on to praise the East Side playhouses "that draw for their patronage on one-tenth of New York's population, and offer amusement and diversion to perhaps the hardest working people in the world."

Just as the Yiddish theater entered its grandest era, a grand personage made her entrance: Bertha Kalish, an elegant beauty with a lilting voice, formerly the prima donna of the Budapest stage. In 1880 in Lemberg, now the Ukrainian city of Lvov or Lwiw, eight-year-old Baylke Kalakh saw a production by Goldfaden's troupe and was lost forever to the theater. In her memoirs, she describes the early Jewish stages. "At that time they had eight-foot lamps which would cause the actor's noses to become full of lamp-black," she wrote. "The scenery was painted on the curtain; if the scenery was a room, the furniture was painted on the backdrop, and the drop would come down on the stage with a bang. We dressed behind partitions, and crossed a bridge to the stage, where there was a little space for about 20 of us waiting to go on, and a space for horses etc. It was all very primitive."

Kalish's husband, Leopold Spachner, was also her director and business manager. In 1899, when the actors Kessler, Mogulescu, and Feinman rented the Thalia themselves, they made Spachner their business manager, and his wife their leading lady. Gordin was commissioned to write a play for the troupe and its star Bertha Kalish; for her he produced the shockingly modern *Safo (Sappho)*.

Set as ever in Russia, the play tells the story of a beautiful, fearless young woman called Sofia, who is pregnant by her fiancé Boris, and who discovers that the young man is secretly wooing her sister. (Again, so often repeated, heartless betrayal by a sibling.) She tells a celebratory gathering of friends and family the shocking truth of her pregnancy and, even more shockingly, refuses to marry the baby's father, insisting that he marry her sister instead. As those in the room react in horror to her confession, she cries, in Nahma Sandrow's translation:

> If I am to be a mother, I can care for my child by myself. Nothing frightens me. I will be free and honorable in my actions, honorable the way I understand it . . .
> *(All Sofia's friends get dressed to leave.)*
> You're running away? You're already ashamed of me too? Ha ha ha. A little pinch in the dark is all right with you, but open love, open, as our true feelings command us—that's a scandal. Yes, it will be very bitter for me to know that people are ashamed of me. But it would have been much more bitter to feel that I should be ashamed of myself . . . Only it's hard for me to feel that all I hoped, all I waited for, all my sweet dreams—Oh, Oh!
> *(Lets her head fall onto the table, and weeps bitterly.)*
> CURTAIN.

In act 2, she is working as a photographer to support her parents and her fatherless child. Fate throws her a kindred spirit: Apollon, a sensitive musician and poet whose musical education has been paid for by a fishmonger, in return for a promise to marry his patron's half-witted daughter. He and Sofia commune with talk of Wagner and Chopin, of duty and freedom; the young man, when he renames her Sappho, delivers Gordin's usual literature lesson, this time about the Greek poetess. The friends are soul mates, but they cannot be together; Apollon goes through with the marriage, and heartbroken Sappho vows to leave the city and make a fresh start. But Gordin allows a rare conventional ending for his unconventional heroine: Boris returns after his wife's death, and Sappho accepts his offer of marriage. If she does not have great love, at least her son will have his father.

Gordin was flinging out a number of subversive ideas for a nineteenth-century immigrant audience to digest all at once: unashamed pregnancy out of wedlock, love without marriage, and most difficult of all, female self-determination. His play's portrayal of love, motherhood, and unwedded independence not only challenged Jewish law but many centuries of Jewish tradition. In the statuesque person of Bertha Kalish, however, the character Sappho became not a revolutionary symbol but a tortured female soul.

Though this was purportedly the theater of realism, the first entrance of the play's star was anything but realistic. An English-language review reports that when Kalish walked onstage on opening night, she was greeted by a storm of applause. Cut flowers rained down from the balconies, and the orchestra struck up a flourish of trumpets and a roll of drums. Kalish, the review continued, "is an artist, emotional to the tips of her slender fingers, sparing of gesture and motion to the point of parsimony—natural to a degree beyond which even Duse does not venture—yet every instant in perfect command of her audiences. She is reputed the most capable and intelligent actress on the Yiddish stage in Europe or America. And as nearly as one could judge, knowing only the most obviously German elements in the jargon she spoke, she would shine forth an artist in whatever comparison." This role was a triumphant milestone for Kalish. Now a star, she began to look uptown, toward Broadway.

Despite the relative success of *Sappho* and Mme. Kalish's personal popularity, the play provoked a flurry of scandalized criticism in the Yiddish press. Gordin dealt with his critics in a lengthy essay published in the paper *Free Society,* in which he responded to a series of negative letters supposedly from outraged audience members. It takes little perspicacity to realize that they were actually written by Gordin himself. The playful writer gives us, for example, a letter from "An educated woman from Hoboken," disappointed with *Sappho* because of its self-evident theme. "She" wrote, "What kind of news are you telling us? That women are also people? That they should also have rights? That they should not be treated badly? And that's enough to entice people to come all the way from Hoboken, to keep them awake the whole night, and in the bargain take 3 quarters from them?" Gordin replied that the task of every poet, every writer, is to struggle against old dogmas, and to enlighten the people. One of the lessons of the play is that moral laws should apply to everyone equally. We can't have one moral law for whites and another for blacks, he noted; one for women and a different one for men.

A male correspondent wrote that as he watched, he cried for brave, unlucky Sappho, though "I know that a man doesn't cry." But then he realized that his wife and daughter were also watching and continued, "Maybe Sappho is right, but if my wife or my daughter, Heaven forbid, behaved that way, I would go mad! Don't you think this play is too radical, it is too early to perform such plays in the Yiddish theater?" "The quiet, thoughtful, devoted Russian woman is the greatest revolutionary in the world," responded the playwright. (Surely he wasn't thinking of his wife, the most quietly devoted and least revolutionary of Russian women.) Gordin urged women, for their own sake and for their children, to fight the social hypocrisy crushing them, and then, a New Age man before his time, he continued, "You needn't be ashamed that you, a man, wept in the theater. Those are good tears, my friend. The greater shame would have been if you hadn't wept."

And at the end of the long series, a "counselor at law" explained that because of the racy title *Sappho* he had attended the Yiddish theater for the first time, in order to see "some naked Jewish flesh." Instead, "I got Sappho, a naked spirit . . . unlawful and immoral ideas! Shameful to hear!" The appalling lawyer contends that Sappho would have been more moral to abort or even murder her baby rather than bring up an illegitimate child.

Gordin did not stoop to respond. His conclusion: "Many of us are radicals in theory, but when it comes to practice, we are all weak and stupid, part of the large blind mass." Surely, despite the first person plural, he was not thinking of himself.

While providing a hit for Kalish, the playwright had not neglected loyal Keni Lipzin. In the fall of 1899, he gave her another of her greatest roles in *Di shkhite (The Slaughter)*, a play noted for being Gordin's first without any of the music or vaudeville additions demanded by his audiences; even *Sappho* had featured songs and piano solos intermingled with poetic recitations. *The Slaughter* attacked the old-country custom of arranged marriages. Lipzin played a young woman who is not permitted to marry her love, the *shoykhet*, the ritual butcher, and is betrothed against her will to a wealthy lumber merchant whom she hates because he is crass and insensitive, as the rich, except for Mirele Efros, always are in Gordin's plays.

Again from Gordin's pen came a tragedy of unrelenting darkness, apart from a single scene: in one critic's words, Kessler's "buoyant, dirty, coarse, black-bearded, deep-voiced, greasy husband" finds out from his father-in-law—a meaty role for Mogulescu—that his wife is pregnant, and there is, briefly, joyful celebration. Near the finale, the writer gave his favorite actress yet another opportunity to demonstrate her skill at fits and hysteria: in a fine histrionic denouement, she staggers onto the stage dazed and maddened, carrying one of the butcher's knives, dripping with her husband's blood.

Cahan, who was still writing for *The Commercial Advertiser*, came to see the play. As his memoirs tell it, he went backstage afterwards and muttered his criticisms to Mogulescu, among them a complaint that the character Rivka, a village girl, "declaims poetical words to a lamp!" On hearing of the critic's sarcasm, Gordin apparently began his habit of mimicking and insulting Cahan from the stage, in defense of his plays. The problem with this story, as with so many others, is that it appears only in Cahan's memoirs, so we have only his word for its veracity.

•   •   •

A Russian writer called Leon Kobrin, nearly twenty years younger than Gordin, was struggling, after stints as a sweatshop worker, a cigar maker, and a baker, to emerge as a playwright. Theater managers treated him the way all *yolds* were treated. Told by one that the theater produced only dramas, Kobrin reworked his comic play into a drama and brought it back, only to be told that the company, in fact, performed only comedies, and never by unknown playwrights. He took his play to Kessler, who wouldn't read it because he didn't like either the title or the playwright's accent. "What kind of play can come from a Litvak?" scoffed Kessler, no doubt in the middle of a meal.

Doggedly, in 1898 Kobrin entered a competition of the Free Yiddish People's Theater with his play *Minna*, based loosely, though he denied it, on Ibsen's *A Doll's House*. When *Minna* was read aloud at a meeting, Gordin liked it but thought it had problems. Kobrin knew that without Gordin's approval, it would never be performed. When the play received a staged reading, Gordin left during the first act, but at a subsequent meeting told Kobrin that he had found the play interesting. "Then why did you leave?" asked Kobrin.

"It was poorly read," replied Gordin. "I couldn't listen."

"What do you think about putting it on?"

"You know what I think; as it is, it can't be performed. It has to be completely reworked."

At that meeting an argument erupted about the play, some members in favor of producing it, Gordin and his followers against. Finally, a woman shouted to Gordin that he was being unfair. "Madame, if you weren't a lady," he retorted, furious, "I'd answer your accusation. But Jacob Gordin doesn't argue with ladies. I'm leaving the organization." He walked out, and most of the group walked out behind him. Within six months, despite the efforts of Kobrin and others to keep it alive, the Free Yiddish People's Theater was no more.

But at his next encounter with the younger playwright, Yakov Mikhailovich went out of his way to make peace. The entire Russian community of New York came together every year at a New Year's Eve ball, a tradition begun in 1882. Transplanted Russians shouted and bear-hugged during a wildly nostalgic night of Russian music, food, dancing, talk, and drink. Most Russian Jews, like Jews of all nationalities, were usually not heavy drinkers, preferring endless scalding glasses of tea.

At the ball on the night of December 31, 1898, sponsored by the Russian Social Democrats at Grand Central Palace, Kobrin was laughing with a group of friends when he felt a tap on his shoulder. It was Gordin, smiling, stretching out his hand to the young writer, who was confused because he was sure Gordin was angry at him. Soon they were drinking a toast together. A few days later Kobrin received a postcard from Gordin inviting him to visit. "You have a good play, why should it lie around?"

The two men decided that Kobrin should rework *Minna* under Gordin's direction, sharing credit and profits. Kobrin wrote:

> Gordin works out the scenario of an act. Then I fill in the characters and the action according to the set scenario. I remember how impressed I was when Gordin handed me the scenario of the first act, written in Russian. Each scene, from the beginning to the end, was worked out mathematically, and everything was noted—even the main words the lead actors had to say. We work on the play act by act. When Gordin shows me the scenario for the fourth act, I don't like it. He wants Minna to dance a tarantella [a frenzied dance also performed by the heroine of Ibsen's play.] I don't think it is in character. He says he'll write the act himself, and he does.

How indicative of the man that even after completing more than two dozen Yiddish plays in his seven years of playwriting, Gordin still did his creative thinking, his plotting and planning, in Russian.

In a meeting at the Windsor Theater, Gordin read the coauthored play to Adler, who bought it for $150, $75 at the time of signing and $75 on the first night. When the contract was signed, Adler's business partner Edelstein took out a wad of one-dollar bills and counted seventy-five of them out to Gordin, who handed them on to his collaborator. Kobrin asked him why he didn't take his half, and the older man replied, laughing, "You need it more than I do; your shoes give you away. I'll get my share when we put on the play. Take, take. When you're offered a few dollars in the Yiddish theater, take them and run." Then he took Kobrin by the hand and said, "Come, friend, we'll wet your first payment from the Yiddish theater with a glass of wine."

They went to Zeitlin's, Gordin's haunt at 126 Canal Street, where a "regular supper" cost twenty cents and a "regular supper with poultry" cost a nickel more, and where Gordin's friends and *patriyotn* waited for him in the evenings. Kobrin, anxious to show "the treasure in gold" to his wife, didn't get home till 3 A.M., "happy, drunk, full of warm feelings about Gordin."

But the warmth did not last. Not long after, the younger man was distressed to see an announcement that the Windsor Theater would present a new play, *Minna, or Nora of the Jewish Quarter,* written by Jacob Gordin from an "idea by Leon Kobrin." Kobrin asked angrily what had happened to their partnership and quotes Gordin's testy reply: "If you're already running around town shouting that I took over your masterpiece, I'll take full ownership for it."

"Politics were involved in this," writes Kobrin, whose memoirs speak with fondness and respect of his mentor. "Gordin's friends must have told him that my friends were making a fuss about the way he took over my play. He got fed up, and decided just to take credit for the whole thing."

The newspapers joined the fray, with the anti-Gordin *Daily Page* printing an accusation of theft against him. At the premiere, all eyes were on the embattled playwrights. Kobrin, excited and nervous, sat with his friends in a box on the right of the theater, and Gordin, with his friends, in a box on the left. As he watched the first act, Gordin kept stroking his beard and glaring at Kobrin's box. At the end of the act, which was well received, the actors took their bow, and then Gordin appeared in front of the curtain for his author's bow. Voices on all sides shouted, "Kobrin!" and Adler pushed the younger man onto the boards. Both writers bowed, after each act, from opposite ends of the stage.

"I am sure that Gordin at no time was out to claim 'Minna' as his own play," concludes Kobrin. "Had he meant to, he wouldn't have hesitated to come in front of the audience at this first performance and tell them it was his play. He wouldn't have let the article in 'The Daily Page' appear without an answer. Gordin was not that kind of person. He [responded to me] in a moment of anger, and I'm sure he was sorry afterwards."

Though the two men renewed their friendship, a rivalry had been established. Overnight, Kobrin had become so well known that Kessler commissioned a play from him. In response to Kessler's great success in the new playwright's *The East Side Ghetto,* the Thomashefskys commissioned a rival "ghetto play" from Gordin. He delivered it to them forty-eight hours later, changing and adding to the script as they rehearsed. But his play was an utter failure, writes Bessie. "We then performed Kobrin's play 'Lost Paradise' which was a success. In our theater world one heard rumblings that Kobrin was overtaking Gordin."

On December 31, 1899, as the old century spilled into the new, the atmosphere was particularly festive at the Russian community's New Year's Eve ball. The Gordins, too, had reason to be joyful: their first grandson, William, had just been born to their daughter Sophie Greenspoon. Almost ready for production was *God, Man, and Devil*, destined to become one of Gordin's most long-lived and far-reaching plays. His war with Cahan was in a state of truce; although they weren't speaking to each other, Gordin sat at his table loudly praising a series of articles recently written by his former friend, who was sitting within earshot, nearby. In his memoirs, Cahan paints Gordin at this time with some sympathy: "His pride and explosive sensitivity caused him to make a few enemies in the Russian colony. But he also had many good friends and staunch supporters—a group of intelligent doctors, lawyers, dentists and business people. When he attended a dinner party or the annual New Year's Eve Ball, his tall, broad-shouldered figure, proud face and long beard were the center of a group of followers."

But even as he laughed and told jokes that night, Jacob Gordin was in no way a contented or settled man. As uncomfortable as ever in the United States, a land he would always consider rapacious and shallow, he was still dubious about his life in show business. Not long before, he had written without pleasure about his profession. The Yiddish theater may have an audience of hundreds of thousands, he wrote, but "the majority of its authors are people like me, who have become dramatic authors only by chance, who write plays only by force of circumstance, and who remain isolated and see about them only ignorance, envy, enmity and spite."

Did he really spend eighteen years writing for the theater only because he had no choice? How sad if it is true, and if it isn't, how sad that he saw his life that way. Because paradoxically, here in America, in the theater, he had found his calling. With Gordin as leader and guide, the Yiddish stage, its workers, and its writers were now enjoying enormous power and prestige. Around two million audience members had begun to fill the Lower East Side theaters each year, at hundreds of performances—an astounding rate of growth for a theater that had not existed at all just over twenty years before. In 1904, sounding not unlike a satisfied capitalist, Gordin would boast to a reporter that the four Yiddish theaters, with a fifth being built, gave about 1,500 performances yearly with a combined attendance of three million people, bringing in an annual income of half a million dollars.

As the theaters grew, actors enjoyed the rewards. At the turn of the century, Adler and Thomashefsky lived in the same Lower East Side tenement at 85 East 10th Street, where, every morning, Adler would shout affectionate abuse up the dumb waiter to his rival. In 1900, in a time of general economic prosperity, the two popular stars moved to the bigger People's Theater, with a guarantee of increased revenues and, before long, much more luxurious living quarters. But Jacob Gordin had no guarantee of anything. The company at the People's Theater opened with *Sonya of East Broadway*, by his young friend and rival Leon Kobrin.

Though Gordin didn't realize it, other competitors had launched an invasion from which the legitimate theater would never recover: five- and ten-cent movie houses—nickelodeons—and vaudeville houses were springing up throughout the city. Soon fourteen-year-old Isidore Itzkowitz, renamed Eddie Cantor, would win an amateur night competition at a Bowery theater, followed not long after by an assortment of madcap brothers by the name of Marx. In 1905 Adler would complain, "There is a variety theater on every other corner in the Yiddish district."

And this year came another change with unforeseen negative consequences: in 1900 the Hebrew Actors Union of New York was founded and made part of the American Federation of Labor, twenty years before the formation of Actors' Equity. Established Yiddish actors immediately created a closed shop that was almost impossible for new members to pry open, thus granting themselves a modicum of stability and security. Little of either, however, was accorded to playwrights. Because of new regulations guaranteeing cast sizes, large-cast shows like Gordin's became increasingly expensive, and thus even more risky, to mount. The ironclad rules of the union worked against the man who had helped put them in place. His plays, however, continued to feature large casts. Despite the onerous union regulations, he always remained loyal to the chorus and the bit-players.

In 1899 Leo Wiener, a Harvard professor of Slavic languages, put out a learned tome entitled *The History of Yiddish Literature in the Nineteenth Century*. There is a copy in my library. On both inside covers are stamped the words "Jacob Gordin's Library," the same stamp that appears in thirty or so leather-bound books that I inherited from Great-Aunt Helen. Inside the back cover of Weiner's book is written in Gordin's hand, in pencil, "Mar. 20/99." So my great-grandfather had read what the author, who admired Yiddish writers but feared for their future, concluded about the Yiddish theater. "It is very doubtful," Weiner wrote, "whether the Jewish theater can subsist in America another ten years."

He was wrong. The Jewish theater would go on. It was that theater's most famous playwright who would endure barely a decade more.

• • •

Jacob Gordin's turn-of-the-century play, *Got, mentsh, un tayvl (God, Man, and Devil),* is one of his most formidable works, and his own favorite. The plot echoes both Goethe's *Faust* and the Bible's tale of Job, a point Gordin clarifies in the prologue, where God and Satan argue over the corruptibility of man. God singles out as exemplary His beloved servant Hershele Dubrovner, a pious scribe and a pauper; Satan offers to attempt to corrupt the man, to prove that all men are venal. Gordin's literature lesson of the day (in Nahma Sandrow's translation):

> GOD: What do you think you will use on him?
>
> SATAN: You permitted me to test your loyal servant Job by means of sorrows. Nowadays a Jew is used to sorrows. The learned Dr. Faust sold me his soul for an instant of pleasure. But such deals work only with Gentiles; no Jew would pay a high price for pleasure. Almighty Lord, permit me to try him with money; yes, with money, with coins . . . Just let me at him with a bag of gold, and you'll see what becomes of his piety, goodness, righteousness, family life, friendship, and all the other virtues you brag about.

Satan, disguised as a lottery ticket seller, arrives in Dubrovner's serene home, where the scribe, his wife and two nieces lead simple lives devoted to God and to each other; as Dubrovner's wife says, "In poverty people are closer to each other." The righteous man is persuaded against his better judgment to buy a ticket, and when he wins, the selfish concerns of profit and power quickly corrode him. Not only does he become the greedy owner of a factory making prayer shawls, but he stops playing the violin, the sweet voice of his soul, and divorces his loving but barren wife to marry Fredenyu, his beautiful young niece.

Fredenyu, at the start, is a pure unspoiled girl who loves music and spurns finery, always the sign of an exalted spirit in Gordin's plays. "Clothing is silly," she says. "It is a very great sin for Jewish girls to get so many dresses when they marry. Expensive beautiful clothes are unnecessary." (I hear, behind this homily, the concern of a father who has four unmarried daughters at home.) As Hershele's rich and indolent wife, however, Fredenyu deteriorates to the point of near-madness. "Looking in the mirror has become a habit of mine lately," she muses distractedly. "I have nothing else to do. I am totally preoccupied with myself." Her sister Tsipenyu, on the other hand, marries a poor man for love; though they have no money, they have children: "Children are our only comfort, our joy, our contentment. There is no greater happiness than children—according to us paupers. The baby hums in her little cradle like a pigeon. Now that is wealth, that is holy wealth. You get it from God, and you give it back to God's world. Yes—children, that is a true fortune."

The devil continues to spout his poisonous credo, which sounds strangely like Gordin's damning view of capitalism. "The richer you are," croons Satan, with his forked tongue, "the freer and stronger and smarter you'll be. You'll have more honor, more pleasure. You'll be able to make yourself happy, and your children after you."

At the denouement an accident in Dubrovner's poorly maintained factory kills Tsipenyu's husband. Realizing, at last, that he has lost his soul, Dubrovner plays a haunting melody on his long-neglected violin, picks up a bloodstained prayer shawl, and hangs himself. Satan is forced to concede defeat: "So much money in the strongbox, and all the same he didn't want to live any more. What, then even the power of gold has its limits? You can seduce a man with money, corrupt him, deform him, but you can never utterly destroy his soul? In that case, I seem to have lost my bet." Man has redeemed himself. After a battle with the Devil of greed and venality, the God in the Man—conscience and goodness—is triumphant.

Directed by Kessler, the play opened at the Thalia, starring Kessler himself as Dubrovner and Bertha Kalish as his niece. Morris Moskovitz, who later found renown as a Shakespearean actor on the English stage, made of the smooth-talking devil one of the greatest roles of his career. The last minutes of the play are Gordin's gift to his actors. Kessler had a magnificent monologue as he prepared to die, but the other actors, too, had their moment in the tear-soaked spotlight.

The play had limited success at first. During its first week, Gordin lectured his audience between the acts, informing them, with his unique logic, that it is harder to write a play like this that audiences don't like, than one they do. "Hurwitz's plays please," he intoned. "My plays, and those of my colleague Ibsen, do not please." Audiences only want to be amused and aren't ready for serious subjects, he went on. They haven't realized that the theater is a place not for amusement but for teaching. "Truth is the teacher, and therefore," he announced, with a smile, "I will continue to provide serious plays until you acquire a taste for them." Surely never before had an audience been admonished directly by a playwright, even a smiling one, to change its taste for shallow entertainment and gravitate to him. Gordin's speech worked. The play went on to become a success.

Not unqualified, however. Louis Miller, one of the most important agitators on the Lower East Side, a lawyer described by a contemporary as "a witty and energetic socialist and writer," had criticized Gordin before and did so again with this play, complaining that it was not adapted but stolen from the Book of Job and *Faust*. Wounding accusations of plagiarism such as Miller's sliced at Gordin throughout his career, though he made no attempt to conceal his sources, and in fact highlighted them in the dialogue of the plays. The playwright responded by pointing out that most writers, including Shakespeare, lift their ideas from elsewhere. On this occasion, he and Miller quarreled, and it was a few years before they made peace. Later still, they became the best of friends.

In Europe, impresarios didn't care if Gordin had stolen his ideas; they were too busy stealing his work. His plays, in productions based on smuggled or copied manuscripts, were now being mounted regularly by the growing number of touring Yiddish troupes. *God, Man, and Devil*, making its clandestine way over the sea, was eventually played in Russian, Polish, German, Hebrew, and English. No royalties were forthcoming.

As if to test his own phenomenal energy, Gordin now embarked on one of his most time-consuming and admirable enterprises. Determined to counter what he felt was the pernicious influence of the Educational Alliance, the school started by the *Yahudim* for immigrants and their children, he founded an institution called the Educational League, targeting the same constituency. Gordin and his cofounders, a group of "physician-philosophers" who had been his friends in Russia, felt that the popular Al-

liance was designed simply to turn immigrant Jews into American con-
formists and consumers, whereas their League would provide the broad
education required of well-read world citizens. Gordin's school was an
enormous undertaking, teaching up to five hundred people during its
busiest years, in a style and a range of subjects—from basic arithmetic and
spelling to Attic tragedy and the philosophy of Neitzsche—approved by
the founders. He himself devoted countless hours to teaching, fundraising,
and recruiting teachers. The school devoted to "knowledge for its own
sake" survived at least a decade, though it did not long outlive its founder.

My great-grandfather also chose this time to start another ambitious
newspaper, *The Theater Journal and Family Paper*, which in its premier issue
deplored the low cultural level of Jewish audiences, and undertook once
more to educate the theater-going public. Gordin's friend Alexander
Harkavy, the well-known lexicographer and author of the first Yiddish-
English dictionary, wrote a typical article titled, in Yiddish, *"Teater—a
shul."* *Shul* could mean either "school" or "synagogue"; to the Jews of New
York, the theater was both.

An early edition of the paper noted that "the new theater season
opened in the two largest Yiddish theaters with the best pieces of the Yiddish repertoire: *The Jewish King Lear* at the People's and *God, Man, and Devil*
at the Thalia." It announced that both theaters had achieved a new dignity
by forbidding the sale of selzer, apples, and bananas.

Though this paper lasted only about a year, Gordin continued as always to write voluminously for other newspapers, including a lengthy series of scholarly articles about the great plays of the world, which he would
later come to regret. He produced a few not-so-great plays himself this
year, including *Der mamzer (The Bastard, or Lucretia Borgia)*, adapted from
Victor Hugo and called by one critic "a sensationalist, foolish play", and
his only operetta, *Di sheyne miryem (Beautiful Myriam)*, with music by
Mogulescu.

His next play, a more abiding work called *Di shvue (The Oath)* from
Gerhart Hauptmann's *Fuhrmann Henschel*, was written for Keni Lipzin as
star and Thomashefsky as director. In this play, a man on his deathbed
makes his wife swear she will never marry again, but she has been consort-
ing with his steward whom she marries one year later. When her grieving
son drowns, and she discovers that her brutal husband is having an affair

with the maid, she goes mad and burns down the house with herself and her new spouse inside. "Crude in form as these plays are," concluded American critic Hutchins Hapgood, "and unpleasant as they often are in subject and in the life portrayed, they are yet refreshing to persons who have been bored by the empty farce and inane cheerfulness of the uptown theaters."

Hutchins Hapgood wrote his drama reviews for *The Commercial Adver-tiser,* where toiled his brother Norman Hapgood, also a respected theater critic, and Abraham Cahan. The paper's urbane editor was Lincoln Steffens, who considered himself almost a Jew, "as infatuated with the Ghetto as eastern boys were with the wilds of the west," with a mezuzah—a sacred container that consecrates Jewish homes—nailed to his door. He liked to put reviews of the Yiddish theater front and center in his paper, where he felt they belonged. "The Yiddish stage," he once said, "was about the best in New York at that time both in stuff [plays and productions] and in acting."

His employee Hapgood—Hutch, as he's called by Steffens—did the research in 1901 for his estimable book *Spirit of the Ghetto,* which came out the following year. Hutch was a clear-eyed but affectionate and enthusiastic reporter who, like his brother and his boss, was enamored of Lower East Side life in all its forms, yet aware of its excesses and deficits. Fascinated by the intellectual and artistic life in this dense, dark, bustling quarter of the city, Hutch actually moved in; he lived in the University Settlement at the corner of Eldridge and Rivington, listening, watching, and reporting. He especially liked to hang around the little Canal Street cafés, admiring "the somber and earnest qualities" of the actors, socialists, musicians, journalists, playwrights, and poets of the quarter, who talk for hours "over their coffee and cake, about politics and society, poetry and ethics, literature and life."

Hapgood went to the Gordins' rented home in Brooklyn to interview the well-known playwright "of uncommon intelligence and strength of character. He is Russian in appearance," he reported, "a large broadheaded man with thick black hair and beard. As he told me, in his little home in Brooklyn, the history of his life, he omitted all picturesque details, and emphasized only his intellectual development."

O great-grandfather, couldn't you have let slip a picturesque detail or two? Imagine what he could have told or even shown Hutch, there in the tiny house at 365 Fourteenth Street, crammed with nine children (Lizzie, twenty-seven, was now married): Sam, twenty-four, who would never leave home; petulant Alex and sweet Vera, quiet Jim and easygoing Mike doing their best to blend into the Brooklyn high schools; my future grandmother the imperious Jeanette, twelve, her mild-mannered younger brother George, and the two American babies, Leon who even at six took nothing seriously and Helen, five, who was serious about everything. Oldest daughter Sophie Greenspoon's marriage was in trouble, and she was considering a move home with her children. Where would she put them?

Aneuta, who never made demands on the time of her preoccupied husband, was in the kitchen, feeding and raising this hungry gang. Gordin's producers paid him in cash at the theater, and he was always reaching into his pocket to peel off dollars for groceries and doctor's bills, counting them out in Russian. Aneuta was working, too, to educate herself and to learn English. One night, awakened late with an earache, Helen went in search of her mother, whom she found at the kitchen table poring over the *New York Times* with a dictionary, looking up the words she didn't understand. "I'm married to a brilliant man, darling," she told her daughter, "and I have to keep up with him."

"And then," said Helen, "she took care of my ear."

Some outside the family saw Anna differently than did her devoted children. A sharp-tongued writer of the time opined that she was "a buxom woman, somewhat dull, who would mutter behind [her husband's] back, despairing of ever having him think of domestic affairs." Gordin's wife, said another, "was a short, stout, typical daughter of Israel, always ready to receive guests, at no time showing any interest in intellectual questions." She was, he said, "a woman with mournful eyes."

But no, no picturesque details. Hapgood was able to pry loose that although Gordin was "in comfortable circumstances," making "a good income from his plays, which grow in popularity in the quarter," still he felt great contempt for the United States, particularly American politics, and intended someday to return to Russia. And yet, wrote the American, he "longs to have his plays translated and produced on the English stage."

When Hapgood interviewed Gordin in his comfortable circumstances in 1901, neither could know that these very years—1900 to 1903—were the zenith of the playwright's career and life. As proof of his professional and personal success, Gordin was about to be inundated, in two huge celebrations, with the gratitude and love of his public. Would these temper his "great contempt" for the land where he now lived?

The first round of festivities took place in November 1901, the tenth anniversary of *Siberia*, his first play for the Yiddish theater. A full week was dedicated to honoring the playwright, organized by "The Committee of One Hundred," one hundred—one hundred!—of the East Side's artists, doctors, lawyers, merchants, and intellectuals. The revelry began on Sunday, November 10 in the auditorium of the Educational Alliance, the institution Gordin was doing his best to undermine. Professor Felix Adler of the Hebrew Institute had organized a "Literary Evening tendered to Mr. Jacob Gordin by Literary Societies of the East Side and other Friends," with fifty prominent men (and, strangely for these socialist feminists, it seems not a single woman) in attendance. The audience enjoyed a violin and piano duet, a piano solo, a violin solo, and songs. The Hebrew Orphan Asylum Military Band played eight numbers.

When it was time for speeches, the toastmaster announced that each of the speakers could use the tongue that came most easily to him, as it was assumed that everyone present would be able to understand any language. The result was that the after-dinner speeches were delivered in English, Russian, Yiddish, German, and Polish. Among the speakers were Winchevsky, the director of the Educational Alliance David Blaustein, and the doctors H. Solotaroff and Abram Caspe, two of the socialist medical men closest to Gordin.

The following two nights, Monday and Tuesday, were given over to the performance of Gordin's greatest plays to date: at the Windsor, *Mirele Efros* starring Lipzin, and at the Thalia, *God, Man, and Devil*. Gordin, presiding from his box, was the guest of honor at each. Winchevsky provided a special prologue for *Mirele Efros*, intoned by Keni Lipzin, in honor of "our author, who has shown us powerful images, faces, hearts and souls . . . his dark world full of wonder; he who in countless plays/ has shown us our community changing, growing."

At the end of the second evening, a parade of Gordin's best-known characters marched onto the stage, stopping to make a humorous speech to their creator, or to banter with the audience as if their lives had continued, uninterrupted, after the end of the play in which they appeared. One character, for example, a notorious leech, tried to borrow money from the onlookers. The speeches, of course, were written by Gordin himself.

On Wednesday, November 13, Keni Lipzin offered "an informal banquet," on Thursday a banquet was given by the Thalia Theater Company, and on Friday the devoted Lipzin delivered "an elaborate banquet." The final celebration was held on Saturday, November 16, an event sponsored by "Mr. Gordin's non-professional friends," presumably everyone on the Lower East Side who hadn't been at the other six. The feast was held in the reception room of the Terrace Gardens at 145 East Fifty-eighth near Third. The menu was elaborate and extensive, from Bluepoint Oyster Cocktail with Amontill Sherry, through Kennebec Salmon and Fresh Beef Tongue with St. Julien, on to Roast Tenderloin of Beef, followed by Sorbet Punch with Niersteiner. Then the lucky guests enjoyed Philadelphia Roast Capon and Roast Young Duck with Compote and Salad, followed by "Ice Cream Fantasie, Mottoes, Bon-Bons, Tartlettes, Assorted Cakes, Raisins, Nuts, Almonds, Café Noir." The cost of a ticket to this banquet was $2.00, which included the wine.

One article about the festivities is headed "Lion of the Jewish Stage; Jubilee Honors Lavished on Playwright Gordin." It reports that "the program is, beyond a doubt, the most elaborate that has ever been arranged in this country to do honor to a noted person of the theater."

In a warning of things to come, however, another paper ran an article entitled "Did He Deserve a Celebration?" The answer was the negative, because Gordin's pen is "enlisted in the service of anarchist propaganda . . . replete with denunciation of Judaism and Jewish morality . . . With Jacob Gordin in their ranks, the anarchists conspire to capture the Yiddish stage."

Though it scarcely seems credible, in the midst of all this adulatory activity and plotting of takeovers Gordin was writing his next hit play. His son Alex, quoted on this matter because of a lawsuit about royalties, says that his father began writing "during the first week of November, and finished the 17th of December."

According to Bessie Thomashefsky, Gordin was sitting one night in the women's dressing room, watching the actresses make up before a show, when he remarked on Bertha Kalish's long, dark hair. Turning to him, she said teasingly, "Yakov Mikhailovich, have you heard of the writer Tolstoy? He wrote a book with a heroine who had beautiful hair like mine. Why don't you write a play for my hair?" Stroking his beard, Gordin growled, "Yes, madam, I've heard of Tolstoy." And he wrote *Kreytser sonata (The Kreutzer Sonata)* for her.

The title of the new play caused some confusion, as it is the same as a composition by Beethoven and a subsequent novella by Tolstoy, a literary work particularly admired by the Russian intelligentsia for its dark portrayal of the abyss of marriage. In the novella, a husband suspects that his wife, a pianist, is having an affair with her friend the violinist because of the sensuous way they perform the Kreutzer Sonata; murder and tragedy ensue. In Gordin's play, the sonata is played by an adulterous pair and the heroine reads, and explains, Tolstoy's book, but otherwise Gordin's drama does not resemble his mentor's. Many in the audience would have been excited by the title, however, knowing that the book was originally banned by the tsar. Gordin's characters, as usual, deliver a lesson in art and literature as they discuss Beethoven and Tolstoy, his favorite composer and writer.

The first act is set where almost all first acts were, for Gordin's audience as well as his characters: in Russia. Miriam Friedlander—Kalish—is the heroine, thoughtful and good; we know this immediately because she enters "very plainly dressed, with a book in her hand." Miriam recently committed two unpardonable sins: she fell in love with a gentile, a Russian army officer at that, and she agreed to baptism in order to marry him. Convinced, however, that he and his Jewish lover would never find happiness, the wretched officer has just killed himself, without knowing that his lover was carrying his child. To contain this double scandal, Miriam's distraught father Raphael has arranged for her to marry Gregor, a poor musician to whom Miriam tells the truth. Raphael gives Gregor a large dowry and sends the barely acquainted couple off to America.

When the second-act curtain rises, Gregor, Miriam, and her sensitive young son David now live in New York. Gregor, who has become a violin teacher, mistreats both his long-suffering wife and his hated stepson, and is pursuing a long-standing affair with Miriam's conniving sister Celia. The rest of Miriam's family, her parents, brother, and faithful old nanny, have followed the couple to America and are living on a farm in the country.

There Raphael, Gordin's spokesman, struggles vainly to assert the honest rural values of the old country as around him his loved ones are corrupted by the new one. The old man and his grandson David are especially close (as the playwright was close to his Greenspoon grandson William, now three, and soon to David, born that very year.) At last Miriam is driven mad by the crassness of America and by her callous husband's affair with her sister. In a blazing denouement, she shoots them both and ends the play in madness and grief, calling for her nanny, who holds her close as the curtain falls.

On first reading, I thought Gordin's tale of lover's suicides and murder absurdly overheated, but then I learned of a few tormented love affairs among the intellectuals and artists of the time. A well-known anarchist called Aaron Lieberman so adored a cousin of Winchevsky's that he followed her to the United States and shot himself when she reunited there with her husband. Chaim Zhitlovsky, critic, commentator, and a future debating partner of Gordin's, left his wife, the mother of his six children, when she became pregnant with a young student's child. Though the youth then shot himself, Zhitlowsky did not go back.

At the age of seventeen, Boris Thomashefsky's sister Emma eloped with the director Moishe Finkel. When Emma then left him for a younger man, Finkel shot her, her lover, and himself. Emma survived, but was left paralyzed; she made concert appearances singing from her wheelchair. Her nephew, Boris Thomashefsky's son Teddy, once remarked that in the Yiddish theater there was "every form of degeneration you can imagine: murder, suicide, drugs, sex deviations of all kinds." Its denizens, he wrote, "made the Left Bank of Paris look like a convent." He knew from firsthand experience.

Besides graphically illuminating the violent end of unfaithful spouses, Gordin's latest melodrama moralized, as usual, about what happens to Russian Jews when they land in the country of conscienceless greed. Whenever Miriam's foolish brother Samuel opens his mouth, dark-edged Americanisms pour forth: "What you want to learn is the American commandments: First, father, respect your sons. And the second one is, everybody do as he pleases. And the third is, whatever you learned in Russia ain't so."

Miriam's mother Rebecca, as she sweeps from the farm to the glittering city, spits at her husband, "And as for you, you'll learn that in America the father of a family is nobody!" This theme of daughters, and especially sons, pushing away the wisdom of unjustly spurned fathers is so prevalent in the play that I'm sure it was not just a general concern of Gordin's but one he was living daily. His own sons Alex, Jim, Mike and George were twenty-two, eighteen, fifteen, and eleven now, shooting into American manhood, the natural tensions of their adolescence exacerbated as their father tried to pull them back toward the profound truths of his own past. Paradoxically, a man who had spent his youth in Russia battling the intransigence of traditional ways was now battling his own sons, and his own people, in an effort to transplant some of those ways into the resistant soil of America.

His play aches with nostalgia for Russia. Over and over, Gordin mourns his lost land, his lost youth. Looking out at American snow, the nanny says: "Do you remember Christmas in Krementschug, child dear? Snow—just like this!—but more, and whiter—yes, the snow in Russia is whiter, it falls quietly, too—it takes its time to fall. This American snow is just like everything else in America. Hurrying and flurrying!" Even if this overwrought reflection and others in the play were meant satirically, the underlying nostalgic thrust was Gordin's. In his rosy memories, even the Russian snow was better.

From this play, as from *Sappho,* issues a staunchly modern, pro-female view of women's lack of rights in conventional marriage. In the play's climactic scene, when admirable, brave Miriam furiously confronts Gregor and Celia with their faithlessness, her husband attempts to calm her with an affectionate, "You are mine." She snarls in response:

> Yours? Yours? Yes, I'm your chattel. My body belongs to you and must belong to you till I die. When you want my body, you say you love me; and when you say you love me, you want my body. I have lived with you ten years as your servant, and no day of that ten years but you have trampled and derided me, deceived and betrayed me. Yes, and you have struck me. I was silent, and I endured, for his sake, poor little child whom I brought into this vile world. Enough! I'll no longer be humiliated, deceived, betrayed. No—no more!

And she shoots. This was an extreme feminist manifesto for a Jewish immigrant audience. Yet the play did very well; Winchevsky wrote happily in the *Forward* that the theater was selling standing room only with extra seats at the sides, and the author and actors were called out three or four times after every act. An article by writer Louis Lipsky reported that it had been playing to crowded houses for eleven weeks, three performances each week, "a run unprecedented in the history of the Yiddish stage." The play ran, eventually, for four months, until the season ended.

Louis Lipsky is an interesting player in the saga of the Lower East Side, a critic and writer in his early life and later a Zionist leader. In 1962, an old man, he published a fascinatingly snide book called *Tales of the Yiddish Rialto,* which presents censorious, semifictive stories about the Yiddish theater world in the early 1900s. Lulla Rosenfeld thought he exposed more of his own unpleasantness than the theater's and spoke of him with loathing; understandably, when you read his particularly nasty portrait of her grandfather Jacob Adler, whom he paints as stingy, self-centered, and philandering, an actor who merges with the persona of his one Broadway role, Shylock.

But then, Lipsky's portraits of all the players of the time are ungenerous; his portrayal of my great-grandfather as a theater-loving thug is relatively mild. Gordin, Lipsky writes, was "the first man of intellect and education to intrude into the Yiddish theater . . . the first writer who had the will and the physical strength to break the bones of any actor or manager who interfered with the text of his plays. If God had not given him this strength and courage, the new drama would never have found a place in the Yiddish theater."

A more empathetic writer of the time, Morris R. Finkelstein (later known as M. R. Fink), reported for *The Echo* from Gordin's "cozy little library filled with the choicest works of many languages." Writing in the spring of 1902, he marvels not at Gordin's ability to break bones, but at his output: in only eleven years, the playwright has brought out sixty-three plays, some 517 sketches, and innumerable articles. "In the opinion of critics of the first rank, like Norman Hapgood," reported Finkelstein, "the plays of Mr. Gordin rank easily with the best produced in America."

The two men chatted in the cozy library about good and bad theater, Gordin lamenting that instead of performing Shakespeare, "the student of human nature," theaters are opting for Alexander Dumas, "the student of the sensational." Worse, Gordin said—reflecting not only on his own time, but on ours—the theater is in the hands of businessmen, whose maxim is always "Art is uncertain, but sensation is sure."

According to my idealistic great-grandfather, every American city should have publicly owned and run municipal theaters, students should be admitted cheaply to all theatrical events, and schools should include modern plays on the curriculum. He considered the Germans and the Norwegians to be "the only nations which have today a true drama," ignoring Russia where, he said, plays are so much more easily censored than novels—where, although Gordin could not have known it, his countryman Chekhov had recently finished writing *The Three Sisters*. "Our interviewer tried to persuade Mr. Gordin to speak of his own work," wrote Finkelstein, "but Mr. Gordin's modesty could not be overcome."

"Not that he was humble," wrote Lipsky, in his *Rialto*. "On the contrary, he was one of the rudest and most arrogant of all the intellectuals."

•   •   •

1902 was a slow year for Jacob Gordin; after the gratifying success of *Kreutzer Sonata*, he did not have another hit for some time. He and Adler fought bitterly after the actor's rejection of a subsequent work; "a lawsuit, the question of royalties, hot insults exchanged . . ." says Lipsky. All of the plays traced to this year disappeared instantly. Another of Gordin's projects, though, has endured. On the ashes of the Free Yiddish People's Theater arose the Progressive Dramatic Club, begun in a basement on East Broadway, and designed "to develop a public for the theater and a theater for the public." The club, about a decade hence, turned into the Yiddish theater troupe Folksbeine, which produces to this day in a theater on East 55th, which produced, in fact, the *Mirele Efros* that once so entertained me and not my uncle.

Perhaps Gordin's life was actually calm, for a moment or two, and so needed to be jarred once more into war. In January 1903 the lead article in the *Future*, which had just begun publishing again after a hiatus of six years, was a battle cry by my great-grandfather revving up his campaign against the Educational Alliance. He compared the bourgeois uptown Jews to "mixologists," the fancy new name for bartenders, because the jumble of courses at the Alliance was comprised of a bit of this and a bit of that: gymnastics, English, and Hebrew classes shaken together in an effervescent brew, nothing taught effectively or in depth. He charged the Alliance with bureaucratic bungling, amateurishness, and avoidance of any progressive teaching on the East Side, "lest the Jews become too radical."

Gordin's attack went much further this time than last. At a benefit in support of his Educational League, before a delighted audience of two thousand, he ridiculed the *Yahudim* in a playlet called "The Benefactors of the East Side." A rich philanthropist invites to his mansion others concerned about the downtown East Side. Among the characters are "Mr. Hutchins Fish Lobster, a Gentile who belongs to the smart set; Mr. Morris Goldberg, celebrated agitator and friend of labor; Mr. Moses Herring, a prominent divorce lawyer; the Rev. Dr. Knobel, who came from Germany by way of Schnipeschoch, Russia; Mrs. Zoken, a rich widow interested in reform and cookbooks; Mrs. Spriggl, an esthete who would save the hungry, needy and ignorant by classical music; and, of course, Mr. and Mrs. Joske, the philanthropic hosts."

As remedies for downtown vices, Gordin's uptown characters propose everything from "legislation to compel every downtown Jew to use the punching bag" to "the performance of the music of *Thus Spake Zarathustra* in all the halls of the district." My great-grandfather was having fun with this set-to. All of the characters were based on real people immediately known to the audience: Joske, for example, was clearly the wealthy Jacob Schiff. Hutchins Fish Lobster the gentile was perhaps based on Hutchins Hapgood. The composite character Morris Goldberg, Gordin's representative in the play, was played at the benefit by Joseph Barondess, one of the best-known Lower East Side agitators, not an actor (though he had once wanted to be one) but a labor organizer who had recently been refused permission to speak at a meeting on the Upper East Side. He and his friend Gordin relished their theatrical revenge.

The important spring of 1903 brought joy to the Gordins. The patriarch's May Day birthday was always feted royally with a large crowd of family and friends. In a note at the YIVO, Edwin Markham, a famous poet of social protest and important public figure, let his host know that of course he would be attending the dinner in May, as he did every birthday. This year, as Jacob Gordin turned fifty, the event was even more widely acknowledged. Once again, telegrams flooded the Gordin house.

Shakespeare Ibsen and Hauptmann Commission me to Congratulate their Colleague and wish him fifty More. J. E. Eron

Accept my cordial good wishes on your growing power for increasing the heart-life and mind-life of the people. Edwin Markham

Best congratulations from the depth of my heart for your life already past and the one you now start. Philip Zeitlen [of Zeitlen's Café]

You should always brighten the stage with the light of truth, with the light of knowledge, and not forget the one who was the first to offer his hand in welcome in this country, and who will always remain your friend. Jacob P. Adler

And a mass of others—"The Social Democratic Educational Club," "The Principals of the Manhattan Preparatory School," "The Voice of Labor," "The Shakespeare Young Men's Benevolent Association," "The Peoples' Culture Club," "The Pupil's Society of the Educational League."

In time for this convivial event, Gordin had at last amassed the resources to buy his own house. He confided in an interview that he was earning $5,000 a year, a respectable but modest figure given his large family and the constant outflow of charitable donations. For about $4,000, the pater familias was able to acquire a pretty four-story brownstone at 256 Madison Street in the Bedford-Stuyvesant section of Brooklyn, where some of his family remained for nearly twenty years. There was urgent need of the additional space. As Helen told it, her sister Sophie's husband was "a *no-goodnik,* a womanizer who used to come to Papa for money all the time. One day Papa hit him, and Sophie and her three babies came home to Mama." Sophie and her babies would remain with her parents for the next five or six years. Many articles about Gordin mention that he had fourteen children. During these years, he did.

Nearly eighty years later, in 1986, I sought out the childhood home that both Helen and Anna Greenspoon Richmond spoke of with a nostalgic warmth bordering on reverence. Though 256 has been torn down, the row of which it was an end unit is still there, an unbroken façade of well-built, compact brownstones. I laughed when facing it; it is located right next to the Boy's High-school of Brooklyn, which in the early 1900s was one of the best high schools in New York. With five educable sons under his roof, not including Sam, and now two grandsons as well, Gordin made sure that even at home, his boys could hear the school bells ring. The girls went to the Girl's High-school of Brooklyn, also close by, "a very fine school, like a private school," said Anna.

The neighborhood in 1986 was primarily African American; in place of one large family in a thirteen-room home, several families lived in apartments. In 1903, according to Helen, their street was populated not with fellow Jews, but with gentiles. "Oh yes, we celebrated Christmas, not Chanukah. We didn't keep kosher, ate ham, all those things. Mama used to say, 'My parents must be turning in their graves.' She and Papa both came from very Orthodox homes so they were glad to break away, they'd had it up to here. There was a reason for those kosher laws. What use were all those rules once the Jews got iceboxes?"

Aneuta once told her youngest daughter that she and Yakov Mikhailovich had gone to the other extreme because their parents had been so religious. When Helen asked to be allowed to go to temple and to church with her Christian friends, her mother replied, "You can be a lovely, well-rounded person and not go to church. You abide by the Ten Commandments, and by the Golden Rule, and that is the most beautiful religion you can live by. You don't have to go to church. Let your home be your church."

This house and its garden were Aneuta's place of worship; she loved to garden. In front was her flowerbed; the backyard was sweet with rose bushes, lush honeysuckle, and white and purple lilac trees. Lilac was Gordin's favorite flower, and on his May 1 birthday every year, he was sated with the smell not only of his favorite Russian foods—borscht, kulebiaka, piroshkis—but of thick masses of mauve and white blossoms. Enjoying the lilac was as close as Gordin came now to farming.

Helen had indelible stories about her mother. "We were never hit, we were never spanked," she said.

The only time Mama threatened to hit me—we had Russian or Finnish or Polish girls helping in the kitchen. I was sitting on the stoop with my buddies and when the Polish girl came out with a sweater I didn't see Mama standing there. One of my little friends said, "Who was that, Helen?" and I said, "Oh, that was my servant." A child, you know, what did I know about servants? Mama walked down the steps, and her face was as red as a beet, and she said sternly, "Don't you ever say that again, Helen, we have no servants in our home. She is our friend." I never forgot it, and I've never treated a servant like a servant. They sat at the table with us. I eat with my girls now, always fix lunch for the both of us.

The heart of the house lay in the basement kitchen, where Aneuta, with her "friend," spent her days at the two stoves, one gas and one coal, preparing vats of soup not only for her family but for the many friends and admirers her husband brought home every day. She never knew how many would appear. Next to the kitchen was the pantry, and then the dining room with the samovar and the big oak table. When the boards were put in, there could be as many as forty people for supper, artists and intellectuals, politicos, actors, Jew and gentile alike. At the end of the meal the men, or at least Gordin, would light a cigar; the Tiffany lamps were turned down and the guitars were brought out. Family and guests would pour brandy into spoons, set them alight, and sing Russian songs in the glow of the burning spoons. Gordin loved music and had an acute ear for a man who didn't sing or play an instrument. According to Morris Winchevsky, all his friend's senses were exceptionally sharp.

Anna told me, "Anna Pavlova, Nazimova, they were guests at the house. Pavlova was not a very good-looking woman but she could dance. Stalichnikoff, one of the architects of Carnegie Hall, he was a friend of Papa's, and a professor from Columbia, Dr. Hamilton, and Butensky the sculptor of Papa's statue. When he was making his statue at the house we were all fussing around with clay." Jules Butensky was an old friend who had known the Gordins in Russia.

On the second floor was Gordin's library, where he worked in front of the fireplace. He wrote erratically; when an order for a play came in, he sometimes did nothing for weeks and then would write for eighteen hours at a stretch, stopping only for meals. He smoked cigarettes constantly while at work and drank glasses of tea. The walls of the library were lined with wreaths given him by admirers and his famed collection of ten thousand books.

Among the few dozen left me by Helen, there is not one novel, but there are a disproportionate number of tomes about the French Revolution. (In 1905 the Lower East Side Public Library on Chatham Square was the busiest in New York, ranking first in the city for circulation of works on history, science, and sociology, and last for novels.) There are collections of poetry including Browning, Shelley, Tennyson, and Edgar Allen Poe, many volumes of social history such as *The History of the Commune of 1871*, translated by Karl Marx's daughter Eleanor Marx Aveling, and the complete works of Lermontov in Russian. There are books about Balzac, Thomas Jefferson, George Eliot, Dante, Aristotle, and Victor Hugo, books by Darwin, William Morris, and Maeterlinck, and a seven-volume *Complete Works of*

William Shakespeare. These last are leather bound, beautifully preserved except for one volume that is falling apart: the one containing the tragedies, including *Hamlet* and *King Lear.* "He was reading all the time. He didn't believe in children having too many toys, but lots of books," Helen said, and Anna reiterated, "Even if there was no money for presents at birthdays and Christmas, there was always a book for each child. Papa would tell us to wash our hands before we started to read." There's a well-known story that Gordin took one of his friends into his library to point out his many books of plays, from Aeschylus and Sophocles to Wilde, Shaw, Hauptmann, Sudermann, Chekhov, and Gorky. "These are my masters," he said. "From them I take my themes, subjects, and actions," though his characters, he said, lived their own lives while they propagandized his ideas.

His big desk sat in the center of the library, bracketed by Morris chairs, and in a little adjoining room sat the human Xerox machine, the person who was copying his manuscripts. Children who were being punished were made to sit quietly in that room with a book, monitored by Gordin who also kept an ear on the children's piano practice next door. He had a "whistling tube" in his study, so that he could talk downstairs to the kitchen. Once when Anna Greenspoon cut short her practice and crept downstairs, she was startled by his voice over the whistling tube, telling her to come back and start again.

Through beautiful folding glass doors embossed with flowers was the living room. Against the door was a Hardman concert grand, on which my grandmother, her sisters, and her niece had their all-important lessons. Two green velvet couches faced each other, and velvet and mahogany chairs; there were art works, statuary, and a chess set, hand-carved on a wooden table, sent by an admirer. Helen recounted, "After Papa died Leon asked for the chess set, and he sold it! I could have murdered him. And there was Papa's bust—your grandmother took that."

"Upstairs there were bedrooms, lots of simple rooms," she went on. "I shared a room with Leon for many years. I remember one Christmas Eve when I was six or seven, I couldn't sleep for excitement, waiting for Santa Claus. Late at night our door was pushed open and in came Papa in his pajamas, with Mama outside the door, watching. I pretended to be asleep. Papa put a toy at the foot of Leon's bed, and then a doll at the foot of mine. Then he picked it up again and put it gently in my arms."

Anna Richmond told me that her Gordin aunts and uncles loved "amateur theatricals," which meant they made up plays and performed them. One day a group of actors gathered at the house to hear Gordin read a new work. When the reading was over, they climbed up to the attic where the children had prepared a full-blown performance. "They had such a good time, the actors and actresses, watching us children perform. To us, Papa was a playmate," she said. "He used to sneak outside and ring the front door bell, and we'd say, 'Oh, there's someone for Papa,' and we'd go up-stairs, and there he was, large as life."

It is not surprising that Anna called her grandparents Papa and Mama; for some years, they were her parents. "Papa was fascinating to us; we thought of him as a king," she said.

When her grandfather came down in the evening for supper, he would sit on the big leather sofa or in a rocking chair in the dining room, and the younger children would swarm and tumble around him. They'd sit in his lap, and he would tell them stories in English. Helen told me that her mother and father spoke to each other in Russian, switching to Yiddish only when they didn't want the children to understand "or when actors were in the house." Aneuta spoke to the children in Russian, but their father practiced, and made the young Gordins practice, speaking English. How difficult he made communication with his children, by his insistence on speaking a language that was foreign not only to him but to most of them.

After the evening meal, the patriarch dressed for the theater. Occasionally, his wife went with him, and more occasionally still, his children, who rarely attended their father's plays because they didn't speak Yiddish. Helen and her older brother Leon, aged six and eight, were once brought to see *God, Man, and Devil*. Terrified by the flash effects at the devil's entrance, Leon screamed and had to be taken home. "Papa was annoyed. He said we shouldn't come back till it made sense," Helen remembered.

Under his beard when he was in evening clothes there was a silk tie. He was very tall, Mama very short. There was an evening ritual, every night—he'd have his dinner and take his bath and then get into his evening clothes—and he'd come down for her to tie the black bow tie. He'd say, "I'm here, Neuta," and bend to her height. She'd look at him with such love, raise her arms and hug him and kiss him and then make his tie. She'd tell him to bundle up, don't stay out too late. He always came home late, she had the evenings to herself, she was alone. She always waited for him, with a glass of tea, a cup of milk, to talk.

In our many hours of conversation, Helen didn't utter a single criticism of her father or offer a hint of any family trouble. "I never heard an argument between my mother and father," she said once, adding, "They quarreled only about the children." I thought it wise to take everything she said under advisement, although Anna, whose frankness made her more trustworthy than her aunt, was also filled with praise for him. It is difficult to see Gordin as the genial prankster and gentle husband their stories portray when we're so aware of his critical self-righteousness. It seems he could be a playful grandfather and father, to the girls at least.

With his sons, however, perhaps as his own father had been with him, he was aloof and exacting. Leon, aged nine, spent all one winter day shoveling snow for the neighbors and was proud of the money he had earned. Gordin called his only American-born son to his study and scolded, "You took money from our neighbors for helping them? If you do a favor for a friend, you don't accept money!" There were *pushkes*—tin charity boxes— by the front door, one for the Jews and a Salvation Army one for gentiles; Gordin made Leon divide the money and put it in the boxes. Then he asked his daughter, "Yelenychka, why did he want the money?" She told him Leon wanted a new cannon for his lead soldier set, and Gordin sent someone to buy a whole new set of soldiers, with a cannon.

The same rigor was applied even to his youngest. One day the daughter of a visiting acquaintance admired Helen's favorite doll. Gordin overheard and on the spot, asked his child to give the doll to her guest. Helen complied, weeping. She told me that many years later, she learned that the little girl had never been able to enjoy the gift, unable to forget the tears of its original owner. But my great-aunt recounted the tales of the doll and the *pushkes* as praise, not criticism. "He wanted us to be kind, to share," she said.

Gordin sounds like a father who may be operating from the best of motives and with the most well-meaning of theories, but who isn't dealing with the flesh and blood children standing in front of him. It was easier to be a playwright, moving his characters around as he saw fit, than a father, faced with all these personalities who refused to conform to his Olympian ideal of moral perfection. Or simply to be just like him.

.   .   .

On May 1, 1903, in their own home for the first time, Aneuta and her children were determined to make the patriarch's fiftieth birthday party unforgettable, and they did. "It was the happiest birthday," reported Winchevsky.

The front page of the newspaper, however, cast a shadow on the day. That very evening, the *Forward*'s headlines were blaring out the latest horror, the most devastating pogrom so far in Russia. It was an event that would have far-reaching negative consequences, even for the Gordins in New York.

The masthead of the *Forward* showed that the job of editor had recently been bestowed on a man who had returned to take permanent hold of the Lower East Side. Abraham Cahan was back, for good. This also was bad news for my great-grandfather. Luckily, as he ate and drank and listened to Russian music on this happy day, he did not know it yet.

DENOUEMENT

With several newspapers fighting on each side, and with thousands of
admirers making monster demonstrations in favor of Gordin, and the
most intelligent people flocking to his defence, the East Side was stirred
from end to end by this strife. And the event will surely be recorded as
one of the most thrilling chapters in the history of the Yiddish stage.

—English-language newspaper, 1904

AT THE END OF APRIL 1903, on Easter Sunday, the Jews of the Russian
city of Kishinev were subjected to one of the most barbaric pogroms in
Russian history. Forty-five were killed, eighty-six badly wounded, hundreds raped, tortured, and injured, their shops and homes destroyed. Despite worldwide protests against the tsarist government's involvement in
the pogrom, Jews throughout the Pale now saw that there would be no end
to persecution and starvation. Thousands, eventually hundreds of thousands, encouraged by the stories of *landslayt* already over the sea, decided
that the time had come to get out.

Immediately after the Kishinev massacre, wave upon wave of Russian
Jews began to wash into the Lower East Side. In 1902 the number of Jewish
immigrants had dropped to 58,000. By 1904 the number had doubled, and
two years later again, in 1906, nearly 154,000 Jewish newcomers stood
filled with hope on Ellis Island, waiting to go ashore.

Though some of the new arrivals were intellectuals and activists who
had at last given up on Russia, most were simply folk pushed beyond endurance, in search of safety. With a structure of immigrant life in place,
now, to guide them, they settled into American life more quickly than
those who had come earlier. Attending the theater for the first time in their

lives, they weren't interested in the ponderous issues and plain talk of realism; they wanted escapism and fun: singing, dancing, jokes. That is, if they could afford the theater at all. The United States was burdened once again with a depression, and those with a bit of money to spare wanted comedy to lighten the heart.

Anxious to define themselves in their new land as Jews, the greenhorns were eager to hear specifically Jewish stories. Humanist playwright Gordin, like his radical comrades, did not define himself as a Jew but as a citizen of the wide world; comedies with Jewish folk themes held no interest for him. If my great-grandfather had been a more amenable man, he might have sensed the changing times and shifted accordingly, even if slightly. But he had achieved what he had with supreme, inflexible force. A man who has battled his way to the top is not inclined to bend.

As the hoards of newcomers poured in, established Jewish citizens had begun their inevitable journey out, from the ghetto to Harlem, the Upper East Side and West Side, Brooklyn, Queens, the Bronx. The average Jewish family took only ten years to make enough money to move on. I cite the other side of my New York family, the Kaplans, to show how quickly impoverished Russian Jews made good in America.

My tall, fair-haired great-grandfather Yakov Kaplan, perhaps originally named Avram Kaplowitz, emigrated in 1885 from a shtetl near Minsk and became a New York tailor who trudged to an exhausting workday each dawn, sewing machine on one shoulder. His sharp-tongued wife Yetta, who arrived just after the Blizzard of '87, was equally skillful at tailoring. She had no sewing machine but she had scissors, which she used to cut material into pattern shapes for men's suits, selling these bundles of ready-to-sew suits at a slight profit from the family's tenement apartment at the corner of Clinton and Grand. Family lore says that she was haggling over a sale when labor pains forced her into the back room to have the next of her eight babies, of whom seven survived, and then she rose to hang out a load of laundry.

With their first bit of extra money, the family bought not new clothes or a bed for the youngest, who slept on two chairs pushed together, but a piano, so the girls Belle and Ann could learn to play, as cultured girls all did. My grandfather Mike, born the second son in 1894, took an accountancy degree at night school. When the dress firm for which he did the books—Sandra Sage Dresses, another ultra-gentile pseudonym—had to declare bankruptcy, the insolvent but ingenious bookkeeper managed to acquire the firm for himself. In short order he helped his piano-playing sisters make good matches, brought his brother Sol into the firm with him, helped put his younger brother Bill through medical school, and the youngest, Leo, through law school. By then they had all moved to the Bronx.

The upwardly mobile Kaplans of the Bronx, blessed with a doctor, a lawyer, a rabbi son-in-law, and a lot of free dresses, were not interested in paying to see the problems of tormented families in Russia or of new Jewish immigrants bedeviled by capitalism. Jacob Gordin's audience had begun to make a profound shift, and not in his favor. The change instead would benefit Yiddish newspapers, which were greatly in demand downtown by the new arrivals and could be bought all over the city by the old.

This was good news for Abraham Cahan. After leaving the *Commercial Advertiser,* he had been bird-watching in Connecticut and freelancing for the East Side papers when a committee from the *Forward,* which had been losing money and readers, came to beg him to return as editor. This he would do only if he were guaranteed "absolute full power," which meant complete editorial control to implement new ideas he had brought from the American press.

To the chagrin of his opponents, Cahan's changes to the paper were immediately popular: big sensational headlines like those of the American "yellow press," personal-interest stories in chatty, colloquial Yiddish to replace pages of nitpicking socialist polemics, the self-explanatory "Gallery of Missing Husbands," and later, most outrageous of all, a well-loved column called "Bintel Brief" ("A Bundle of Letters") in which immigrants asked advice about personal matters and received thoughtful replies.

His former colleagues were livid at what they saw as an abasement of their paper, a pandering to the lowest common denominator; but the readership was steadily climbing, and anyway the paper they had helped found was no longer theirs. It was Abraham Cahan's.

Far from backing away from controversy in uncertain times, my great-grandfather courted it. His plays had always been targets for the Orthodox papers, but in October 1903 his new work for Bertha Kalish, *Khashe di yesoyme (The Orphan* or *Khasia the Orphan)* pushed them into frenzied attack. It portrayed a poor young country girl sold into a kind of slavery to her unfeeling wealthy relatives; abused, seduced, and neglected, she commits suicide. The play was so provocative that audience members pro and con scuffled with each other on opening night, and a turnip was thrown at Madame Kalish during the second act.

Gordin stormed out in front of the curtain to denounce the conservative press and appeared again after the third act "to excoriate his critics," according to the *New York Herald*. The paper reported that Bertha Kalish "pulled the play out of the fire. In the last act the actress displayed such power that those who had come to scoff remained to weep. It is likely Mrs. Kalish will make *The Orphan* a success." Like the Cinderella story without fairy godmother or prince, said one positive English language review.

But even Bertha Kalish, though she believed in the play, could not counter the negative forces now unleashed. The orthodox press reviewed the premiere with shrill disgust. "Putridity parading as realism," snarled the *Jewish Daily News* about "this emanation from the Gordinic brain. A dramatic cess-pool . . . Gordin's ravings and vituperations . . . the dominance, the bulldozing tyranny of the so-called 'realistic' school which has paraded the vilest instincts, the most unsocial and immoral theories as dramatic motives . . . the homicidal tendencies developed in a certain Class of our ghetto population directly attributable to this realistic school."

A few nights later, speaking during an intermission, Gordin was lambasting his critics when to his fury he saw Kasriel Sarasohn, the publisher of the most virulently anti-Gordin newspaper, the *Daily Page*, sitting in complimentary seats with the *Page*'s theater reviewer. Pointing at them, he raged, "Look, there they are, the bastards—and they haven't even paid for their tickets!" Under the hostile glare of Gordin's *patriyotn*, the two men stood up and marched out.

As expected, the next anti-Gordin diatribe swiftly appeared in the *Daily Page*. Entitled "Who Is Digging the Graves? The Suicide Epidemic among Jews," it opens with fearful statistics about the sudden rise in suicides among the Jews of New York. Why all these tragic deaths? Because, the paper accuses, Jacob Gordin has undermined Jewish family life for years by "preaching filth and lewdness through his plays." He portrays married women who disobey their husbands as idealists, their men as charlatans, and girls who take up prostitution as moral; thus the purity of the Jewish family has been destroyed. "A forward young man who wants to seduce his girl," the *Page* is sure, "need only take her to one of Gordin's plays, and he'll be successful."

> This author has portrayed suicides as the best people, and youngsters have learned these terrible ideas from him. Hundreds of Jewish parents lament their children who have committed suicide, and their tears fall on Jacob Gordin. Thousands of girls have sunk to the lowest depths and they can thank him. The happiness of thousands of Jewish families has been ruined as a result of the licentious teachings of this man. Who knows how far this will go if the Jews of New York don't destroy the pen of the man spreading this filth? It must be brought to an end.

All the papers, on both right and left, used sensational, libelous invective; "a Yiddish newspaper's freedom of expression is limited by the Penal Code alone," one uptown editor had remarked. But this level of malice was unparalleled.

The anti-Gordin outpourings continued. Louis Miller, the editor and lawyer, now rushing to Gordin's side, fired back at the editors of the *Daily Page*, who, it was rumored by the left, ate ham sandwiches on the Sabbath as they scribbled sanctimonious editorials about Jewish law. Gordin's circle loathed their opponents as hypocrites whose political and religious convictions "change color according to the shekels coming in," wrote one Gordinist. (John Paley, editor of the *Daily Page*, was reportedly in sequence a socialist, a Christian, a Jew and a conservative Jew.) Louis Miller submitted to the *Forward* a ferocious defense of Gordin's play that ended with the rallying cry, "Jacob Gordin writes the brightest chapter in the cultural battle against the dark clouds of the past. Where there is a Jew with a heart, with ideals, a Jew with a hope for a better future—he will stand beside Gordin."

Cahan was not interested in using his paper for this skirmish; in his earlier stint as *Forward* editor, he had refused to print Miller's sniping at enemies. By now Miller, and Winchevsky too, had disagreed so often with Cahan about editorial policy that both men were no longer on speaking terms with him. Still, Cahan's strained relations with Miller and his dislike of Gordin were so overt that he was forced, as an indication of fairness, to publish Miller's pro-Gordin article. Shortly afterwards the editor was happy to print another article of Miller's, which gleefully exposed the *Daily Page*'s underhanded involvement in a Tammany Hall scandal.

But then Cahan stopped all coverage of the *Orphan* controversy, shrugging in an editorial that the *Daily Page* was simply using Gordin as an excuse to attack socialism in general. Although he continued to goad the conservative paper, he refused to mention its ongoing campaign of vituperation against a writer of whom he was not fond.

On October 22, an extraordinary event: a mass protest meeting against the *Daily Page*, with loyalist speakers Miller and Drs. Caspe and Solotaroff. The following week, at another rally, Joseph Barondess the labor leader and Gordin himself spoke. A call was sounded for all progressive organizations to join the struggle; rallies were organized in other cities. Twenty-four-year-old Alex Gordin, teaching at the Baron de Hirsch Agricultural School in Philadelphia, received a letter from his father about these events, one of the few of Gordin's letters extant. "You should have seen the protest meetings . . . in New York and in Brooklyn. Thousands, tens of thousands expressed their sympathy for me and their complaints against my enemies," Gordin informs his son. "In the Forward and in the Herald hundreds of resolutions from various organizations are printed. Those against me can see how many are for me."

He tells his Sasha that the people's response has given him "the highest form of satisfaction," but continues with his worries. "After The Orphan I hurriedly translated Gorky's *Summer Folk*. Thanks to the attacks it played several times, but now there's again nothing to perform. Business at the Thalia is poor, and my position is not enviable. I'd like to answer all my critics with a good play. The devil only knows whether that will happen or not."

Unfortunately, a man under siege is unlikely to find the time and concentration to write a good play. Gordin had sailed into an all-encompassing artistic, religious, and political dispute, provoked by conflicting notions of how to reform Jewish life in the United States. The religious traditionalists focused on the old-fashioned good they wanted to encourage; the socialist realists saw the flaws they were intent on changing. A published letter from a Gordin supporter that December attests that Gordin "is helpful not so much by giving new ideals of what to do, as by giving warnings of what not to do."

Other writers coming to inspect this quarter of the city marveled at the feuding carried on continuously between one paper and another, one branch of Judaism and another, and especially, then as now, between the various factions on the left. American publisher Lincoln Steffens relished this era among disputatious Russian Jews. Cahan took him to the cafés where the debate was raging at every table and to the theaters where, wrote Steffens, "the realists hissed a romantic play, and the romanticists fought for it with clapping hands and sometimes with fists or nails. . . . A remarkable phenomenon it was, a community of thousands of people fighting over an art question as savagely as other people had fought over political or religious questions, dividing families, setting brother against brother, breaking up business firms, and finally, actually forcing the organization of a rival theater with a company pledged to realism against the old theater, which would play any good piece."

As Steffens pointed out, my great-grandfather was now not only the playwright at the Thalia, he was a producer "pledged to realism" as well. Kalish's husband Spachner had offered Gordin a partnership in forming their own company if he also provided two plays a year and two or three translations. Now when his plays were performed, he was backstage at first, dealing with costumes, props, entrances and exits, before appearing in the house for the third act as the author. The partnership meant that he was even more involved financially in the success or failure of his work. For his next play, he accepted no fee as playwright to boost the profits of Gordin the producer. But increasingly, there was less profit for either.

Before the next premiere, however, an important remount brought him a thrilling new prestige. For the first time an English-speaking audience, en masse, flocked down to the East Side to attend the theater, at a special presentation of *God, Man, and Devil.* Part of the orchestra and the first balcony of the Thalia were filled with students and professors of literature, philology, and German from Columbia University, Barnard College, and City College. The rows of outsiders, according to one critic, looked like "bands of gold in the audience." The day after, an exhilarated Gordin described the event to Sasha. "The special performance went famously," he wrote. "We had a lot of friendly calls. After the fourth act, though the performance dragged on rather late, the audience was in no hurry to leave. I was called out a few times by the students with the college yell. I was very moved by that. The ovations were picked up by all the old-timers under the parterre; I noticed one old chap fanning himself with a rolled-up program yelling with the students, 'Rah! Rah! Rah! G-O-R-D-I-N! Excellent!' "

The uptown press were also in attendance, reporting back like wide-eyed anthropologists observing the natives of the rainforest. Under headlines like "The Bowery Sees a Sacred Play with Angels in It" and "This Satan Incarnate an Artistic Creation—'God, Man and Devil' Rendered in a Manner Worthy of More Exalted Thoroughfares," the writers enthused about their recent trip downtown, where they had understood only the broad strokes of the actor's physical work. To figure out the action on stage, they had consulted their English-language programs, which contained an act-by-act summary of the plot.

The *Morning Telegraph* enjoyed the Thalia Theater itself, "where the audience doesn't chatter while the play is going on, and where hundreds of high-browed men sit in the house at every performance and mentally dissect the dramatic offering with a discrimination which is rare." Another critic found the dialogue "extremely curious from a sophisticated point of view. Long discussions as to the rights of man, the freedom of the will, the value of honesty as a policy and so forth were listened to with breathless attention."

Town Topics praised the ensemble work, assuring its readers that "the honesty and unanimity of spirit that prevail on the Yiddish stage are just what the Broadway stage needs—what it must have before we in the upper end of town get real, indigenous drama in our theaters." Noting that Gordin was as well known on the Lower East Side as playwright Clyde Fitch was uptown, the writer concluded, "No American dramatist has got so close to the spirit of American life as Gordin has got to the life of his people." The comparison with Clyde Fitch was in retrospect an unfortunate one for my great-grandfather. Fitch was the most popular Broadway scribe of his time, astoundingly prolific—once called "the Ibsen of the champagne set"—and yet his works have been consigned to the dustbin of theater history.

The Mail and Express compared Gordin not to Fitch but to Shakespeare, as both worked "for a humble and absolutely unconventionalized public which knows perfectly well what it wants and is not afraid to ask for it. I believe there is nothing so fundamental, so thoroughly serious in spite of its abounding buffoonery, so vital in its revelation of a whole people's habitual thoughts, aspirations and weaknesses on the American stage today as this 'God, Man and Devil.' " The writer finished, with mournful insight, "I felt . . . that I was assisting at the birth of a dramatic literature. The Yiddish drama is so good that it deserves to live. But nothing can keep Yiddish alive very long here, because those who speak it do not long have any daily use for it."

The problems of the evening were brushed aside. Kessler as usual did not know his lines, but a lone review noted only in passing that he and other actors stopped regularly to hear the prompter. One critic spent most of his piece admitting that he hadn't understood a word. He knew that the rest of the audience enjoyed the play thoroughly, however, because when the theater cat wandered onstage during the first act and remained center stage for five minutes until carried off by one of the characters, no one in the audience noticed. I imagine my great-grandfather, not an animal lover at the best of times, raging in the wings as the cat strolled about under the lights.

The playwright himself came in for a great deal of attention. Several critics remarked that because he attended his own plays so frequently, he knew the audience well and was well-known by them. *The Modern View,* which under a photo of his usual solemn profile printed "the Goethe of Yiddish Dramatic Literature," was of the opinion that "Gordin is a genius. He knows humanity."

The Mail and Express admired the playwright's eyes, "like still blue pools far back beneath the shadows of his shaggy eyebrows. They are very eloquent eyes, having the look of melancholy often seen in men who think, as well as in men who have suffered." (Gordin's eyes, unfortunately for the simile, were brown.) The review ends with a grandiloquent flourish: "The cold gloom and the settled melancholy and the half barbaric sweep of passion that is Russian, in combination with the acquiescent suffering and the persistent striving that is Jewish, appeal singularly to the imagination."

Shortly after the performance, the dramatist received a gracious fan letter from William Addison Hervey of Columbia's Department of Germanic Languages, expressing the wish that Gordin reach a larger audience "beyond the limits of the people to whom you have hitherto spoken." That was also Gordin's great wish. As further encouragement, he heard from critic Simeon Strunsky of the *New York Times*, who had been at the Thalia. "I consider you as one of the best modern writers for the stage," wrote Strunsky, "a master of his craft, comparable to some of the contemporary German dramaturgists. It is my considered opinion that if the world outside the ghetto had the opportunity to become acquainted with your art, you would be accepted as a leading American playwright."

Gordin's critics have targeted what they brand as an overweening pride in his own skill and importance, but it is easy to see how this pride bloomed with such encomia strewn onto his path. Actors covered him with sycophantic accolades. When he had finished a partial draft of his next work, as per his contract with Spachner, he wrote to tell Sasha about its reception:

> Yesterday I read my new play *The Truth* to the actors. They want to present it this coming Friday, and I have only three acts. But I'm not worried—I'm doing my part and I think not badly, and they'll have to work it out, I can't add much to it.
>
> While I was reading the third act, a tragi-comic scene took place— they all cried. Feinman's head fell on the table, and he started to scream, "I can't stand it! I can't stand it!" The actors predict that it will be successful.
>
> If it isn't, my boy, it's all over.

Did the Gordin family live as close to the edge as that? I believe it to be so.

Di varhayt (*The Truth*), written for Kalish, is one of Gordin's few plays set from first act to last in the United States. The playwright highlights two questions that fascinated his countrymen: what are the fundamental differences between Jews and gentiles? Can intermarriage be successful? The play introduces Leah, a poor but bright and sensitive Jewess, to a wealthy, magnanimous gentile called William. Despite the horrified entreaties of both families, they fall in love and marry, but as time passes the gulf between them grows steadily more apparent, especially in matters concerning their son Ben. At the climax, Leah's dignified old father staggers bleeding through her front door; some boys jeering anti-Semitic slogans have wounded him with stones. The terrible truth is revealed: Ben himself led the attack without knowing that it was his own Jewish grandfather he brought down. With regret and relief, the couple separates.

In the translation I've read, woodenly done, as are several in my library, by Sasha, Gordin attempts to give a balanced analysis of both the Jewish and the gentile soul. As he did not know many gentiles, this must have been done more through hearsay, observation, and guesswork than personal acquaintance. He sets up the two sides and has them argue, refute, and rebut, in the process setting out his own strongly held beliefs on a myriad of domestic and philosophical subjects. Though not unsympathetic to William, the writer's heart is with Leah, who plays Chopin on the piano and dresses sensibly so we know she's the heroine, and with her brother Daniel, the Jewish version of a Greek chorus.

Over and over, Gordin makes points for his audience to assess and contemplate, imparting so many opinions that the play bursts with concerns, large and small. Aware that the uptown papers deplored the filthiness and smell of the Lower East Side streets and inhabitants, Gordin explains the quarter's lack of hygiene: Jews are so "beset with cares and tribulations" that they have no time for cleanliness. Unlike gentiles, he frets, Jews don't know how to care for plants and flowers and are "estranged from Nature." Gentiles exert themselves too much, and Jews not enough, in sports and exercise. Jewish youths stray far from their families and are more distanced from their parents than young gentiles, who unlike young Jews have at least one common point of interest with their parents: "the baseball game."

Husband William speaks about Jewish proclivities with Gordin's ambivalent affection: "You people are slaves of extremes. Either you burst into unnatural gaiety and noise, or you sulk in melancholy and discontent. Some of you cover yourselves in jewellery from head to foot. Others parade all winter without an overcoat in order to be sure of a seat at the opera." Gordin later spoke fondly about a young poet of his acquaintance, probably Abraham Leissen, who had done exactly that—sold his winter coat in order to buy tickets to the theater.

The playwright replays some of the battles of his own home. When Leah objects to William giving their son a dime, and he shrugs that the boy is only going to save it, Leah bursts out in the voice of her socialist creator, contemplating his snow-shoveling son: "Saving is worse than spending. Is it necessary to awaken in the child an interest for money, to teach him to hoard it up and stint himself? By the time he grows up, he will be greedy enough for money, without these premature lessons."

Leah's strong feminist sentiments echo still a hundred years later; she complains to her husband that "while we are your sweethearts, you spare no efforts to please us," but that after marriage, women are expected to grow "daily more attractive, while you, on your side, never care whether you are agreeable or not." Gordin portrays Leah's immigrant parents as vulgar, closed, and fearful, but her husband William and particularly his cold, snobbish mother and sister are just as narrow-minded. "Your cooking, much as I like it," sniffs William, "has a peculiar foreign taste."

The playwright leaves us with a hopeful speech; Daniel envisions a day "when all barriers and prejudices will be swept aside. Then the one great sun of truth will light up the whole world, the whole humanity!" But it is clear the writer doesn't hold out much faith for the imminent rise of the great sun of truth.

An American critic in the audience on opening night describes the effect on the audience of the dramatic third act, the bleeding grandfather, the taunts of the child. "There are tears in Mr. Gordin's eyes now, the audience is weeping manifestly, it is a riot of emotion," he writes.

> Dramatically, it is a stirring scene, but as it appeals to the Hebrew the effect is beyond description. It is several moments before the audience comes back to itself after the curtain falls. The glare of passion in their faces, stained with tears and drawn with emotion, is striking. Then, suddenly, from all over the house, come the wild shouts of "Gordin, Gordin, Gordin!" The play has gone and the house hails its hero.
>
> There is a certain pathos in the awkward squat figure that comes slowly forward; his eyes are fixed not on the audience, but on the roof; there is a strong suggestion of the ancient prophet in the stern face, the sweeping beard and the glowing eyes. Three times the crowd clamors, three times the figure moves solemnly across the stage and vanishes, then Gordin returns for the inevitable speech. For three minutes, in rapid incisive Yiddish, he addresses them sternly, almost angrily, still the teacher, the law-giver almost; then he retires. For him it is another truth sent home.

The play was well received. Under the headline "J. Gordin's New Play—Realism's Latest Success," the *Forward* ran a positive front-page article, though perhaps as much to annoy the *Daily Page* as to support the playwright. An English language review, dubbing *The Truth* Gordin's most mature play, found it "remarkably interesting and wonderfully well acted" and—damning with faint praise—"without the sauerkraut rankness, the tendency to sensationalism not infrequent with him." From one review, a discussion of stereotypes that are still in place today: "Gordin is entirely non-partisan. The Christian criticizes the Jew, finding him too sensitive, too argumentative, too high strung, too serious. The Jew criticizes the Christian as too complacent, too bourgeois, too conventional, too physical." Another presented slightly different stereotypes: "The Christians are represented as athletic, comfortable, rather unintellectual persons. The Jews are philosophical, introspective and melancholy. But the playwright nevertheless tries to play fair. He makes the Christian far less profound, it is true. But he also makes him more tolerant than the Orthodox Jew."

Extraordinarily, this play presaged an actual mixed marriage a year and a half later. In July 1905, the Lower East Side gloried in a fairy-tale wedding. Rose Pastor, a poor but bright and sensitive immigrant Jewess whose mother in Poland had been carried to her own wedding by force, worked for eleven years in a cigar factory before becoming a journalist for the *Forward*. When she interviewed Graham Phelps Stokes, a gentile socialist and the millionaire son of a banker, the two fell in love and married. We don't know if the couple argued about houseplants, cleanliness, and the foreign smell of her cooking, but, just as in Gordin's play, they eventually divorced.

Before the premiere of *The Truth*, a feverishly positive article about my great-grandfather appeared in *The New Era*, "An Illustrated Magazine Devoted to Humanity." The piece was signed "Judith Herz," the pseudonym of Mrs. Mary Dunlop McLean, an ingenuous, emphatically non-Jewish woman who seems to have been a sort of Lower East Side groupie. Though she didn't speak Yiddish, she had seen a number of works by Jacob Gordin, the "greatest dramatist" of the ghetto, and spent considerable time breathlessly interviewing the playwright, of whom a full-page photograph appears, again above the words "The Goethe of Yiddish literature." The Yiddish Goethe is much better padded than in previous photographs, as he regally puffs on a cigar in his study.

Though Gordin is suspected of being a linguist, reports McLean, "he is the most modest of men and declares that he speaks a little very bad German, and a little very bad English. His English, despite his disclaimer, is careful and scholarly." (He did, in fact, speak or at least understand six languages: Russian, Ukrainian, Hebrew, Yiddish, German, and English.) "He is hampered to a certain extent by his unfamiliarity with American life. And moreover, how large a public have even his masters, Ibsen and Hauptmann? He produces nothing unworthy, and caters to commercialism only in rare instances when it is forced upon him. For a man owes food to his children as well as truth to his art."

The perspicacious McLean was aware of the difficult situation in which Jacob Gordin found or, more accurately, had placed himself: as a man who spent his days and nights immersed in the immigrant Jewish corner of the Lower East Side, he could not write well about the realities of the golden land because he encountered them so rarely. She saw, too, that with his overflowing household and diminishing box office returns, he was a man who could ill afford the inflexibility of his principles.

• • •

In 1904, fortunes changed in the world of serious Yiddish drama. Jacob Gordin became director of the Thalia Theater, and for many reasons—the unbroken stream of heavy works, the changing tastes of the East Side audience, his preoccupation with various controversies near and far at the expense of his writing—he failed. Jacob Adler became owner and operator of the first theater built specifically for the Yiddish audience, and there made a glorious success. The theater of the day was always more about actors than playwrights; more about eyes and physique and declamation than words.

In one of the best-known photographs of the early Yiddish stage, the two-thousand-seat Grand Theater, at 255-57 Grand Street near the Bowery, rises gracefully behind the crowd gathered in front, with its own water tower, its ornate creamy brick façade inlaid with busts of theater artists, and rows of curliqued oval windows. Over the marquee is written, in light bulbs, "Jacob P. Adler," and underneath, "THUR NIGHT KING LEAR." Though the first hit at the new theater was *Broken Hearts* by Z. Libin, who had two more plays produced by Adler that first season, the fact is that for Adler the Libins came and went, but *The Jewish King Lear* was forever. The *Forward* theater critic M. Katz concurred. His review of Libin's opening night compared the broken hearts of the characters on stage to the broken hearts of the disappointed audience members as they walked out of the theater.

Adler had recently rejected a new play by Gordin during one of their arguments and instead adapted, produced, and starred in his own version of Tolstoy's *The Power of Darkness*—a big risk for him, and very successful. This play, said the poster, was "true art, not false, not imitative, not distorted," wording that the actor admitted later was aimed directly at Gordin. The playwright came to the opening night, however, and sent flowers backstage afterwards, full of praise.

Not long before, Adler had suffered a wound to the heart. On a trip to Europe to recruit new performers for his company, he had bribed his way into Russia to visit his family. In Odessa he tried to persuade family members, especially his mother, to come back to America with him, and was devastated when she refused. Seriously ill on his return, the actor announced to the press that he was dying and requested his *patriyotn* to come to the hospital one Saturday afternoon to bid him farewell. The great eagle—Adler is German for eagle—proved his point. Thousands came to weep outside the hospital, and the Yiddish theaters, for that Saturday matinee, were empty. The actor speedily recovered.

In 1904 Adler produced and, to great acclaim, starred as Shylock in a translated *Merchant of Venice*. The following year, he was invited to play it on Broadway, with the star performing the title role in Yiddish and all the other parts performed by Broadway actors in English. On his first entrance he was showered with rose petals, and the next day he received good reviews from the American papers, including the *New York Times:* "A master of all the mechanics of his art, Mr. Adler has also abundant temperamental force, much magnetism, and a fine sense of dramatic values." After his bilingual *Merchant,* Adler was happy to go back downtown to stay. His talented children, on the other hand, would go far.

Eminent visitors were now making the trek to the theaters on the Lower East Side. German historian Karl Lamprecht attended a production at the Grand, where he found the playing of the Yiddish actors comparable to the "religious consecration" in the playing of ancient Greek drama. "Criticism is absent here, for drama is still a form of worship," he wrote, having obviously not read the *Daily Page.* Prominent German sociologist Max Weber, too, visited and lauded the Yiddish theater; in his opinion "the acting was . . . magnificent," the actors "the best to be found in America."

A third European writer ventured down in 1904 to see the sights on the Lower East Side: Henry James, author of *Portrait of a Lady* and *Wash-*

ington Square among other famous novels, an expatriate American on his first visit back to his homeland in twenty years. The fellow writer-in-exile who met James, dined with him, and escorted him to the theater was my great-grandfather.

I wonder if the two men found some common ground; my guess is that they did not. Writer Stefan Kanfer describes the two men as "the most unlikely literary couple in the history of the city." As Gordin approached, James saw with trepidation "a great bear of a man with a black Assyrian beard and an air of flamboyant yet aristocratic Bohemianism characteristic of Russian artists," as he was described at the time. James, on the other hand, an inhibited, tight-lipped, closeted bachelor with no hair on his face or pate, must have been for Gordin a creature from a cold, distant planet, a thriving but cautious writer "as Gentile in his way as the other was Jewish," writes Kanfer.

The gentile writer did not fall in love with the Jewish quarter, as had Lincoln Steffens and the Hapgoods. Quite the opposite: he was offended by the noise, the language, the "swarming . . . the signs and sounds, immitigable, unmistakable, of a Jewry that had burst all bounds," he wrote in *The American Scene*. Learning that his host had eleven children could not have reassured him about "the Hebrew conquest of New York." He found the fire escapes clinging to the tenements "a little world of bars and perches and swings for human squirrels and monkeys." James dined in a tenement apartment near Rutgers Street with "my friend, the presiding genius of the district" and "a trio of contributive fellow-pilgrims," probably Winchevsky, Louis Miller, and one of Gordin's doctor friends. Though he attended the theater with Gordin, the novelist left after one act, not because of the language but because of the smell. Wrote James, "There was also, I recall, a snatched interlude—an associated dash into a small crammed convivial theater, an oblong hall, bristling with pipe and glass, at the end of which glowed for a moment, a little dingily, some broad passage of a Yiddish comedy of manners . . . then our sense of it became too mixed a matter—it was a scent, literally, not further to be followed."

The "Yiddish comedy of manners" was probably Gordin's *The Truth,* in which, ironically, the gentile characters recoil in exactly the same way as Henry James. It is to be hoped that Gordin, who must have been honored by the famous writer's visit, was unaware of his companion's delicate nostrils. I wonder if he knew that ten years before, James's play *Guy Domville* had been such a spectacular failure in London that the playwright was booed from the stage.

Another visit in the fall of that year was an unqualified success. Christian Waldemar Svensen, a Norwegian playwright, was befriended by the Yiddish dramatist, who wrote to invite Lillian Wald to meet his guest. The altruistic Miss Wald was the saint of the East Side, a young German-Jewish nurse and founder of the Henry Street Settlement, a nursing clinic for the poor and sick where she lived and worked. From 285 Henry Street, Lillian Wald replied:

> My dear Mr. Gordin:
>
> We will be very glad to meet your Norwegian friend, and would like to have you bring him to dinner some evening next week . . . Ibsen was absent from Norway when I was there, and I did not have the pleasure of meeting him, though I did meet the family of Bjornsen, his colleague. I hope . . . that you will keep us informed as to when the readings will take place.

It was Bjornson, incidentally, not Ibsen, who later won the Nobel Prize for Literature. We don't know about the dinner or the readings, but we do know that Svensen enjoyed his visit, for he sent an effusive thank you letter to Gordin. "I have been sitting at your feet and listened to you," he wrote, "and I must thank you for every new thought you have brought me, for every step you have helped me forward and for every stone you have helped me over, giving me your kindly hand."

There is no doubt where Svensen sat at Gordin's feet, or where the older playwright shared his thoughts and lent his kindly hand: his friendships were almost all nurtured before or after the theater, in the cafés. It was to the cafés, the crowded, smoke-filled centers of Lower East Side intellectual, political, and artistic life, that Gordin took Henry James. His guest did not appreciate the experience, dismissing the bright, noisy restaurants reverberating with exclamatory Yiddish as "torture-rooms of the living idiom." But in those rooms, Gordin was at home. Winchevsky, Kobrin, Hapgood, and others have all written about Gordin in Zeitlin's café, where he was so much part of the landscape, such a good friend to the management that Philip Zeitlin, the proprietor, later accompanied him to

Europe. Night after night the playwright sat in the café surrounded by his friends and admirers: intellectuals, writers, musicians, doctors, radicals, community leaders. With his "extraordinary imperial manner," he reminded Leon Kobrin of a leader of biblical times with his apostles: "With what reverence they look into his eyes—they are thrilled with every word. If he takes out a cigar, half a dozen hands reach out to light it. And if Gordin tells a joke, everybody laughs."

Once, as he sat in Zeitlin's with his tenth glass of tea, Gordin began to speak to the group about the memories dearest to his heart, thoughts of Russia, and Tolstoy. All noticed that as he spoke his eyes softened; he sounded lonely, heartsick, almost vulnerable, almost weak. But when a young member of the group contradicted something he had said, suddenly he sat straight, stroking his beard, and his eyes flashed fury. He immediately "demolished the other, who must have felt like a small boy who had been whipped," reports Kobrin.

Another writer describes the actors arriving with hearty appetite, washing down caviar, eggs, and potato latkes with huge goblets of Rhine wine and seltzer. But Gordin neither ate nor drank to excess. The cafés were more than his place of leisure; they were his classroom. He watched the actors to match them to the roles he was writing, and he gave them acting notes, pushing them always to be more realistic in their work. If an actor was angry or joyful in the café, Gordin would say, "Now, why can't you act like that on stage?" And on stage, in rehearsal, he would tell them not to work too hard, not to act, just to pretend they were with him in the coffee house. As they so often were.

The king of the theater was now founder and editor of yet another newspaper, *Dramatische Velt (Drama World)*. His articles appeared regularly there and also in other papers, including a long piece on the hotly debated issue "Realismus un Romanticismus" in the *Future*. (Abraham Cahan had published an article on the same topic, but his was entitled "Romanticismus un Realismus.") Gordin went on the road to lecture; early that year he went to Philadelphia to speak and to visit his son Sasha.

He did not, however, tour the Jewish communities of the south, as did, at this time, another tall man with a black beard who had "a very prepossessing appearance and a haughty mien," according to a newspaper report. The imposter introduced himself as Jacob Gordin and lectured on

Gordin's dramas in Chattanooga, Knoxville, Nashville, and Atlanta. How much the Yiddish theater must have meant to Jews far from New York that it was worth someone's time to impersonate the famous playwright.

The real playwright had made himself visible throughout the country with a torrent of one-act plays, written specifically for amateurs and seized upon by community groups. One that year had a professional production: "The Bundists" was produced by Adler at Grand Central Palace in honor of the first American convention of the Bund, or the Jewish Workers' Federation. Bundists were Jewish socialist revolutionaries from Eastern Europe, organizing to fight for workers' rights. Gordin, watching the idealistic faces argue and discuss, must have remembered his own counterculture youth and the days of his brotherhood, so very far from this American life.

At the beginning of 1904, another uptown newspaper, the *New York Sun*, came downtown to interview the fifty-one-year-old "Yiddish Shakespeare," the author, it says, of "70 plays, twenty-five of which were popular successes." (Would it were so.) Gordin informs the *Sun* that the one thing he aims for is to always tell the truth, no matter what the ultimate success of the play may be. "The truth always hurts somebody, but it lives longer in the end," he says.

"He speaks English fairly well," comments the interviewer.

Gordin concludes the *Sun* interview by boasting, "The American stage will at some near date want to produce my plays." He was right, but his first attempt at an American production was a disappointment. The experienced Broadway producer Daniel Frohman, then manager of the New Lyceum Theater on Forty-fifth Street, would with his brothers produce hundreds of Broadway plays, and less than a decade later become Adolph Zukor's right-hand man in the creation of Famous Players. Frohman came to see *The Kreutzer Sonata* and subsequently sent a letter rejecting it, in translation, for his theater. "My dear Mr. Gordon," he began, misspelling the name as many did, and would continue to do. "As a dramatic work, your play is a powerful and well-ordered work, intense, compact and strong; but the subject is one which drags forward so much moral ugliness, so much unhappiness, dealing so much with sordid traits, and vicious qualities, that I fear it would not prove a financial success with my audiences. . . . If the play . . . had a happier, or an animated plot, free from a gloom which the sad story imposes, it would have a better chance with an English audience."

Like Ibsen's dramas, Frohman explains, the play would be favorable for special audiences at special performances, but it was not up to the long commercial haul. By the end of the year, however, the producing team of Wagenhals and Kemper had bought the English-language rights to the play, and a playwright from Columbia was hard at work translating and adapting. We know this through two of his agonized letters at the YIVO. The young writer, Clayton Hamilton, made the mistake of sending Gordin an uppity letter reminding the playwright of the billing credit he had accepted as translator, in lieu of "larger financial remuneration." "I need the advertisement to help me in selling my own plays, and I want you to be sure to see that I get it," he had the temerity to write.

Gordin's bellow of rage can be reconstructed from Hamilton's cowed and groveling reply, in which he reveals what it was like to work with my great-grandfather. "I don't claim that my work was very good," he pleads, "but I want you to believe that it was careful. I read my revision to you page by page and line by line. I strove to take advantage of all of your suggestions; and I revised my revision in your presence until I thought it suited you."

For all this revising of revisions, the man had received one hundred dollars, for which, he says, he was amply satisfied even without billing credit for his work. He is sorry that Gordin thought him unsympathetic. "You have always been so kind to me," he says abjectly, "and I have so many sweet memories of your many, many favors to me, that it grieves me more than I can say to feel that you consider me ungrateful. To a young man like myself, just starting out, the influence and the friendship of such a man as you are among the most beautiful things that he can know."

When Great-Aunt Helen listed Gordin's dinner guests and friends, she remembered "Dr. Hamilton from Columbia" among them. Perhaps Hamilton was forgiven, allowed back to Gordin's hearth to continue his work, but the English-language script I was given by Helen, published in 1907, is by Langdon Mitchell, an accomplished translator; another version was translated by Samuel Schiffman, adapted by Lena Smith and Mrs. Vance Thompson. My great-grandfather no doubt overreacted to the young scholar's request, although Hamilton does reveal himself, in a lengthy arti-

cle he wrote the following year about the Lower East Side, to be both admiring and insultingly condescending about the quarter.

But there was another reason for Gordin's lack of perspective: he was
having a very bad year. Shut out of the Grand, except for *Lear* to which
Adler owned the rights, Gordin was desperately trying again at the Thalia.
He, actress Keni Lipzin, her husband Morris Mintz, and Morris Maashkoff
(the new but temporary stage name of the actor Morris Moscovitz) signed
an agreement with the landlords to rent the theater until August 1, 1905.
They agreed, among other expenses, to pay $450 for steam heat. About this
era, Bessie Thomashefsky wrote cynically "In the Thalia Theater they
played only Gordin—Kessler, Kalish, Lipzin, Moskovitz and the rest—and
with these plays they made their fame. But we at the People's Theater
were making fortunes. Well, the poor actors at the Thalia were not to
blame that the great Gordin had made them great. Soon enough they became envious of our big houses, threw away their art, sent God and Man
to the Devil and began to deliver the goods to Moishe—to the esteemed
and worthy audience."

With so much at stake, did my great-grandfather the producer do as
Bessie suggested and "deliver the goods," opting for the safe route and
pleasing Moishe with a charming comedy or musical? The answer is easily
guessed. On September 2, a month after signing the producing contract,
Gordin opened his new drama, sarcastically entitled *Tares ha-mishpokhe (The
Purity of the Family)*, a mocking reprise of the theme of the *Daily Page*'s attacks. The play, a "family drama in 5 acts about Jewish life in the USA," was
a tale of unhappy couples and tortured families, including a satiric view of
the arranged marriages of the nouveaux riches. Once again, the honest,
sensitive characters who dare to rebuke society's laws by loving who they
must are persecuted for their honesty; the heroine is forced to leave her sensitive soul mate and return to a violent, soul-destroying marriage. Those
who spout conventionality and orthodoxy in public while violating every
rule in private, like the *Daily Page* editors, live lives of wealth and privilege.

The play was a call to arms. Assembled at the premiere were all the socialist warriors of the East Side, including Abraham Cahan, seeing his first
Gordin play in years. The *Forward* editor came to the theater now not as a
fellow socialist, however, but as a theater critic. Specifically, as a Gordin
critic.

There were two surprises for the downtown population in the *Forward* the next day: that Cahan had disliked Gordin's play and that he said so with such relish and in such vituperative detail, in essence defending the *Daily Page*'s attacks. He began by dismissing the need to write the play at all. Gordin shouldn't have wasted time trying to expose Orthodox hypocrisy in America because "the religious hypocrite is not really a hypocrite at all here. He is nothing more than an example of American *chutzpah.*" Besides unnecessarily dragging up issues that had been settled months before, he wrote, *Purity of the Family* was badly written and conceived. Gordin didn't portray the arguments; he simply loaded his characters with sermons denouncing his enemies. "The leading feminine role was not a role at all. Madame Lipzin, who played this role, had nothing to play. Her task on stage was to propagandize; instead of acting, she had to make speeches." Cahan praised the male lead not for the writing but because of an excellent performance by Mogulescu, assailed the writing of the secondary roles as no better than Lateiner's work, and concluded sweetly that he hoped Gordin would write better plays in the future.

I wonder why Cahan chose this moment to launch his stinging provocation. Was there something in this play, particularly, that offended him? Or did he simply feel so confidant now in his position as East Side editor, writer, and polemicist that it was time to take on his rival? His shocked compatriots knew that Cahan's review was a gauntlet, thrown down in challenge. If only my great-grandfather had been able to shrug his shoulders and turn away. If only he had refused to register this barbed critique and instead had gone back to his study with an idea for a new play, which he would take his time to develop. He had dreamed of writing his masterwork when time and money allowed; now was his chance. Lost in his stage world, he wouldn't even notice when Cahan's vendetta fizzled out, ignored. His new play, produced with the luxury of time and concentration, would be a triumph, eventually made into a silent picture, and Gordin's reputation and finances would be golden forever.

But that was not my great-grandfather's personality, not his story. He was a combatant who could never turn away from what he saw as an insult or an injustice. "They were great haters in those days," said Lulla Rosenfeld. The Lower East Side was like a Western frontier town under the rule of two gun-slinging sheriffs who disagreed violently on how the place

Jacob Gordin circa 1906.

should be run and were ready to shoot, no longer at their mutual enemies, but at each other.

And so the next round began. Gordin denounced Cahan from the stage as a man of poor education and even poorer taste. Louis Miller again wrote an article in defense of the play, but this one Cahan refused to print, ordaining that the *Forward* didn't print discussion about theater reviews even when written by one of the paper's founders. Miller's article found a place in Gordin's own *Drama World*.

Published there too was Gordin's furious denunciation of his rival, exposing their most profound disagreement: how to teach their *landslayt* good socialist principles. Each man was trying, in his own paternalistic way, to lead his perplexed Jewish flock. But Cahan saw Gordin as a bombastic, overrated, nostalgic self-promoter. Gordin saw Cahan's attempts to ease his readers into the American way as a hypocritical sellout of everything he should stand for as a Russian, a Jew, and a socialist. Gordin fumed,

> I cannot reach any accord with him because he is my principle detractor, because whatever I build, he tears down, because whatever I've been doing all my life, he negates. We are working for the sake of the selfsame people. But I want to lead them forward, and he drags them backward through the Forward. I say to them, a man must be upright and defend his principles unequivocally; he teaches them to be politicians. I say, a revolutionary should not be two-faced. . . . He says, you have to keep the circulation in mind. I say, you have to lift the masses up to your level. He says, you have to stoop down to the level of the masses, cater to them, and accommodate yourself to their basest instincts.

Here is the core of the battle, the old way versus the new: one lifts, the other bends. The Russian playwright strove to elevate his audiences, once amenable but now more reluctant to make the effort to meet him. The American editor had learned to identify what they would like; he gave it to them and ran a profitable newspaper for decades. Both styles of leadership have intrinsic value and drawbacks. But there was no room on the Lower East Side for both.

Cahan's attack, and Gordin's counterattack, opened a chasm throughout the entire Jewish community of New York and beyond. Everyone took sides, for Gordin or for Cahan, some believing that Cahan's writing was petty and vindictive, others that he was justified in illuminating Gordin's faults. The division in the community was so profound, the atmosphere so charged with tension that family members stopped speaking to each other. Either Gordin or Cahan could do no wrong; there was no middle ground. It is hard to imagine thousands of readers and theatergoers now becoming emotionally, viscerally involved in a skirmish between two local writer-intellectuals, as if Noam Chomsky and William F. Buckley embarked on a savage war of words, leading thousands to demonstrate in the streets.

In a series of maneuvers, Miller and Winchevsky tried to oust the editor and regain control of the paper, but they failed. Cahan had secured his platform from which he would reign for half the century. Winchevsky was busy as editor of the revived *Future,* but Miller immediately founded a new paper, *Di Vahrhayt (The Truth)*, which waited only one issue before pouncing on the *Forward*. The new paper became the forum for the Gordin wing of the radical left on the Lower East Side.

Some commentators of the time felt that the true struggle was between Miller and Cahan as rival newspaper editors, and that it was Gordin's friendship with Miller that condemned him to Cahan's wrath. Whatever the reason, the flexibly socialist *Forward* remained locked in awkward alliance with the conservative religious papers against the reviled playwright.

In the midst of bloody skirmishes right and left, Gordin enjoyed a brief, memorable encounter with a youth who would one day become one of the greatest actor-managers of the Yiddish stage. A teenaged theater fanatic called Maurice Schwartz, a *patriyot* of David Kessler's, despaired as he watched the burly actor, week by week, losing popularity to Adler. The angry, self-defeating Kessler was often in cafés eating and playing pinochle rather than learning his lines, and so, besides always needing the prompter, he was getting fat.

Idealistic Maurice went to the theater as part of "a committee of five" of Kessler's most fervent admirers, to urge him to change his ways. According to Schwartz's biographer Martin Boris, when the committee arrived, Kessler was sitting in his dressing room clad in a toga, eating a plate of Chinese food. When warned that he was losing his fans, he moaned, "Woe to the deserted star who has lost his *patriyotn*; without *patriyotn* a play is no play, a role no role, a curtain call no curtain call!" Then he threw them out to finish his dinner.

Schwartz decided that only one person could save Kessler, and the next day he accosted Jacob Gordin at the ferry slip to Brooklyn. The nearly constructed Williamsburg Bridge loomed above; until it was completed, Gordin still ferried and walked back and forth from his home to the Thalia. (Louis Lipsky wrote that when money was tight Gordin "would walk from East Broadway to Brooklyn, lacking the fare, and never speak of it.") Schwartz begged Gordin to write a play or two for Kessler, so the actor could improve himself.

Impressed by the young man's appeal, the playwright led him to a nearby candy store "where he ordered seltzer for the boy and a dish of chocolate ice cream for himself," Boris tells us. Afterwards he invited the youthful *patriyot* to take the ferry with him, so they could continue their talk. Watching the waves, Gordin mused about the sad waste of Kessler's talent, thrown away on hot dogs and pinochle.

As the ferry docked on the Brooklyn side, Gordin spoke again. "Boy, go home and don't get involved in theater," he told Schwartz. "Even composers and actors die of hunger in the Jewish theater. I pity those children who lose their way. The stars exploit them and become famous, while you are ruined." Schwartz ignored Gordin's advice and went on to become one of the greatest stars in the history of the Yiddish theater. His first big break as an actor came when he was hired by David Kessler.

That day the playwright was on his way home to finish his latest play, *Di emese kraft (The True Power)*, which was bought by Adler in a friendly lull with his favorite writer. Gordin took to heart Schwartz's plea: the lead role of the doctor was played by Kessler, and Adler the producer took for himself the small but rich role of the doctor's assistant. Lulla Rosenfeld's mother Fanya, thirteen-year-old Frances Adler, was taken to Brooklyn by her father to hear the playwright read his work because the child role was for her. Fanya remembered Gordin reading it "like a genius, an acting genius."

The play opened at the Thalia in November, with Kessler as a kindly doctor and generous friend of the poor, a widower who marries an uncultured, materialistic yet lively young wife, played by Kalish. Her ignorance and thoughtlessness, not to mention her near-affair with his brother, so distress the doctor that one day, just after treating a patient infected with typhoid, he picks up his beloved young daughter. When the girl falls ill and dies, husband and wife, afflicted with guilt and grief, are reconciled.

The True Power, not often performed after its initial run, is a solid drama, though it is hard now to know how much is actually Gordin's. Lipsky writes that in rehearsal the play, which he describes as "realistic, high-class, literary," was "expanded, condensed, revised, and refined to suit [Adler's] whimsical and erratic ideas." Some of the characters are the "types" Gordin had to write to please both audience and actors: the innocent little girl, the greedy businessman, the intellectual who's a short-sighted snob, a part played with such panache by an actor named Schacht that the audience went mad for him on opening night, and Adler recast the part the following day. We know that the wife Fanny is not a satisfactory human being when she complains, in the dramatist's private joke, "I'm bored by good plays. There's not a song or dance in them."

As in so much of Gordin's work, we are shown the almost desperate love of a father for his daughter. In a tender scene with his little girl, Goldenweiser murmurs, "If my Birdy flies away from me, it's 'Finita la commedia.' I am done with life." At the premiere, the final curtain came down after one o'clock in the morning, to the sound of robust applause. But the play did not run long.

The following month, however, compensatory excitement: the American actress Blanche Walsh opened in Chicago in the first Yiddish play ever translated into English and performed on the American stage, *The Kreutzer Sonata.*

Though her press release called her "one of the foremost emotional actresses of the American stage," Blanche Walsh was a B actress on Broadway, heavyset and plain, attempting something daringly new in this ferocious melodrama by a playwright unknown to American audiences. On December 5, 1904, opening night in Chicago, as they waited to be introduced to some of the great talents of the Yiddish theater, the expectant multitudes had a lot to read in the program besides the synopsis of the play, the cast list, and the almost invisible name of the author. "McVicker's Theater," they read. "40 exits. The Safest Theater in the World." This was an important boast as only a few years before a theater fire in the city had killed six hundred people.

They perused advertisements for "a la Spirite Corsets," "Electric Lighting Outfits for Xmas Trees, no grease, no dirt, no danger," and for "Prof. Roach Dancing Schools—skirt dance, buck and wing dancing, sand jig, genteel song and dance." As the musicians warmed up, the audience read, "Dr. Charles Flesh Food. Produces Firm, Healthy Flesh. *Develops the immature bust.*"

And they learned about the next play to be produced in the theater, opening on Christmas Day and written by Jacob Litt, who was, coincidentally, the "Proprietor of the Theater." He announces his "World-Famous Success—'In Old Kentucky,' " and tells us that the story results in the "confounding and punishment of the villains in the play, while sweet and darling Madge Brierly, handsome Frank Layson, dear Aunt Alathea, the distinguished Colonel Sandusky Doolittle, 'of Kentucky, sah!,' and quaint old Neb are left in quite a glow of boundless felicity when the curtain falls. Then, too, there is the jolly band of pickaninnies—a source of never-ending pleasure to theater-goers—to make laughter and good humor prevail throughout an audience." Litt knew his audience; this jolly play was to run for twenty-seven seasons. And then the crowd closed their programs as the curtain rose on *The Kreutzer Sonata.*

Four acts later, Blanche Walsh and the company received an immediate standing ovation and eleven rapturous curtain calls. The reviews the next day were all guardedly or even wildly positive, if bewildered by the unusually febrile nature of this artistic event. One of the papers made a great deal not of the play but of the audience. After describing the prolonged standing ovation, it commented, "An overwhelming majority of the auditors last night were of the Jewish race. They nearly filled the boxes and the seats on the lower floor, as well as the upper part of the house, and their delight in the presentation of the Yiddish playwright's offering was beyond question."

The rest of Chicago, used perhaps to tales of boundless felicity, was taken aback by Gordin's tragic tale of hopeless love, suicide, pregnancy out of wedlock, family strife, marital discord, adultery, and murder. One headline announced, "A Terrific Drama of Hideous Realism and Intensity" with "Extremely Good Acting," its author a "Whirlwind of Emotionalism and Philosophy." Another queried, "TRAGEDY TOO 'BALD' as to world's evils FOR YOUNG PERSON?" Some critics were driven to rhetorical extremes. "Yes, the play is crude, but so is nature crude," wrote one. "This Jew writes with a dagger on the primeval rocks."

"The new playwright, at least new to translation, comes as a kind of fascinating, venomous and powerful menace," said another. "He rips open the common lies of decent silences with a shining machete, uses a morbid power vehemently and rips philosophies out of loathsome conditions as rare as they are hideous."

The *Chicago Daily Tribune,* unused to the Jewish style, complains about the incongruous alternation of comic with highly dramatic scenes, and wonders whether the overdrawn, extravagant emotions are in fact the "true to nature portrayal of the emotions of the people whose habits and manners are unfamiliar to us." Better than our melodramas, is the verdict. Yet another paper opines, "Gordin has taken the material for three plays and a melodrama, and has welded it together with brutal, masterful hammer-blows. A word as to the 'sensational' aspects of the play, which have been touched upon in advance notices: It contains much plain speaking, but not one word that was written in a questionable spirit."

The *Post* writes in a strangely disjointed way; perhaps the critic was a Yiddish speaker: "Gordin deals with primitev [*sic*] beings, with the great passion, in a fearless manner; he never endeavors to gloss over, to refine. He has a gloomy picture, spreads it over a tremendous canvas and puts the color on thick." One Chicago critic quoted "an intelligent and popular actor" in the audience, who remarked as he left that *The Kreutzer Sonata* was "one of the most unnecessary plays he had ever seen." The reviewer went on, "The criticism was just. The play is unnecessary. So was the Lisbon earthquake. So was the destruction of Pompeii. So was the Galveston flood. So is all the tragedy of life. But what would be the value we should place upon heaven were it not for hell?"

Well-known critic Burns Mantle takes time to reflect. "A daringly frank problem play, with the problem neither diluted nor even delicately presented, but deliberately and even brutally at every turn," is how he opens his review. He asserts that the play, dealing as it does with the smashing of the Sixth and the Seventh Commandments, is not for young people, or even for "your sister, some other fellow's sister, your mother or your mother's friends." He does not admire Blanche Walsh.

> Miss Walsh has become what might be termed a "healthy" actress, physically robust, mentally assertive. Her countenance has lost the mobility it once possessed, and the changing expression of her face is now limited to an opening and shutting of the eyes. If they are lightly shut, it means resignation. If they are tightly closed, it conveys a stifled "My God." ... Her outbreak in the last act was well within her scope and excellently handled, and so good a shot was she that, after she had killed her husband and his mistress, she received half a dozen curtain calls.

As for the author, Burns Mantle guardedly approves. "There is neither time nor space at this writing to discuss this, to us, new playwright as fully as interest in him prompts," he wrote. "That he is an author of consequence and one whose work is worthy of analysis, no one will deny. Should this, his first play to be translated, prove a popular success, it will be because it deals openhandedly with humanity, with neither apology nor euphemistic frivol."

A contest to rename the play was announced, because of its confusing title, but the winning entry, "The Mills of the Gods," was never used. Titled as it was, the play proved enough of a popular success to interest the legendary producers Sam and Lee Schubert, who put together a tour that spent the early months of 1905 traveling to far-flung cities like Louisville, Kansas City, Indianapolis, and Toronto, and to less populous cultural centers such as Schenectady, New York; Evansville, Indiana; and Lima, Ohio. Although its official Broadway opening was scheduled for the following year, it did play the Manhattan Theater in New York for a week in August and the Astor for a week in October, where it earned Gordin a royalty of $331.34—5 percent of gross. Following this success, Blanche Walsh's manager put out a press release announcing that she "will be seen in a new Clyde Fitch play this season."

Grande dame Bertha Kalish was watching all this; it was she, after all, who had originated the leading role, and she had a special love for the work. She told the *Sunday Telegraph* in 1904 that Gordin "was the greatest of all playwrights" and that *The Kreutzer Sonata* was "the greatest play written in the last 20 years." Though Madame Kalish continued to act in her native tongue, she was improving her English as fast as she could. At one point that year, during a brief revival of *Sappho,* her crowd of *patriyotn* grew so large that the police were called in to control them. Because many fans were unable to buy tickets, Kalish spoke to the audience between acts, promising to play again.

In an interview, explaining her admiration for the "socialistic or anarchistic ideals" in all Gordin's plays, she spoke of *Sappho* as a work in which "Gordin has presented a type of woman, not as she is, but as he believes, and as I believe, she will some day be. Yet she is intensely real . . . a woman of perfect independence and of perfect goodness." I wonder if it was Gordin's fantasy or Kalish's romantic notion that a woman of perfect independence and goodness could be real.

In the spring of 1905, as Adler appeared uptown as Shylock, Kalish too made the foray to Broadway, in the title role in Victorien Sardou's *Fedora.* The subhead of the *Times* review read, "AN ACTRESS OF MUCH POWER, But Somewhat Lacking in Polish and Method—She Has a Slight Accent That is Not Unpleasant." Next she triumphed in *Monna Vanna,* by Maurice Maeterlink. In September the star came back downtown, took over the old Windsor Theater, renamed it the Kalish Theater—"The Only Classic Jewish Play House in New York"—and opened with *The Kreutzer Sonata* in Yiddish. She continued with *God, Man, and Devil* and a translation she had commissioned of *Hamlet* in which, like Sarah Bernhardt, she played the title role.

But she was most interested in playing the translated *Kreutzer Sonata,* for which she believed she held the rights although she was aware that Jacob Gordin believed he had given sole rights to her rival, Blanche Walsh. As the *Kreutzer Sonata* debacle boiled over, Gordin must have wished he had been more systematic and businesslike in his dealings. Helen told me that her father often did not write formal contracts with actors and producers but would note an agreement on the sleeve of his shirt. When the shirt was laundered, the numbers and signatures disappeared.

•   •   •

In a huge burst of creative output, Gordin wrote three important plays for the Adlers in the theatrical season of 1905–6. *Der meturef (The Madman)* was actually written for Thomashefsky, but it was rejected by him and bought by Adler for himself and Sara. Branching into new territory, Gordin then produced a drama of ancient history, *Elisha ben Avuya,* and he followed that with the more traditional *Der fremder (The Stranger)* from Tennyson's "Enoch Arden." Though Adler was given three very different and superb roles, and he loved all three, only one was a financial success for the fiscally prudent producer, and so the season exacerbated the ongoing difficulties between actor and playwright.

The Madman is one of Gordin's most unsentimental and complex plays. Gordin's hero Ben Zion is an eccentric who despises money and improves himself by constant reading, not unlike his creator. His father, a soulless merchant, and his inane older brother Ezra scorn him as a melancholy misfit. His industrialist father's factories have poisoned the town's water, and by making public this and other unpleasant truths, Ben Zion enrages his family. Living in exile with an understanding aunt and uncle, the idealistic but impractical young scientist invents a perpetual motion machine that he hopes will provide a never-ending source of nonpolluting power. The play makes much of the importance of scientific discovery at a time when the concept that science rather than religion might save the world was exciting and novel.

Ben Zion loves Lisa, the daughter of his father's rival, though she has been promised to his brother Ezra. Pragmatic Lisa prefers the penniless genius but goes through with a marriage she finds repellent—as marriage so often is, in Gordin's world.

> LISA: I'm not keen on marriage, but how can a woman avoid it? We must be born, we must die and we must get married *(sighs)*.
>
> EZRA: Marriage should be looked on as a sound and practical business deal, ensuring a woman's material well being for a lifetime.

When after her wedding Ben Zion asks if she knows his brother well, she scoffs, "If men and women knew each other too well before marriage, there would be no marriage *(laughs without constraint)*." Her callow husband berates her for not appreciating his skills:

> EZRA: You may know how to drum on the piano keys and parley in French, but you can't appreciate business ability. My mother is a plain woman, but she understands and respects my father and me because she's no fool.
>
> LISA: Yes. If I could see you with your mother's eyes, I would be happier. And if she could see you with my eyes, she would be just as miserable as I am.

In *The Madman*, Gordin is again tackling his *Daily Page* enemies. As Ben Zion dreams of a future of peace and happiness for all mankind, his untested invention is stolen by religious neighbors, who think it is the work of the devil. The curtain falls at the end of act 3 to the sound of his machine, his life's work, being smashed to pieces. He collapses; lying at death's door in convulsions, he cries, "I'm going . . . the herd will trample me down . . ." When he is dead, the townsfolk and his family realize what they have lost. His neighbors remember how good the young man has been to them, and his father reveals a deep and hidden love for his son. But it is too late.

Though again featuring the destruction of a pure-hearted outcast, like many of Gordin's plays, the playwright's next work moved in such a different direction that it might have been composed by another writer altogether. Elisha ben Avuya was an actual Jewish heretic in the second century, a historic figure who died not for his faith but for his loss of faith. In his play *Elisha ben Avuya*, Gordin's hero Elisha, though based on the historical man, is his most autobiographical character. Like the writer's other champions, Elisha spurns adornment and money; loves books, music, truth, and mankind; lives misunderstood; and ends unhappily, hounded for his integrity and ethical vision. But this protagonist, most of all, exposes the pain and frustrated love behind Gordin's generalized philosophies.

Living in the era of early Christianity, Elisha is a respected Jewish leader who is gradually losing his belief in organized religion. He rejects not only his own faith, the rigid rabbinic Judaism of his ancestors, but also, even more firmly, the developing new Christianity. Because of his apostasy, Elisha is excommunicated by Jewish religious leaders; his house is burned down, and his only child, his beloved daughter Nomi, is lured away by a Roman officer. Persecuted for his heretical clarity, like Jesus, Elisha also encounters a Mary Magdalene figure, the beautiful young prostitute Beata who falls in love with him. The married Elisha protects and even loves her but will not touch her; rejected, she becomes a fervent Christian and spouts life-denying claptrap. In the last act, betrayed on all sides and flooded with despair, the hero takes poison. His daughter returns filled with love for him, just before he dies.

Elisha ben Avuya is an explicit depiction of Gordin's mental and emotional state at this difficult time. The playwright can feel his audience turning away and the forces of religious traditionalism and the press arrayed against him. Perhaps, too, he senses his health starting to fail. Feeling victimized and alone, he spills everything in his heart, his entire philosophy of life, into one play. Gordin is calling specifically to fellow Jews. When young Nomi snaps at Elisha, "You yourself laugh at the Jews, and suddenly you want me to wear Jewish clothes," he replies, "I laugh at the Jews because I don't want to show how my heart cries out to them. I laugh at the things that make the Jews look ridiculous." His pride in Jewish traits is revealed through the eyes of the critical Christians:

THE ROMAN INQUISITOR (surveying Jewish slaves): Don't let them sing. Jews shouldn't sing; songs bring out the revolutionary spirit.

ABNIMUS: Why do you behave differently to the Jews than to others?

INQUISITOR: The Jews are the worst enemy to government. Not only are they always dissatisfied, they plant ideas of dissatisfaction and protest in others.

ABNIMUS: Roman, their nationalism has great power you will never

conquer. Visit their many schools, meeting houses, read their writings—in
that lies their great strength.

The play is Gordin's love letter to the Yiddish theater, which he fears is
leaving him. Once again he portrays an intense bond between father and
daughter, but here I think Nomi, Elisha's flighty daughter, represents the
theater. Elisha tries to teach Nomi his high standards, but she cannot hear
him, running off, instead, to her ruin. "I want her to think and feel as I do,"
her father despairs, "but one mother has more influence on a child than ten
thousand fathers." Possibly a symbol of commercial interests in the Jewish
theater, Nomi's mother, Elisha's nagging, disloyal wife, subverts everything her good husband stands for. When Nomi returns, wiser from bitter
experience, the girl is penitent: "I was lonesome for you and for mother. As
I went further away, mother became smaller and smaller until she disappeared. You, however, were the opposite. You became bigger and bigger,
until only your figure was before my eyes. And when I was far away from
her, you became so big and so dear. Papa, it was from the distance that I actually saw you." This is the wishful thinking not only of a playwright but
of an increasingly estranged father. And of a forlorn warrior, who writes
with transparent wistfulness of the admiration and sympathy shown to Elisha but not to his creator. Elisha "pretends to be proud," explains a follower, elucidating what Gordin himself surely would have liked to
overhear. "Actually, he's good to everybody. You can't condemn a great
man like Elisha. Often we can't understand what a great man is doing."

Most clearly expressed are Gordin's thoughts about his lonely position
as self-declared iconoclast and infidel. Over and over comes the theme: he
who leads the way to change and enlightenment will know nothing but rejection and unhappiness. He discusses this with his pious disciple.

MEYER: Isn't it best to join your people for the common good?
    ELISHA: Yes, child, it's heroic to join your people, for your people. It is
more heroic to go against your people, striving for their greater happiness.
    MEYER: Why is that more heroic?
    ELISHA: Those who go along with the people are loved and honored
as long as they do nothing important. Those who go against the people,
even if they perform great deeds, are hated and dishonored. Do you think
it's easy for me to go against everyone? I want to open their blind eyes. Do

you think it doesn't hurt me to decry all they think is holy? I try to awaken their sleeping thoughts. He is honorable who tells the truth, and derives his happiness this way.

Gordin had often said exactly the same thing about his own life.

What interests me most in the play, besides the depiction of Gordin's obvious pain, is the relationship between Elisha and the fallen woman, Beata. Unlike Elisha's petty wife, Beata needs and wants him, but he won't allow himself intimacy with her until it's too late; he courts her only after she has embraced Christianity and rejected earthly love. I wonder if these scenes are a middle-aged man's fantasy—Gordin was only fifty-two, but he appeared much older and had been married for thirty-three years—or was it a declaration, as in *The Brothers Luria* more than a decade before, to an actual woman in the audience? Or to a vital memory?

When they first meet, Elisha the feminist acknowledges Beata's intelligence and need. She tells him that he is the first man who has ever spoken to her not as a woman but as a person, and she asks him to be her friend. Elisha responds with honesty that he can be her confidant and protector, but not her friend. "A healthy honorable man," he tells her, "only becomes the friend of a woman if that way he can mask his true feelings." Later, as Beata waters the flowers, in itself a sign of enlightenment, she enthuses, "I'd love to see his room, where he sits and studies—his books that give him so much pleasure—his desk. I would kiss the desk where the noble hand writes." This is almost exactly what Marussia wrote in her impassioned love letter, more than a decade before.

In their longest scene, Elisha allows himself to reveal to the loving Beata how lonely he is, how hurt by his solitude, with no real love or understanding, "an outsider, an outcast." Beata cries out her admiration and support: "Let me see the real you, not as you show yourself to others. I know that beneath the surface of that solitary, proud, angry, critical, aloof person is buried someone else—a good man, loving, tender, good-hearted, sensitive. You are locked into yourself. Open your heart to me, love me." These powerful lines were later quoted by Winchevsky to reveal the true soul of his best friend.

"Oh child," Elisha says in response, "because you love me so, and understand me, that alone would make me love you!" He draws her to him and then forces himself to push her away. Love in unfavorable circumstances, he mourns, only brings pain. His wife enters, angry to find the fallen woman near the husband she claims as hers. Beata rages in response.

> He's yours? Why? Do you know him? Do you love and understand him? Are you interested in his knowledge, his greatness? Does your heart bleed when he's sad? His lofty thoughts, his great spirit, his iron will, his courage, is all this worth anything to you? When Elisha speaks his golden words you yawn; when he's with the gods in the heavens you're busy with your pots of soup. You've been beside him for twenty years and yet you're as far away from him as the earth is from the sky. If he's yours, why are you a stranger to him?

If my great-grandmother, who had spent her whole life busy with pots of soup, was sitting beside her husband at the premiere, I hope she understood Elisha's wife as a metaphor and not as a portrait.

The opening night performance went on for nearly four hours. An English-language review, though positive, remarks dryly, "From a Gentile point of view, the performance would have been better had the dialogue been greatly condensed." The choice role of Shlomo Hoots was another triumph for Mogulescu. Adler, the review notes, "was as superbly impressive as ever." After the third act, the actor received numerous floral tributes and made a long speech about his problems with the actors' union.

But Gordin had predicted that *Elisha* would not be a hit, and he was right: it was a devastating flop, running less than a week. "Put it on after my death," he advised Adler bitterly. "Then it will be a success." Again, he was right. Following Gordin's demise, Adler mounted *Elisha* again. According to one perhaps exaggerated report, it ran for a year.

The *Forward* review was a caustic piece by Cahan's then friend and colleague M. Baranov. Though Baranov admitted, with unusual warmth, that Elisha was "one of the finest and most powerful roles our talented dramatist-poet has created," he went on to belittle the play, disagreeing with Gordin's portrayal of early Christians and ending, "What started out as a grandiose tragedy ended up as a comedy. The heart ached for the play and its author."

Gordin was deeply hurt by the failure of a play so linked to his soul, and was further displeased that his next play, *The Stranger*, which opened in April 1906, was in comparison so successful. As was now habitual, he scolded his audience one night during the run. "I gave you a play, *Elisha*, and you didn't like it, though I liked it very much. Now I give you another play—you like it, and I, not at all," he said, again surely unique among playwrights in publicly dismissing his own most recent work. "Why do you run to see a melodrama like this? What pleases you about it?"

After Gordin's speech, Adler was furious. "Mr. Gordin, what have you done?" he cried. "You're killing my success!"

"I told the audience the truth," replied the intractable playwright.

Adler's act 2 entrance in *The Stranger* is described by his granddaughter as the greatest moment in all Yiddish theater. Adler played Naftali Herz, a soldier who goes off to war and vanishes. His wife, left with two children and pressured to remarry, waits six years for his return. Finally she agrees to wed her suitor and go with him to America. In the second act, set naturally in the new country, the seemingly happy wife still hears her former husband's voice calling her. At the end of the act all is quiet on stage; the new husband sits working at a table, listening to sad music. A knock at the door. "Come in." Silence. Another, louder knock. "COME IN!"

The door is slowly pushed open; Naftali Herz stands there, haggard and aged. He doesn't reveal himself and is so changed that his own wife doesn't recognize him. The stranger, as the family calls him, begins to frequent the house; he meets his own children. In act 4, the young daughter is called on to recite a poem: Tennyson's "Enoch Arden," about a husband lost for years at sea, who returns to find his wife happily remarried and who renounces his right to his family in order to preserve their happiness. The girl stands center stage, speaking first in English and then in Yiddish, so that all the characters in the play, and everyone in the theater too, could understand. A pause.

And then the wife, the great Sara Adler, turns to the stranger with tears in her eyes. "Naftali Herz. I recognize you," she says, and calls her children to meet their father. "I'll go with you," she cries. "With you, I don't care if I'm the most unhappy woman on earth, because I was once the happiest." And husband and wife are reunited.

Adler played the work intermittently, reviving it in 1924 after his stroke, a broken man playing a broken man. When that production arrived in Toledo, police were on hand at the theater to control ten thousand people vying for tickets. At Adler's entrance, "such emotion broke out in the theater, there were such tears, such shouts of his name, that he wept aloud, and the curtain had to be lowered," wrote his granddaughter.

The play was produced again that same year, at Kessler's Second Avenue Theater. The audience sobbed throughout Adler's short first scene, and called him out eighteen times as the first act curtain fell. When he broke down in his dressing room after the final curtain, his wife tried to console him. "You made them cry as they have never cried before," she told him.

"But it was not my art that made them cry," replied the actor. He would die two years later.

The Stranger did well, though the *Forward* review, written once more by Baranov, attacked Gordin personally. "The play, in general, is better than most melodramas playing on the American stage," he wrote. "If Mr. Gordin didn't consider himself a Jewish Shakespeare, we would say he did the best with his small talents . . . But for a man who has the nerve to compare himself to Shakespeare and Ibsen, we expect a lot more."

Despite this string of powerful roles, in a September interview Adler disparages his long-time colleague. "We have but one strong Yiddish playwright, Gordin," he says, "and he is too independent to write." In Adler's summation of his colleague's skills, Gordin ranks with Ibsen and Maeterlinck but is not as good a playwright as Sudermann. "When [Gordin] first came to America, he was poor and announced that he would furnish his house with plain furniture, and without carpets, following a mode of life similar to Tolstoy's. But after he had tasted American success, a change came over him. His gold watch was as expensive as his neighbor's. His dress, his speech, his habits, all denoted the man of the world and consequently his Tolstoy ideas vanished."

Poor Gordin, who had far less money and lived far more simply than his thespian colleagues, to endure sniping because of his gold watch and his carpets! "For myself," the actor grumbles, "I have spent twenty-six years of my life on the stage, and shall remain there until the end of the chapter, but it seems a hopeless task to elevate the Yiddish Theater." In October, he was at the Grand starring reluctantly in *The Businessman, or, The Downtown Parents and the Uptown Children*, while Thomashefsky at the People's had produced a bauble entitled *The Jewish Yankee Doodle*, a "melodramatic musical" with a plot like Cahan's *Yekl*. All the great Yiddish actors, with the exception of Keni Lipzin, had an enviable facility in going back and forth between the didactic dramas of Gordin and his acolytes, and the lightweight work of the *shund* writers and traditionalists.

As the years rolled by, Adler's pessimistic tone was proven right; the serious plays were produced less and less frequently, the frothy ones more and more. The new Yiddish audience wanted money and a new address, and for entertainment they liked sentiment and comedy, sometimes even in English. To indicate how quickly the greenhorns adapted, Hutchins Hapgood wrote that some of them buy only English-language newspapers and converse about prize fights, crime, and business. They also "gradually quit going to synagogue, give up *kheyder* [Hebrew school] promptly when they are thirteen years old, avoid the Yiddish theaters, seek the up-town places of amusement, dress in the latest American fashion, and have a keen eye for the right thing in neckties."

· · ·

My ancestor, at this moment, was preoccupied with more important matters. There was crisis in Russia, and he was fomenting revolution as best he could from afar. On "Bloody Sunday" in January 1905, troops in St. Petersburg fired on thousands of demonstrators bringing a petition to the tsar at the Winter Palace; months of unrest and protest followed. The nation was also, disastrously, at war; after a Japanese attack on the Russian fleet in early 1904, the tsar launched a war with Japan. Gordin hoped that losing the war would bring down the Russian government and "kill the prestige of the Tsar, though I am sorry for the Russian soldiers," he was quoted as saying. "No, I don't think they will win. I desire Japan to win, but for the sake of Russia herself."

In May 1905, the Russians were indeed defeated by the Japanese. A month later, the battleship Potemkin commandeered headlines around the world. When sailors aboard the Black Sea ship refused to eat bad meat, the ship's commander cried mutiny and ordered a number of men shot. The executioners refused to shoot and the sailors took over the ship, killing the captain and other officers. As the Potemkin sailed into Odessa, riots in support of the sailors provoked a dramatic charge by mounted Cossacks, resulting in over one thousand dead, killed by bullets or by the subsequent fire that engulfed the port. The ship sailed on, with the eyes of the world upon her.

Jacob Gordin raised money for the sailors' cause by producing money-making events. At a September fund-raising concert in Elizabeth, New Jersey, Gordin spoke for an hour and a half about the gifts the Jewish and Greek races had given to civilization, and the poor conditions for peasants and Jews in Russia. A reporter at the event described the speaker as "the idol of the East Side, one whose literary attainments and general culture have not disdained him the friendship of eminent men other than his compatriots." I take this to mean that he was so cultured and successful that he actually had non-Russian-Jewish friends. The report concludes, "Gordin, a striking figure of immense frame, burning eyes and patriarchal beard that sweeps to his waist, received a splendid ovation."

This journalist was really swept away by the speaker, whose magnificent beard never grew past his breastbone and who was hardly "immense." The man is described so repeatedly as a "colossus," "a man of massive size," "a giant figure" that I was determined to find out how tall he actually was. Helen told me he was at least 5'11", so I wondered why one of his canes, which is now mine, fitted my hand so nicely. I found out the truth when George Gordin Jr. gave me his grandfather's certificate of naturalization: Jacob Michael Gordin was 5'8½", exactly my height but much taller than the average Eastern European man of the time, who was 5'1" to 5'3". Of course he would seem taller to a young girl. And my great-grandfather stood erect, his spine so straight that when he returned from Europe in 1907, even the ship's manifest at Ellis Island reports his height as 5'10".

The florid writer covering the fund-raiser finishes, "The Liedertafel Society sang and was encored repeatedly. Miss Dora Gordon scored a hit with her performance on the piano. Miss Katy Mararow's clever manipulation of the violin won for her a number of encores. Morris Lessin and A. Greenburg of New York recited." And as a result over $3,000 was raised at this one concert alone.

In October, Gordin received an effusive letter from London, gratefully acknowledging receipt of money "given for the allocation [*sic*] to the International Revolution Committee for the sailors of the crew of the Potemkin." The writer, Lev Deutsch, informs him that the money has been passed to Vera Zasulich, who will one day be a famous revolutionary.

Deutsch himself, only two years younger than Yakov Mikhailovich, later became a leader of the revolutionary movement. With his thank you letter he sent along his novel, asking Gordin to find a publisher for it in the Jewish press.

Shaken by a general strike against the Russian government, Tsar Nicholas II was pressured, on October 17, into passing a manifesto granting a constitutional government with a parliament, or Duma. The very next day, a series of pogroms was triggered by the tsar's instigators, and continued over the next year in more than 650 towns and cities, including Elizavetgrad. The worst was in Odessa: over 400 dead, 1,600 Jewish houses and shops damaged. Although Plehve, the tsar's hated minister of the interior, had been assassinated by socialist revolutionaries the year before, his hideous words lived on. "We must drown the revolution in Jewish blood," he had said. If Russian peasants were busy blaming and slaughtering Jews, they wouldn't notice hunger, landlessness, incompetent government, and the disappearance of the Duma.

Once again, it was clear that though life might improve for their Russian brethren, for Jews the horrors would not, would never abate, and yet another tsunami of immigrants from Russia landed in New York City. Gordin was made aware of the latest assaults not only through the Russian newspapers but in the mail he received from home. There are so few personal letters among his papers at the YIVO that these are treasures: a string of imploring missives in Russian, almost all confusingly undated, from his sister Eva Liaznova.

There is tragedy in these letters. Eva, the mother of two girls and three boys, lived in the southern Crimean town of Melitopol. She never mentions her husband, although an enclosed photograph in one envelope shows her and her spouse with one of their sons. Gordin's other sister Masha lived in the town too with her husband and children. Someone called Doina or Doyno is always mentioned in passing, perhaps a cousin or aunt, or possibly a non-Jewish former servant or nanny; forward-thinking Russian Jews, like Aneuta in New York, made efforts to treat home staff almost as members of the family. Melitopol, interestingly, with its large Jewish population, was a center for idealistic Tolstoyan agricultural colonies; another letter was sent to Gordin from a former Brotherhood follower now living there. I wonder if his sisters had attempted to follow his dream of communal farming.

Eva's heartrending correspondence dwells on daily concerns, her poverty and fear, and begs for Gordin's attention. It is clear she thinks her brother in America is comfortable and successful while she is suffering terribly in Russia. Why doesn't he write back? she wonders, and so do we. In the first letter, written around 1904, Eva expresses her fears for her oldest son, who despite his bad leg has been drafted again, a grave concern now that Russia has declared war on Japan. And then her litany begins: "It has been a long time since I've heard from you, and now I've decided to send you a letter and to share my sorrow . . . Will I ever see your family, Yasha, or you? So many times I have asked you to send family photographs, but you never fulfill my request. I am keeping my hopes up to see you and Aneuta in person, but only God knows whether we shall ever achieve this goal. People often tell me what the Jewish newspaper writes about you."

In the next letter, not long after, she still has not heard from her brother. As her words show, the ban on Yiddish theater was rescinded this year.

> I beg you to write—I know that you are busy and have no time to write, but we so seldom write to each other. I've heard much about you in the last little while. A Jewish theater troupe was in town and staged your plays. King Lear was staged, as well as The Oath. Dear brother, you cannot imagine the pleasure I received! And Masha as well! It was as though we saw you in person. And heard your wise words. When they staged King Lear, all the men were in tears. How painful it is to have such a famous brother, and not see him!

And then, in 1905, her world explodes, as Russia heaves around her:

> I must inform you of some unpleasant news, something that happened in Melitopol. During April 18th and 19th, there was a pogrom. This horrible word pogrom is heard very often in Russia these days. And now we had to experience this horror.
>
> We were waiting for it on the . . . second day of the Easter festivities. And at six o'clock in the evening, people started running all over the place, and I heard screams, "Beat the Zhids [kikes]!" I will never forget that terrible long night. Yes, the pogrom lasted the whole night and the next day. When we saw our friends again after these two days we had all aged considerably.
>
> Two of my sons, not sensing any danger, were going for a walk in the

city, and when the pogrom began they joined the resistance movement, made up of armed Jews. Only at 3 a.m. did I finally see them. They came home to calm me down, and told me what was happening in the center of the city. The thugs destroyed a drugstore, and began demolishing a shop. But the Jews started shooting in the air. And the crowd changed its direction and headed for the church, where the bells were ringing to call people to service, but the thugs continued looting. Forty-four stores were burned, and then they started looting private homes. All the streets were covered in feathers. Some people were left with nothing.

The next day the crowd got so violent and angry at the Jews for resisting, that they moved towards the Jewish neighborhood with the idea of killing them. But then the governor came in with the troops. There were quite a few wounded, Jews and Russians. There was such panic and distress, no one has been able to get back to normal. I along with three of my children went to Doina's place, and we were prepared to die together. But thank God, we survived. I honestly thought that we wouldn't have the chance to write you again!

A newspaper of the time reported that the "disturbances . . . began with brawls in the street. A crowd armed with sticks fell upon the Jews, but also damaged and plundered the property of Christians. A row of shops was set on fire. On the arrival of the troops order was restored," but not before thirteen Jews had been killed. There was another massacre that day in Simferopol. The worst occurred in Zhitomir, with three days of rioting and the murder of fifteen Jews.

In Eva's next letter, written around the end of October 1905—just after Gordin had done his fundraising in New Jersey—the political situation continues at the forefront of her sorrows.

We are all very nervous; the situation in Melitopol is very dangerous for Jews. Every day you read in the newspaper that pogroms are imminent— this person was killed, that person. The rumors are tearing my soul apart; waiting for my children to come home from work, I am worried sick. Every day there are leaflets calling for pogroms against the zhids. My God what kind of life is this? How happy you must be to be living on the other side of the ocean. I have many friends in Melitopol trying to get to New York. Their relatives are sending them "shiftkarts." Would you think badly of me if I asked you for a shiftkart for one of my children? I'm begging you not to fail me.

I'm afraid I'm bothering you too much, overwhelming you with my letters and my life. You must be sick and tired of me by now. I'm afraid if you get tired of me you will stop writing to me altogether. If that happened I would not forgive myself but it would be too late.

The *shiftkart* was a ship's ticket sent from America, the most common way for landed immigrants to assist the passage of family left behind. Yet again, she heard nothing from the silent man on the other side of the ocean. In her next missive she mentions the tsar's short-lived constitution, which appeared in October and was withdrawn only a few months later.

November 12, [1905] Melitopol

Dear Yasha:

I see you are not interested in knowing what is happening in our lives. I suppose you are very well aware of what is going on in Russia. Blood is being spilled in oceans. Our Melitopol is still untouched. Measures have been taken and the troops have been called in. People are being recruited for the army. There are many enemies, who instigate beating up the zhids. We are experiencing very uncertain times. . . . There are some people calling for the murder of the Jews. Two of my sons are not in Melitopol. After the strike they lost their jobs. My oldest son left for Simferopol, where he was arrested and spent a whole month in jail. This put a great strain on my health. The younger one left to look for a job and I don't know where he is . . . God only knows what awaits them in the future. God only knows how much blood will be spilled before they reach their goal. How dearly will they pay? This little constitution has cost us so much. I remember how it was greeted with rejoicing. Many of our acquaintances have been killed.

There are many families leaving to go abroad. Of course, they are all wealthy. There's much more to say, but not everything can be expressed, and anyway, to keep receiving these sad letters must be a nuisance for you. You must be sick of this by now. It is time to write more joyful letters. Why don't you answer my letters? Please respond. It has been two years already since we've received anything from you. Not a single letter. Farewell. Be healthy. Kiss Aneuta and the children. Regards from Doina and Masha. Eva Liaznova. My address: City of Melitopol, Station Street, Pashkovsky House.

Helen told me that when her father went to Europe a year and a half later, in the summer of 1907, "there was one sister he really loved and wanted to see, but he wasn't allowed in." If he loved Eva so much, why didn't he respond to her pleas? In the next letter I unearthed and had translated from Russian, I learned that in March 1907, an affectionate young woman called Sarah had come from Russia to stay with the Gordins. Believing her to be one of Eva's daughters, I was relieved to learn that Gordin had at last come through for his sister and her family. On April 10, 1907, in a chatty letter addressed to my great-grandmother Anna Lazarevna, Sarah wrote from the steamer on her way back to Europe: "What are Nadia, Lenochka [Helen] and your little boys doing? What about Yakov Mikhailovich and Sasha? It is sad to think that maybe we shall never see each other again, but still, I'm so glad that I met you. Give my regards to Sonia and Liza. With kisses, Your Sarah."

In one of sister Eva's later letters, however, though I struggled to interpret her words in any other way, it is ineluctably clear that her children have never met their American family. She tells her reticent brother that though it seems he has not received any of her previous letters, she is sending this one with a young acquaintance. Sarah, I believe, was Eva's young friend, who became close to the family but was not related.

Why didn't Gordin try to bring over even one of the Liasnovas? My translator told me that Eva's letters are written in ungrammatical Russian, probably by a poorly educated, somewhat coarse Yiddish speaker. Perhaps Gordin was simply snobbish and didn't want an unschooled sister on his doorstep. Perhaps, after cutting himself loose from his family, he didn't want to become ensnared in the reality of a past he had idealized. Possibly, too, even if he had sent money to Russia through the years, the thought of the financial and social responsibility for his sister and her big family, and then Masha as well, undoubtedly, to follow with her husband and four children, was enough to keep his pen still and his door closed.

On November 23, 1905, just after Eva wrote complaining that for two years her brother had sent "not a single letter," he produced a benefit of *The Jewish King Lear* at the Grand Theater to assist the Russian Jews "murdered and plundered" in the pogroms. The following year, he sent 200 rubles to an old Odessa friend with a physical handicap, who sent back a profoundly grateful thank you. "I am so happy," she wrote, "that you have remained the same person." I can only hope that he was as kind, at the same time, to his sister.

Despite the sufferings of his family, Gordin still had idealistically high hopes for Russia's future, telling an interviewer with "mingled courtesy and reticence" that he believed that in time Russia would be one of the greatest nations of the world, "just as now, Russian music, poetry and literature are great. . . . At the present time the whole of my native country is a prison. But even in that prison you hear the sound of distant words, of music, of song. We cannot imagine what it might grow to be when it has freedom, after the action of politics." Unfortunately, Great-Grandfather, what Russia grew to be after the "action of politics" was indeed unimaginable, though "freedom" does not enter the picture. A nation that could divest itself of the cruel and addled tsars and replace them with a system just as addled and cruel, if not more so, seems doomed to eternal misery. And now, after the disintegration of the U.S.S.R., we read about greed, corruption, and brutal gangsters and see that doom again.

Gordin, extraordinarily, asserts in the interview that "every city in the United States is full of Russian spies." He accuses the tsarist government of killing every freethinking man of genius, citing Pushkin, Lermontov, "Dostoievsky—poor man, after his Siberian exile, broken down, dying, he became a conservative. Turgenev, Stepniak, Kropotkin—here I have them all . . ." He gestured toward his library. "Here they all stand, and I cannot see one, not one, that was not persecuted." But Russia is producing giants of thought and daring, he continues, mentioning specifically how much he admires Gorky. "The great men," he says, "are still coming."

He was right. During his time, Russia surely produced a richer assortment of geniuses in all fields of the arts, in music, literature, visual arts, theater, dance, and design, than any other country, in any era. Toward the end of the nineteenth century and in the first years of the twentieth, Russia produced the exceptional writers he mentioned, as well as Chekhov, Rimsky-Korsakov, Kandinsky, Tchaikovsky, Diaghilev, Stanislavsky, Chagall, Bakst, Andreyev, Prokofiev, Nijinsky, Fabergé, Chaliapin, Borodin, Mussorgsky, Shostakovich, Fokine, and Anna Pavlova. Not to mention one of the greatest artists of all time, Leo Tolstoy, who though elderly was still churning like a battleship.

Great Russians of thought and daring were also arriving, one after another, in New York. 1905 brought Chaim Zhitlovsky, Zionist and delegate of the Social Revolutionary Party, who in October challenged Gordin to a public debate on "Nationalism Versus Assimilation." The scholarly Zhitlovsky argued in favor of creating a state for Jews in Palestine; his opponent disagreed. Gordin's exasperated point was, "It is not enough that we're Jews, we must become Jewish Jews?" Jewish Jews live isolated and apart in their own Jewish country, an incomprehensible picture to Gordin, who believed that a socialist could not be a Zionist. He argued for the bigger picture, Jews as exemplary citizens of the world. He also stated, with not a little humor and foresight, that Jews would not be good at making a country because they're "against organization and group discipline."

A newspaper reported about the debate, "Mr. Gordin was not at his best as an orator. In fact, he is an infinitely better writer than speaker, and on Thursday night he was ill and hoarse. But what he said was profound and showed him to be a man of monumental knowledge. Mr. Gordin quoted from nearly all the writers, ancient and modern, in every European language. He pleaded for freedom for the Jew in Russia, but he would not encourage an ephemeral nationalism that could not result in any good to Jews as a whole."

Chaim Zhitlovsky, a witty, resourceful debater twelve years younger than Gordin, was later described by historian Nora Levin as "a prodigy of intellectual brilliance [who] stirred mass audiences with his eloquence and dazzling erudition." Yet the newspaper concluded, "Mentally, Gordin towers above his antagonist as a condor of the Andes above a black beetle, and the big man—with the weakness of all big men—could not forgo the desire to play with his eloquent but weaker antagonist." The meeting broke up with roars of disagreement from both sides. But there was no ongoing unfriendliness between the men: Zhitlovsky was a eulogist at Gordin's funeral.

Another accomplished Russian, Abraham Goldfaden, "the Father of the Yiddish Stage," had tired of struggling in Europe, and returned in 1903 to New York. After his arrival, for several years, he received a stipend from Adler and Thomashefsky so that he would not starve. This year, 1905, he was lauded at a testimonial in his honor, and several of his comic folk plays were revived. Although an earlier newspaper report noted that "Mr. Gordin paid his respects to Mr. Goldfaden, and spoke in high terms of the beginning he has made for the Yiddish theater," Goldfaden was not won over; he remained a vociferous critic of his rival. "I search out the fine attributes of the Jews, and especially portray fine family life on stage," he jeered, whereas Gordin looks only for ugliness—theft, adultery, murder—in the Jewish family. "What's he doing in the Yiddish theater?" he asked rhetorically. Believing that only someone who hated Jews would portray them in a less than favorable light, Goldfaden, too, accused Jacob Gordin of anti-Semitism.

Also in 1905, actors Pavel Orlenoff and Alla Nazimova of the Moscow Art Theater arrived in New York with their company, which found favor with the Astors and Vanderbilts. The flamboyant, bisexual Nazimova stayed in the United States and was an occasional guest in Gordin's home. The following year, in April 1906, the distinguished Russian writer Maxim Gorky appeared, greeted by a committee of equally distinguished new world writers including Mark Twain. Shortly afterwards a storm of disapproval hit Puritan America, and Mark Twain snorted his disapproval as loudly as everyone else when it was discovered that the woman traveling with Gorky was not Mrs. Gorky, at least in the legal sense.

Suddenly Gorky was persona non grata everywhere except among his Russian compatriots on the Lower East Side. In June, Gordin wrote an article in the *Future*, praising the writer whom he greatly admired for his romantic ability to "poeticize the soul of reality." Gorky was apparently eager to encounter his Jewish colleague, but he took sick and the two men did not meet. In any case, Gordin feared that Gorky only wanted to meet him because of his translations of the Russian writer's plays, not for his own work as a playwright. "If I had written my *Mirele Efros* and [the other plays] in Russian," he complained, "would people like Gorky not have known about me?"

Now Gordin and Adler, too, were more often combatants than colleagues, and so the playwright no longer had a confirmed theater space. His plays, when sold, brought a few thousand dollars, but he was concerned about the future. According to Lipsky, though the playwright "looked like a grand duke, built on a large scale, with huge appetites which were hard to satisfy . . . he was seldom far from starvation. He would not talk of himself or his privations."

But vulnerability enraged him and provoked a caustic piece for the *Fu-*

ture entitled "The Future of the Yiddish Theater." Our theater is still an impressionable child, he chided, corrupted by selfish American values, incapable of mature work. Switching metaphors, he asserted that Jewish theater is a delicate plant, withered by overheated America, where it has no future. "As soon as the spring of freedom comes to Russia," the plant must be sent home.

He attacked Yiddish actor-managers, who should be visionary directors but instead care only for money, disdaining literature, art and the public. Like Adler, he also blamed the restrictive actors' union for the poor prospects of his theater. Youth came in for his disapproval; growing up as vulgar Americans, they only want a theater "where they won't be plagued with poetry and philosophy, where they will be sure to be given sensational stage-effects and tricks." (If he knew what was to come!)

And finally, he presented his last rationale for the jeopardy of his livelihood: Jewish life in America just doesn't make very good drama. "The settled American Jew," he fulminated, "is a dull, plastic object, who deals in real estate, plays poker, gambles on the exchange, and bets on political candidates and racehorses."

Pace Clifford Odets, born that year (1906), and many other dramatists of Jewish life in America. Gordin is so angry now that his good sense is often left behind.

•   •   •

Far from thinking of returning, like delicate plants, to Russia, the great stars of the Yiddish theater were enjoying ever-increasing prosperity. Adler owned a brownstone mansion on East Seventy-second from which Sara went to Paris every spring to buy gowns. The Thomashefskys had three homes: a twelve-room house in Brooklyn, a bungalow by the sea with electric lights and a fountain full of goldfish, and a house on twenty acres in Hunter, New York, with an outdoor theater called Thomashefsky's Paradise Garden. They kept a coach and horses and each of their sons had his own Arabian steed. At the theater, Boris's dressing room was decorated in gold and marble and hung with tapestries.

And what of their writer? Gordin was not going hungry. In 1906 he broke with Adler and signed a contract with Keni Lipzin, to write four new plays for her company at the Thalia during the coming year for an unprecedented payment of $7,000. Soon controversy would erupt and his work for Lipzin would end, only to begin again, but in the meantime the Gordins were feeling flush. Their extravagance extended to having some renovations done on their house.

My great-grandfather wrote the contract himself, longhand, on June 23, 1906. Contractor Israel Perlman agreed to "renovate and renew the complete house of Jacob Gordin," an extraordinary amount of work to be done in only three weeks for a fee of $500, with a bonus of $100 "if the work is well done, with the best materials, and Jacob Gordin is satisfied." Among other things, Perlman was to repair the roof and paint all the rooms except those on the parlor floor, which are "to be papered with the best and most expensive paper." He would clean and repair all windows, ceilings, stairs, and the front stoop. The kitchen was to be washed and painted and a new iron stove "of the best make" to be installed with shelves above. Also to be installed for Aneuta and her helpers, including her daughters and grand-daughter who all had housekeeping chores: a new stone sink and three stone washtubs of the best quality, to replace the wooden ones.

Perlman must tend to more mundane matters, making sure "there won't be a bad smell from the sewer pipe" and "in the basement toilet room, put in a gas line." Finally, he should "paint the two front doors of the house, so that it looks very nice" and then "repair and paint all small items that cannot be noted, but that Jacob Gordin will expect to be done."

This is a contract written by a man acutely aware of his surroundings, a perfectionist used to asking for hard work, whose attention to detail is scrupulous: "Doors on parlour floor—install new glass, same design as before." He expects to live in this house for a long time; or perhaps, instead, he is shoring up his foundations against disaster.

Before the renovation began, Jacob Gordin did something not just un-customary but unheard of. Though he was a man who had never been on vacation with his children, just this once he went to Coney Island and tried to have some fun. We don't know if he rode the Ferris wheel or "Shoot the Chutes," but two extraordinary tintypes, taken in a Coney Island studio in May 1906, show Gordin pretending to drive some companions, among whom is Sasha, seated behind him in a model T car. In one shot Gordin wears a chauffeur's cap, and in the other he sports a cowboy hat. A relative who had seen the pictures told me, "The old man got drunk one night and went to Coney Island with his friends." Yet even in the silly poses, Gordin looks composed and solemn, almost haunted.

What is surprising is that the photos exist at all, when so few were taken of the family. There are a number of formal portraits of the patriarch, almost always with his head angled to show off his favored left profile. There is one shot of him with his sister Eva and her husband before he left Russia, where he sits on a chair set backwards, fixing the camera intently with his black eyes. There is one of him gazing at Sasha and one at Winchevsky, and the most inclusive picture taken a few weeks before his death, with a group of friends and family. And that's all. In comparison, there are innumerable photographs of writers Sholom Aleichem or Sholem Asch with wives, children, friends. Did the Gordins not take group shots because they were ashamed of Sam? Or, more likely, did the head of the family discourage photos as a vanity he didn't want to foster in his children? One year hence, on a trip to Germany, he would criticize contemporary artists because "they put too much of themselves in their work. You see self-portraits, portraits of their wives, their children etc. Can they not find more interesting subjects?"

Groups of young men, youthful members of the Jacob Gordin Literary Circles, were invited these days to spend time in the Gordin home. Their reports indicate that in their eyes Gordin was not a warm family man. The house was full of typical American boys, one writes, who were confused, lost, aimless; it was clear their father didn't spend much time with them. Gordin was only happy sitting at his writing desk or chatting, warmly and openly, with young visitors, "just the opposite to the coldness one felt in his relations with his family." It seems that the pressure on him to produce constantly, the irritation and pain caused by his current difficulties, and the disappointment in his children, who were not doing and becoming what he wanted them to—all had a chilling effect on Gordin's family life.

Joseph Rumshinsky, later a famous composer for Yiddish theater and film, had another view of his boyhood encounters.

There were two different Gordins—the Jacob Gordin in his home, the good-natured, mild, warm person who loved to hear and tell a joke, and the Gordin in the theater—miserable, tough, who would bury five fingers in his soft black beard and make his thin voice sound like a bass. He laughed at this description and told his friends, "I have to play-act when I'm with actors. I have to ask for and insist on respect; if not I won't get it. I don't care what happens personally, but I care what happens to my plays."

His play-acting worked; actors were afraid of him. It is said that he actually stormed backstage after watching one of his plays and struck the actor Finkel, who had been ad-libbing freely, on the back with his cane. He asserts that he was only miming ferocity. Was he miming with his family too? Winchevsky admits that his friend could sometimes be too cruel a tease, especially of children. "There is spite," he wrote, "sarcasm, sometimes forgetting the weakness of the natures around him."

Winchevsky believed that in Gordin's heart the God, his generous and creative side, and the Devil, his critical, destructive side, were always at odds; that Gordin's good impulses came first but were cast aside, out of the shame and fear of being thought too soft. Then he would reveal his pride, irrational anger, and "the greatest modesty," says his friend, "in the guise of so-called boasting." Some, who had felt his mockery and contempt, saw only the Devil side of Gordin.

But Winchevsky asserts that the goodness of his companion's heart always burst through his stiffly buttoned emotions. Gordin always reverted to the God. "The toughness he affects," writes Winchevsky, "melts away with the warmth of his great, good heart." He cites an example: Gordin's telephone rang once at 5 A.M. It was a *landsman* from Elizavetgrad; someone had died, and there wasn't enough money to pay for the burial. "Imagine!" Gordin cried to Winchevsky. "He asked me for one hundred dollars! Am I a millionaire?" Gordin's financial situation at the time was not good; Winchevsky imagined his friend sending the man away until Gordin went on triumphantly, "I gave him eighty, and not one penny more!" His daughter told me that people asked him all the time for money, for rent, coal, tuition. They were never refused. A piano tuner Helen hired once, long after her father's death, turned pale when he saw the portraits in her home. With tears in his eyes, he explained that he had become a musician because Jacob Gordin, whom he'd met as a boy at the Educational League, had taken an interest in him and paid for his music lessons.

But sometimes it must have seemed to Gordin's children that their father was more tied to such strangers, indeed to the whole Jewish world, than to them. In his family, as in his plays, Gordin was always teaching, trying to make humankind better according to his plan. When the time came to relent, relax, soften, at home and at work, he did not know how. Lulla Rosenfeld calls him a man of "suicidal integrity." That was his gift. It was also his undoing.

THE JEWISH KING LEAR

Not a tie, not a bond, but it is loosed here—every good and ancient thing. What in our Russia stood like the eternal rocks, Faith, Family, over here they thaw—yes, thaw, melt and dance away. Dissolution! Chaos!
—Jacob Gordin, *The Kreutzer Sonata*

MY GREAT-GRANDFATHER spent the summer of 1906 embroiled in yet another dispute over the translated *Kreutzer Sonata*. He insisted he had given the rights to Blanche Walsh, whose producers Wagenhals and Kemper were planning a Broadway opening. His former acolyte Bertha Kalish, however, was going ahead with her own English-language production, produced by Harrison Grey Fiske. The feud was reported in the American press; one of the headlines cried, "Agog over Kreutzer Sonata—East Side Theatergoers Side with Gordin and Kalich." Which means that they took one side or the other.

Gordin, in a furious letter to the rival producer Fiske, wrote that the man has done him the honor of turning his dramas into dollars. But how can the producer grant himself the power to issue an English translation, when even the Yiddish text of Gordin's plays is not to be altered? "When writing a play I try to the utmost of my humble powers," he explained, not humbly at all, "to characterize minutely all the participants in the cast, to portray their inner life, to create the atmosphere, to make clear the dramatic situation. For this reason every line, every word, has its importance."

But, he protests, Kalish's husband Spachner has sold the right to adapt the play although he has no right to do so. "Probably you do not know the full meaning of the phrase 'to adapt' in the vernacular of a theatrical manager," he writes. "It means that he hires a butcher and sets him to chop and cut the play at will. Meanwhile, he is spending thousands upon thousands of dollars to make the play cheap." I think many modern playwrights would agree with Gordin's definition of "to adapt."

Blanche Walsh's production, with Gordin's full support, opened at the Manhattan Theater on August 13, attended by many of the writer's friends and associates including Morris Winchevsky, the star Keni Lipzin and her husband Michael Mintz, labor leader Joseph Barondess, editor Louis Miller, and dramatists Kobrin and Libin, but not, it seems, by the playwright himself. David Kessler, who had finally thrown his support behind rival Bertha Kalish, was also not there, nor were Gordin's enemies Paley of the *Daily Page* or Abraham Cahan.

The event, in one of the few favorable reviews, "marked the opening of the present dramatic season in New York. The play is notable chiefly as the work of a singularly gifted playwright, and as a type of a school of drama with which, as yet, the American public is almost totally unacquainted."

Unlike the politely enthusiastic Chicago reviews, however, many of the New York notices were lukewarm, except for the one in the *New York Times*, which was virulent. Under the play's title was written, unequivocally, "An Offensive Theme Which is Handled with No Great Skill. THEATRICAL MIRE AND MUCK. Use of Disinfectant Strongly Recommended for this Latest Effort in Stage Sensationalism."

> In the face of all sorts of threatened legal proceedings, Jacob Gordin's so-called domestic drama was produced last night at the Manhattan Theater. The play is an offense against decency. It cannot be excused even on that ground of last resort—that it is good art, and, therefore, to be considered outside the pale of the commonly accepted conventionalities. Like most plays based upon transgressions of the great moral law, it is not without occasional flashes of power and moments of pathos, but these are almost buried beneath of the mass of shallow talk and cheap sentimentality.

Perhaps it is a badge of honor to be massacred, at least once, by the *Times*. This same year Strauss's opera of Oscar Wilde's salacious *Salome*, mounted by the Metropolitan Opera, met such a hail of protest and such vicious reviews that it was forced instantly to close.

The conservative Yiddish press seized on the English-language reviews. "Our Shame on the English Stage," proclaimed one; "Smut and Anti-Semitism as 'Art.' " Undaunted, the Kalish production opened at the Lyric a month later, on September 10, with Langdon Mitchell's translation. It didn't fare any better and ran for nineteen performances only. The *New York Evening Post* complained of "a foul family skeleton fetched out of its closet and made to stalk up and down the stage, and all to no purpose." The critic for the *New York American* waxed lyrical in his dislike of "these Russo-American pictures—gloomy, squalid, contorted, dark green, maudlin and occasionally madly melodramatic. . . . Everybody said, 'Isn't it strong?' It was. So is Camembert cheese. But an unrelieved and squalid tragedy, ending in bloodshed, needs something more than mere strength."

One more tempered review describes a haunting moment at the end of act 3, when the dispirited father asks his daughter to sing him a song from the old country. As the Americanized family members chatter, steadfast Miriam—Kalish—"sits apart from the boisterous company, and, her body moving slightly with the rhythm of the music, intones softly this prayer, and the woe of a race's age-long lamentation is in the lines, so crude, so simple and so surely the expression of a broken heart and a groping spirit." Though Kalish and Gordin were now estranged, surely he would in those moments have recognized the value of a fellow Jew in the lead role. Almost all the other cast members—Mary E. Baker, Hearn Collins, Gladys Hulette, Giorgio Majeroni, Margaret Reynolds, Josephine Florence Shepherd—did not bear the sort of names usual among his associates.

A bemused English-language paper gave a longer review to the playwright than to the play, describing him as stalwart and majestic, like a character in the Bible: "But he has the gift of energy, humor, and a 'hustling' ability that is truly modern. This journalist and theater manager, who looks as if he were the reincarnation of an ancient prophet, is one of the most bizarre figures of our cosmopolitan metropolis. An American dramatic critic recently dubbed him 'St. Peter.' "

The ancient prophet was squabbling with his stars again. After breaking with Adler to sign with Lipzin, Gordin was outraged that his most faithful actress had hired the faithless Kessler for her company. Under the headline "Big Shake-up in Yiddish Theater," a newspaper reported that because Kessler had recently changed his position and taken the side of the Fiske-Spachner-Kalish combination, "the stern Mr. Gordin has decided

that where he will be, Mr. Kessler will not be." It hinted that the break between Gordin and the Lipzin Company had been purposely precipitated
by Lipzin's husband Michael Mintz, who decided that the troupe would
profit more from the acting of Kessler than from the plays of Gordin. There
were also rumors that the first two acts of Gordin's new play, *Af di berg (In
the Mountains)*, were found to be unsatisfactory for the company.

But *In the Mountains*, a "four act fantastic and symbolic drama" inspired by the symbolic works of Ibsen, was produced that December with
Lipzin and without Kessler. The play tells once again of a sensitive Russian
soul driven mad by the coarseness and corruption of life in America. Before the main action, it features, as prologue, a discussion between a wise
old spirit of the mountain and a young spirit as to the merits of a new breed
of human now invading their domain, the Catskill Mountains. The old
spirit is furious that these restless, frivolous beings are disrupting the calm
of his retreat.

> YOUNG SPIRIT: Israelites, they are called. At this time they can't appreciate
> the beauty and grandeur of nature, they're an unhealthy people with
> wounded hearts, weak bodies and sick souls. But unbeknownst to them,
> they are starting to turn back to Mother Nature. They're getting accus-
> tomed, bit by bit, to know her and to love her.

The American Hebrew gave *In the Mountains* a relatively sympathetic review, speaking almost with regret of a "confusing, unreal and oft times tedious drama, unrelieved by any of the delightful episodes which [Gordin]
knows so well how to draw." It concludes gently, "While the public will regret that Mr. Gordin's new play is not as good as was expected of him, the
actors may congratulate themselves on having a play which gives them
opportunities. It is good to see, also, that Mr. Gordin has abandoned his devotion to plays that cannot be witnessed without the shivers of conservative people, and has written one which is as fresh as the hills which have
inspired him."

In the Mountains was not a hit.

On December 22, shortly after the opening, and immediate closing, of
this play, Keni Lipzin and her troupe traveled to Washington, D.C. They
had invited President Theodore Roosevelt to attend a performance of *The
Kreutzer Sonata* in Yiddish, and although they received a polite refusal—

Mr. Roosevelt undoubtedly read the *New York Times*—key members of the troupe were invited to meet the president at the White House. Lipzin, Morris Moskovitz, and Samuel Tornberg went, as did David Kessler, who was once again with the troupe.

Jacob Gordin, though in Washington with them, did not go to the White House. Because Kessler did? I think that Gordin did not want to prostrate himself before any political leader, anywhere. He spoke instead between the acts of the play, pointing out that the kindness of the president was in sharp contrast to the manner in which Jewish players were treated in Russia.

If they had invited the tsar to a performance in St. Petersburg, he told the audience, they would all have immediately found themselves in jail. This is the first positive statement he had ever made, publicly, about the new world.

. . .

Earlier that year, on May 23, 1906, Henrik Ibsen died at the age of seventy-two. The Norwegian genius must have gone to his death without knowing that in New York lived "The Yiddish Ibsen" who admired and emulated his work; who, earlier that very year, had received an English-language review stating that Gordin's "skills are so immense that to call him the Yiddish Ibsen is scarcely to do him justice." As men, Gordin and Ibsen were opposites, but in their respective theater worlds, the two playwrights played roles that were surprisingly similar.

Described in a biography as "a sensitive hermit freezing in his austere prophet's cave," Ibsen was a shy, withdrawn man who hated public appearances and who credited much of his professional success to his strong-willed wife. As the father of only one son, and thanks to a yearly stipend from the Norwegian government, Ibsen was released from dependence on the daily box office. He was relatively free to experiment with risky and unpopular forms and to live abroad in voluntary exile, spending years in Italy and in Germany.

The great Norwegian was a brooder who spent hours pacing or staring at the sea as characters and plots took shape. His biographer describes him as "prolific" because he wrote a trio of successful plays in five years, each play undergoing at least three separate drafts from the meticulous craftsman. Though he entered the theater more by chance than by compulsion, working first as a poet with ambitions to be a painter, he ended up in his youth working in direction, design, management, and all other facets of the theater except acting. And of course, he was writing in his own language, and for a people with a long theatrical tradition. He and his Yiddish disciple would seem to have almost nothing in common.

And yet in many of their aims and struggles, they were akin. Like Gordin, Ibsen always defined himself as a man in revolution against the dead hand of tradition. Sounding exactly like his fellow realist, he once wrote, "My plays make people uncomfortable because when they see them they have to think, and most people want to be effortlessly entertained, not to be told unpleasant truths. . . . People who are afraid of being alone with themselves, thinking about themselves, go to the theater as they go to the beach or to parties—they go to be amused. But I find that people's eyes can be opened as well from the stage as from a pulpit." (The struggles of art have not changed. Recently screenwriter William Goldman wrote that mainstream Hollywood movies "tell us . . . a falsehood we want to believe in," whereas independent films "tell us things we don't want to know.")

An enormously influential theatrical pioneer, Ibsen opened the way for his successors Chekhov, Shaw, and Strindberg as well as the realists of the Yiddish theater. From the beginning, his plays were often received with outrage and horror. When *Ghosts* received its first English-language production in London in 1891, the *Daily Telegraph* called the play "an open drain; a loathsome sore unbandaged; a dirty act done publicly." The perverse Ibsen, however, seemed to delight in criticism. "Most critical objections," he wrote coolly, "boil down to a reproach against the writer for being himself, thinking, feeling, seeing and writing as himself, instead of seeing and writing as the critic would have done, had he been able." If only my great-grandfather had been so confidently objective.

Ibsen too wrote exceptionally fine parts for women and had to fight actors and management to have his plays performed as written. (A German actress, crying, "I would never leave *my* children!" insisted on a revised happy ending for *A Doll's House*.) Ibsen too wrote about the persecution of the lonely individualist, women's rights, and the need to fight the constraints of the past and the conventions of society. He detailed the miseries of conventional marriage, championing real love as opposed to dutiful love. Though a play like *An Enemy of the People* is written with his extraordinary eye for vivid characterization and his ear for fluid dialogue, it still contains the kind of bold, lengthy rant, a lecture directly to the audience delivered by the mouthpiece character Dr. Stockmann, that was Gordin's stock-in-trade. Stockmann's final message—"The strongest man in the world," he intones, this man who has just outraged his entire community with his uncompromising ideals, "is the man who stands alone,"—sounds just like Elisha and many of Gordin's heroes and heroines, and indeed, like Gordin himself.

The biggest difference between the two men, of course, is that Ibsen was without question one of the greatest playwrights who has ever lived, and Jacob Gordin, without question, was not. Ibsen breathed life into multifaceted, complex characters and then stood back and let them talk. His Yiddish colleague found it hard to let his creations speak for themselves; his urge to teach, his need to manipulate the strings, was too strong.

The accusation of creating puppets and propaganda is often made, too, against playwright George Bernard Shaw who wrote at the same time, although Shaw propagandized and pulled strings with exceptional skill, depth, and wit. Ibsen watched the world with a stern, sour eye, Shaw with an almost macabre glee. But perhaps because Shaw had no children and Ibsen only one son, perhaps because they wrote for a settled people rather than one in the course of a profound transition, the two great dramatists weren't weighed down with a paternalistic sense of shepherding everyone—providing food and wisdom, saving the family from immediate danger. Gordin fathered his audience whether they wanted him to or not.

Ibsen and Shaw had the task of all the best playwrights: to delve into their deepest souls, dare to tackle difficult topics, and bring their ideas dramatically into focus on the stage. Jacob Gordin had to start a bit further back: he had to teach his actors to read. He had to tempt a people who knew absolutely nothing of the theater into the building, to stop them eating and keep them, and their babies, quiet, to show them and the actors how a drama unfurls upon a stage, and to include enough of what the audience had already come to expect of a coarser theater—songs, dances and music, comedy, cheap theatrics, "types"—to satisfy them. He had to write for a specific company, which might or might not at that moment have a comic, a soubrette, a juvenile lead or an elderly character actor, but which most certainly had an actor-manager of volcanic ego and often his equally talented and exacting wife.

And he did this on average four or five times a year. Ibsen wrote twenty-five plays in fifty years, Gordin around eighty plays in eighteen. Even Winchevsky admitted that, because the playwright had to turn out work so quickly, he couldn't write properly. "Even in the last three or four years [when Gordin was ill], he had to write two original plays and two translations every year. There was no time for concentration," he wrote after his friend's death.

Gordin was also working in a language in which he was not entirely comfortable and of which he did not entirely approve, sometimes while managing his own building and his own company, and always while struggling financially and fighting for royalties from the very actors for whom he was writing. At the same time, he was scribbling constantly for, and even founding, daily newspapers and weeklies. He was touring, lecturing, founding playreading groups and schools, teaching, fund-raising for the revolution, discussing deep matters every night in the cafés, distributing largesse to *landslayt,* and supporting a family of eleven children and three grandchildren. It is miraculous not that Gordin wasn't a better playwright but that he succeeded at all.

And according to the Yiddish actors, he succeeded very well. A rival playwright once complained that Gordin created not plays but roles, a skill that endeared him to the men and women of the stage. Bertha Kalish, declaring Gordin better at construction than the French master Sardou, said, "Every part in one of [Gordin's] plays is a real part. Every character has as good a chance as the star."

Bernard Mandelovich affirmed the star's praise. Bernard, who spoke to me on the phone twice from his home in England, began his career in the Yiddish theater in 1933, when he was eight years old. He had performed in nearly all Gordin's plays, and he raved about their richness of language and characterization for actors. Gordin's plays "had a beautiful construction, with a very high level of dialogue. He had a true sense of the theater, one hundred percent theatrical," Bernard told me. "Everyone had a great part; no one was wasted on stage. He knew what the audience wanted and what the actors needed. He knew how to bring the curtain down. There are not many who can do that."

After our second long talk, as I said goodbye, Bernard interjected. "Never forget, Beth," he said, with perfect diction in his mellifluous voice, "that your great-grandfather was the most important playwright in the Yiddish theater."

I will not forget.

• • •

Now sailing into view, in the fall of 1906, was the most likely contender for my great-grandfather's crown as had yet appeared in New York. The Yiddish author Sholem Aleichem had long been anxious to find a way to settle in the new world, and particularly to take his place as a writer of Yiddish plays. A great lover of the theater, he hoped that success as a playwright in the United States would guarantee his financial future. Adler met him in London while performing Gordin's *The Madman* there in July and begged the gifted storyteller to "take Gordin's place during the coming season" in New York.

Sholem Aleichem immediately began work, adapting one of his novels into a play for Adler and another for Thomashefsky. Filled with anticipation, he and his wife set sail for the new world, arriving, to adulation and acclaim, in October. What actually happened there to the man and to his dramatic work is a sad exposé of the deadly factions and rivalries of the Lower East Side. Poor Sholem Aleichem, an innocent from abroad, thought that mere reputation and talent would assure him of success. He didn't stand a chance.

The newest Lower East Side playwright had changed his real name, Solomon Rabinovitz, to the Hebrew greeting that means "Peace be with you." Aged forty-eight in 1906, Sholem Aleichem had been a writer since his youth, in recent years one of the foremost champions of Yiddish literature in Russia. He and Jacob Gordin, both editors and much-published satiric writers, must have known of each other in Russia, but they had never met; the younger man arrived in Odessa just as Gordin was fleeing. As described by his daughter Marie Waife-Goldberg and many others, Sholem Aleichem was wise and loving, full of fun; his stories are filled with humorous, empathetic, yet ruefully sharp insights into human foibles. Two of his characters, in one tale, complain to each other about their aches and pains, until one says, "Enough! This is too sad, let's talk about something cheerful. What news of the cholera epidemic in Odessa?"

Sholem Aleichem was often dubbed the Jewish Mark Twain. Jewish writers, it seems, achieved their greatest status when they were compared to someone else, as Gordin so often was; fellow dramatist Kobrin was called the Yiddish Maupassant, and Libin the Yiddish Gorky. Mark Twain was the only goyish writer to return the compliment; during this visit he referred to himself as "The American Sholem Aleichem." Though acclaimed in Eastern Europe, the Yiddish Mark Twain, like his colleague the Yiddish Shakespeare, was a poor businessman always in need of money, and so he was anxious to satisfy Adler and Thomashefsky in order to make his fortune in America. Thomashefsky paid him a thousand dollars for his play, and the thrifty Adler was forced to do the same.

When the optimistic scribe landed on Ellis Island, he had no idea of the ferocious factionalization that awaited him in New York, in both the theater and the newspapers. As a writer of charming folk-tales celebrating a traditional view of Jewish life, he had been adopted as a figurehead by the Orthodox papers. If the politically conservative papers admired him, it followed automatically that the socialist papers would take exception to his worldview. This had nothing to do with his skill as a playwright, which was, as yet, untested. Even an extremely talented fiction writer cannot leap easily onto the stage, especially for an audience as demanding as New York's. Exaggerated reports of his skills had led to exaggerated expectations. Not to mention that unless the writer sat on sentry duty in rehearsal hall and theater, as Gordin did, the actor-managers embellished the words of any author, famous or not. What chance did a gentle greenhorn have?

Sholem Aleichem himself made things worse with his low evaluation of the work being done on the New York stages. He wasn't impressed after seeing *The Madman* in London, because he felt that "Gordin's characters did not behave like Jews." He wasn't impressed, either, by Gordin's writer colleagues. Knowing nothing of this, the arts community of the Lower East Side, determined to welcome him like a hero, formed a "Sholem Aleichem Reception Committee" of eminent citizens, including Adler, Thomashefsky, and Gordin's bitter enemy Paley of the *Daily Page*. The only Yiddish writer included was Abraham Goldfaden, also not a friend to my great-grandfather. Gordin's foe Cahan was as conspicuously absent as he. Cahan had made his judgment clear: the Russian import would not know how to write for American Yiddish readers. The *Forward* did its best to ignore him, though that was difficult to do.

The first celebration honoring the writing star was held at Adler's Grand Theater on October 31, 1906. The speeches, welcoming the newcomer but also replete with polemics, went on for over three hours before the guest himself was permitted to open his mouth. After the reading came a banquet for 300 people, with many more speeches, lasting into the early hours of the morning.

While the love affair between writer and community flowered, beneath the surface Sholem Aleichem was battling for his words like any inexperienced *yold*. Adler was so enraptured by *Der oysvurf, oder Shmuel Pasternak (The Scoundrel, or Shmuel Pasternak)* that the great eagle cried, "What a golden hand! What a golden language! How he writes! How his characters talk!" When rehearsals began, however, both he and Thomashefsky demanded extensive rewrites, insisting the stories be more conventional, with more comedy, more for the stars to say and do. Adler rewrote the "golden language" exactly as he saw fit.

Thomashefsky went even further with the play *Stempenyu*. A composer brought in to provide some music reported that by the time the show opened, both music and play had been completely changed. "All its folk quality, its Sholem Aleichem charm, was gone," he wrote. "New words were added, so-called lyrics, and new bits of melody injected, which drowned the folk quality . . . The entire piece was drowned in cheap theatrical effects."

Both productions were advertised with more than the usual hyperbole. When Adler's poster appeared emphasizing Sholem Aleichem's fame, Thomashefsky put one out boasting of "Sholem Aleichem's greatest masterpiece, which astounded the whole world and was translated into all languages." The community was primed, and the plays quickly sold out. In order to make sure one star didn't get a jump on the other, the two productions opened on the same night, at exactly the same time. On February 8, 1907, the humorist and his wife, after the first two acts of *Pasternak* in the Grand Theater, had to march briskly over to witness the last two acts of *Stempenyu*, at the People's.

It was at the Grand, speaking in front of the curtain, that Sholem Aleichem made his greatest tactical mistake. He proclaimed, with hubristic confidence, that with his play a new era was about to begin in the Yiddish theater; he continued with negative remarks about the man he was hoping

to supplant. Sholem Aleichem's son-in-law wrote later that his wife's father "ridiculed with direct and indirect allusions the way Jacob Gordin
treats the Jewish way of life." Marie Waife-Goldberg reports her father as
saying that new currents were sweeping the Yiddish theater and that travesty and raw comedy were giving way to art, a sarcastic allusion to Gordin
apparently understood by everyone. She surmises that her father might
have been encouraged to make "this outspoken remark" by Jacob Adler,
"who was then in a fight to the finish with Jacob Gordin."

After his double opening night, unaware of his faux pas and of his precarious position, Sholem Aleichem was elated, sure of success. He had received many standing ovations; audiences had responded to the pathos,
laughed at the comedy. Although he was aware that there were still difficulties on the road ahead, he wrote in a letter home that this was "a big battle from which I hope to emerge as the winner."

And then he saw the reviews. The conservative press used the opening
of *Pasternak*, which they loved, to further excoriate the forces of realism. "It
is a pleasure to turn to such an uncorrupted and entertaining work of art
after the blood and filth with which the stage has been inundated in recent
years," said the right-wing *Morgn Journal (Morning Paper)*, though its ally
the *Daily Page* did complain about *Stempenyu*, horrified because the play
dealt evenhandedly with extramarital love.

The radical papers, which before his speech at the Grand had regarded
Sholem Aleichem as a force of reaction, now advanced with flaming swords.
Even Cahan, uninterested in defending Gordin in any way, went on the attack, dismissing *Pasternak* as foolish vaudeville. Louis Miller wrote that he
had walked out of *Pasternak*. Another Gordin ally, the critic Joel Entin, jeered
that he had never seen a worse play and also derided Adler's work as both
actor and director. The attacks on *Stempenyu* were even more forceful.

The battered greenhorn playwright did some rewrites, changing the
end of an act to please the *Daily Page*. His attempts to fix matters were to no
avail; both shows closed after only a few days and were never performed
again in New York during his lifetime. He tried writing stories for the
newspapers, but he could not simplify his witty style in order to churn out
material quickly, and for demanding editors who paid very little at that.
Not long after, Sholem Aleichem and his wife had to borrow money to
make their rueful way back to Europe.

Their rout is a low point in the history of the Yiddish theater. Had he been able to find the proper support of a company, a place in which to learn the technical requirements of playwriting, Sholem Aleichem's work would have greatly enriched the Yiddish stage. An article in the *Morning Paper* concluded that Sholem Aleichem had been hounded from America because writers such as Cahan and Louis Miller feared losing their power over the masses if a kind of theater other than realism came to the fore. "The Realist plays always assist the Socialist papers in spreading hatred and envy . . . It is, therefore, an old rule that anything slandering the Jewish character, presenting a repulsive Jewish type and ridiculing Jewish leadership [like Gordin's work], is 'art,' and anything unconnected to 'class conflict,' or leaving, God forbid, a good impression of Jews [like Sholem Aleichem's], is *shund.*" Perhaps in this instance, buried in the usual slanderous overstatement there is modicum of truth.

The comic writer was never able to make his finances commensurate with his fame and adulation. In 1913, still poor and now suffering from diabetes and tuberculosis, he returned to New York, again hoping to improve his fortunes, and again, his ambitions were thwarted. On that return visit, he offered Adler his new play, *Tevye,* about a wise dairyman with many daughters, but it was rejected. Though he was eager to write for the ever more successful *Forward,* Sholem Aleichem found Cahan nursing a grudge dating from his first visit. The most famous Yiddish writer in the world was refused work at the most successful Yiddish newspaper.

Sholem Aleichem died in a shabby Bronx apartment three years later, in 1916, at the age of fifty-seven. Also born in central Ukraine, seven years later than Jacob Gordin, his life span was almost exactly the same. He too was honored by an enormous and emotional New York funeral and is buried in Brooklyn. He has had the last laugh on those who denigrated his dramatic abilities. His *Tevye the Dairyman,* in its famous reincarnation as *Fiddler on the Roof,* is the most recognizable and popular Jewish story ever told on a stage. There is a monument to him in Kiev, and in December 2001 a new statue of the writer was unveiled in Moscow, near the city's Jewish Theater. He also has a modern monument of another kind: his own Web site.

In the mid-nineties, I heard that one of Sholem Aleichem's granddaughters, Bel Kaufman, author of *Up the Down Staircase,* would be speaking in Toronto, and I went to hear her. A spry octogenarian, she was full of energy and wit, as I imagine her grandfather to have been. She showed us a photograph of herself as a toddler on her *zayde*'s knee shortly before he died. Humor like his, she told us, has kept the Jews alive. During the question period, someone asked her a question in Yiddish; the audience was astonished when she replied in English that she speaks and reads Yiddish hardly at all.

I stood to ask her if she remembered any of her family members ever mentioning Jacob Gordin, wondering if despite everything her ancestor and mine had become acquainted. A letter to 256 Madison, sent by a European friend in 1907, includes the line, "Regards from Sholem Aleichem; he gave two readings here."

"Jacob Gordin's name was often heard in my home," she replied. "He was spoken of with great respect." She did not know anything about the indirect standoff between our relatives in New York, and I did not enlighten her.

. . .

In June 1907, the same month Bel Kaufman's grandfather left New York to sail to Europe, my great-grandfather did the same. There were two important goals for his journey. He wanted, first, to regulate the flow of pirated plays to European companies, which continually played bastardized versions of his work and paid no royalties. In a letter in May to his Odessa friend Rosenblum, Gordin wrote indignantly that it wasn't losing royalties so much as reading the stolen versions of his plays that was making him sick: "The directors rewrite the plays from memory, make changes, [add songs] that are not mine, they are Goldfaden's and Lateiner's, and discard—and what's left is printed in Russian under my name. I'd be happy to supply the correct text, but they ignore me."

In *The Komediant,*, a recent documentary about a family of Yiddish actors, an elderly stage director boasts proudly that he was able to obtain any play he wanted by hiring a young boy with an extraordinary memory. After attending a play once, the youth could recite it word for word. The director would write it down, change what was necessary for his own company, and presto, just as in Gordin's day, a play ready for performance without an inconvenient authorial encumbrance.

Gordin, born in a shtetl famed for its waters, also went overseas to take the cure in the waters of Carlsbad. He was not well, and the trip was an attempt to banish his illness. Another letter to Rosenblum reveals a new vulnerability. "Several of my friends will be on the ship," he writes. "I'm afraid to travel alone." Traveling with him to Europe were his great friend Philip Zeitlin, the proprietor of his favorite café, and the Yiddish actor Henry Ginsburg. He tells Rosenblum how much he would like to cross into his homeland and visit Odessa, but because "I'm not yet an American citizen, I left that for later, and I'm not a Russian," he fears he cannot. Several of his radical friends, including Krantz, had managed to reenter Russia, but Gordin, on learning that there was still a warrant out for his arrest in Russia, did not attempt it.

Just before departing, he signed a contract with Keni Lipzin and her husband. In return for a generous sum he had already received, perhaps to fund his journey, he gave them the sole rights to the 1904 drama *Der unbekanter (The Unknown)* and promised two new translations by November 2. Then the writer embarked on a trip from which he would not return until August 22, leaving himself ten weeks to deliver two complete plays in translation. This was a feat he did not accomplish.

Gordin and entourage set sail in early June. From Berlin began a series of letters, in Russian, to his wife and children at home. On June 20, he wrote that he had arrived "perfectly happy and healthy," though he gave evidence, once more, of uncustomary fragility and tentativeness: "Ginsburg, who has been very helpful to me, is going off, so I'm left alone. But I feel at home in the hotel . . . I'd like to buy gifts for all of you here, but I'm afraid to go shopping alone. I'll probably do that when I'm with Ginsburg again." This letter from husband and father, headed "Dear Aneuta and dear children," is signed, "My hearty regards to all, all. Yours, Jacob Gordin."

Gordin was also sending back travel articles for the *Truth* with his observations about the sites he was visiting. From Berlin, he wrote of the National Museum and a small gallery where he saw the paintings and sculptures of "the young, the sensationalist, the renegades"—artists showing their work despite the disapproval of King Wilhelm, who had called them a disgrace. "They are called crazy, decadent—fauves [wild animals]. They call themselves Impressionists," Gordin informed his readers. (The year before, at a time of unprecedented upheaval in the visual arts, Matisse had shocked le Salon d'Autumne in Paris with his bold use of color, and this year the young Spaniard Pablo Picasso was painting "Les Demoiselles d'Avignon.")

The writer waded unabashed into the field of art criticism:

> The first picture I saw amazed me—a large white canvas, completely dotted with grey and blue spots, black stripes and a red and blue hill in the middle—a lovely picture, ha? However, when I stood patiently and looked more carefully, I saw a heavy snow falling from the sky in crooked lines; the black stripes become trees, the red and blue hills, two women in red and blue clothing.
>
> This small exhibition impressed me greatly. I saw something new and original—a bit wild, but with talent and real artistry. Colors are combined in a new way. At first the conservative eye is offended, but the artists create a mood and show feelings. Every picture symbolizes something. Each painter expresses truthfully not only what he has seen in the outside world, but also the impression it has made on him. They consider themselves pioneers.

Gordin wrote home on June 26 that he would be leaving Berlin the next day for Lemberg, in Galicia. (Galicia was then part of the Austro-Hungarian empire, comprising southeastern Poland and western Ukraine; the city is now Lvov or Lwiw, in Ukraine.) His stay in Berlin had been a success. "My nerves are so settled that I don't even get angry when the waiter serves me kasha instead of tea. I'm not at all excited, even though I'm taking a long trip tomorrow. I give you all a big hug and kiss."

From the Hotel Bristol in Lemberg, Gordin wrote to "Madame Gordin and all the little Gordins" that as he crossed the Austrian border, surrounded by "porters with hands which had long not seen soap, *muzhiks* [Russian peasants] with shirts over white linen trousers, . . . Jews with *payes* [sidelocks] and long beards and long coats," he was struck with a sense of familiarity. "It hit me, not only in my nerves, but also in my nose, and I unconsciously cried, 'It smells of Russia here!' "

Lemberg was an important trading center, a beautiful city with a population of more than 100,000, a third of whom were Jews. When Gordin arrived at the station, he was met by the Jewish members of the Austrian parliament, along with 300 delegates of various organizations, each with a

banner and slogan. Despite this impressive welcome, Gordin was saddened by the Jewish quarter of the town. In his letters home, he painted
"frighteningly dark and sad pictures" of dirt and ghastly poverty, concluding, "In Berlin, I didn't even want to think about Brooklyn, but from here
I'd run away immediately to 256 Madison Street. Probably our roses are already blooming. When will I finally get a letter from you?"

To the *Truth* he wrote in more detail about the harshness of Jewish life
in Lemberg, in which until 1858 Jews had been legally confined to the city's
ghetto. "Every nation has hardship and problems," he began. "Poverty,
however, is a Jewish specialty . . . They have nothing to eat, but stomachs
full of hope . . . Naked, barefoot children, women clothed in rags, old people in torn filthy clothing. Dirt, hardship, children." New York tenement
apartments are like palaces compared to the dwellings in the ghetto of
Lemberg, "small narrow rooms, lit with a small lamp or candle. A wooden
table, a few old broken benches, 2 or 3 beds with filthy bedclothes. Here
they work, cook, eat and sleep; old and young sleep together, children and
parents, relatives and boarders."

Sholem Aleichem too, through Motl, one of his characters, tells us that
though most of Lemberg was clean and spacious, "there are streets where,
if you walk on them in the summer, you have to wear galoshes and hold
your nose." Though fastidious Gordin was undoubtedly holding his nose,
he didn't reveal his feelings about the town to his admirers. Not so, however, his reaction to their theater.

The intelligentsia of Lemberg was impressed by the émigré writer's
"collegial friendliness" as he held court over a samovar in his hotel room.
But they were taken aback by his behavior when he went to see his play.
The playwright was galled, initially, by the theater space itself. The largest
theater in Galicia "is as much like a theater as a turkey is like a hot air balloon," he wrote. "In the middle of the courtyard, surrounded by a wooden
fence, is a mound of garbage, a few scraggly trees, several broken wooden
benches, a stage—a few planks knocked together . . . If a forest, a hill, a
temple, a ship, a cottage, a castle . . . are required, the same scenery painted
with a few trees is used."

In this inauspicious theater with its inadequate sets and props, Gordin
sat through a production of *The Wild Man* and a week later of *The Madman*,
both starring "American guest artist" Henry Ginsburg, who had traveled

with him from New York. At both he barely had the stomach to remain until the end. The mutilation of his script and the clumsy amateurishness of most of the performances were a travesty, he declared, "a poor effort." He hated the fifth act that had been added to give the first play a happy ending and the pseudo-German—*Daytshmerish*—the actors used instead of simple clear Yiddish. He spoke in front of the curtain furiously and at some length, thanking the audience "for their friendly, warm reception, but advising them that at least 75% of the play was not mine. The audience, the actors, the director," he later admitted, "all were astounded at my undiplomatic speech."

Couldn't Gordin have restrained himself, told a white lie or two? It was obvious, he said so himself, that the Lemberg artists were poor and isolated, doing their best with little. They were nervous working with an "American guest artist," with the esteemed playwright in the audience. And yet, like a judgmental father viewing the flawed work of his children, Gordin could not let the problems pass; he had to point out all the mistakes in order to push the struggling youths to do better.

Then too, he did have to endure a corrupted version of his own work. Playwright Eric Bentley said once that seeing one of your own plays done badly is "one of the most unbearable things in life. Particularly if you think your play is pretty good." And that Gordin did.

As Gordin harangued the crowd, Emil Gimpel, the dismayed producer-director, was tempted to lower the curtain onto his head. Gimpel is an often-cited name in the history of Yiddish theater in Eastern Europe. Ida Kaminska writes about visiting in the 1920s "the musical and talented Gimpel family, grandchildren of the founders of the Lemberg Yiddish theater in the 1880's." She goes on to mourn that almost all her Lemberg friends, including the Gimpels, were murdered in the Holocaust.

Gordin moved on to Varish, close to the Russian border. In Varish, as he did throughout his voyage, Gordin gave money to all who asked, to such a degree that he was thought a millionaire trying to pave his way to paradise. The hopelessness of the Jewish population affected him sorely, as did the experience one afternoon of standing at the border to Russia.

The same sky, the same fields are on either side of the road. Why did my heart start to pound? What did I hope to see in the distance? . . . From this side of the border, as I look over, I look as a foreigner, one who has been ex-pelled, locked out. I look across to the land where I left so many happy and sad memories; where I was born and brought up; where I left the graves of my father and mother, where my two poor sisters still live, where my best and most valued friends still live. I don't know what to call that country. My fatherland? My birthplace? The cemetery of my past? The grave of my future? Oh Russia! I turn my back to my friend, so he will not see my tears.

I find this cry of a man "locked out" of his beloved homeland one of Gordin's most heartbreaking passages. How can he write that his "best and most valued friends" still live in Russia, when standing beside him is the faithful Zeitlin, and in New York Winchevsky, Miller, and his doctor friends sustained him daily? Who were these valued Russian friends who wrote to him rarely, if at all?

On a less emotional note, Gordin pointed out in his article that on the Russian side of the border are trees, gardens, and flowers, but none grow on the Jewish side. Jews have always planted flowers in heaven, he says, but they need flowers here on earth.

By July 14 he had landed in Vienna, the capital of Austria-Hungary, al-though after four days he was ready to depart. His letter home and his arti-cles expounded on how dirty, old, and small Vienna seemed after Berlin. "Tell Burshinski I'm going to kill him," he joked to his wife. "His Vienna has given me little pleasure." This isn't the image we now have of the ele-gant city of Strauss, but when Esther Kaminska's troupe passed through the city ten years after Gordin, her daughter was revolted by the "dirty, noisy, primitive" theater in which they had to play. Gordin was thankful for his gracious Russian host in Vienna, brother of a theater musician who, even as Gordin sat writing his letter, "pours tea for me from a Russian samovar." He was in perfect health, he told them, even his digestion was better, but the weather was terrible, and he still hadn't heard from home.

In Carlsbad, the luxurious spa town west of Prague, Gordin at last re-ceived his letter. The next day, Sunday, August 4, he replied, berating wife and offspring for taking so long to write.

I was certain that there would be letters waiting for me in Carlsbad. I went to the Poste a second and third time and there was nothing there. Madame

Zeitlin wrote to her husband, but I waited for nothing. I was sad and ashamed! A whole week, I went morning and evening to the post, then I realized that there was nothing to wait for. I decided not to write to you anymore, not to buy any presents, but yesterday's letter showed me that it was all because of foolish mistakes, not because of any bad motives.

He didn't feel unwell, but the water wasn't having much effect and he was not losing weight. "So much money thrown away and I'll come back with the same pot belly," he sighed. To this day, the spa's twelve hot springs splash out hope to patients with arthritis, rheumatism, digestive problems, and even to those with cancer. These last included Jacob Gordin, who did not know that he was suffering from cancer of the esophagus, which was spreading throughout his body.

As he drank the waters and wrote his family, he handled a family tiff. "Vera writes (her letter is very loving) that Sasha is insulted because I don't write to him separately. I have written to EVERYONE with love, and nobody wrote to me. Thank you Vera and Leon for your letters. For the others, there's nothing to say thanks for." He ended by singling out Ginsburg, such a fine fellow, admitting sheepishly that he "never expected to find one among Jewish actors."

In his last family letter, written on August 9 from Dresden, "a beautiful German city," he wrote rapturously about German "cleanliness, order, organization." In hindsight, there is a ghastly irony in his conclusion: "No one in the world can live as well, as comfortably, as simply and economically as the German. If I travel to Europe again, I'll try to remain longer in Germany. The evenness and quiet of the Germans works very well on my digestion. The devil! I really wish that the Jews could be Germans and the Germans, Jews."

He was on his way to Leipzig, Hamburg, and then "to a happy homecoming. Yours, Jacob Gordin." He sailed back on the ship *Deutschland*, "the world's fastest passenger ship," still accompanied by Ginsburg and Zeitlin as well as the Yiddish actors Morris Moskowitz and Louis Hyman, who had toured Europe that summer. This time he landed on Ellis Island; his immigration forms are on file there. Interestingly, the reluctant American listed himself as a "U.S.A. Citizen," though he was not, not yet. He also wrote that he owned a house in Brooklyn, the address of which was "Brooklyn Bridge." Perhaps he was having a little joke on the officials. Or perhaps he was weary and unwell, and could not be bothered with bureaucracy.

Even before he sailed, the New York newspapers were speculating about his future: which theater would he join, Adler's or Lipzin's? The *New York Telegraph,* explaining that because Gordin was "the most prominent Yiddish playwright, his activities usually shape the theatrical complexities of the East Side," discussed the matter avidly. "It was said yesterday," the paper gossiped, "that somebody had seen a friend of Mr. Gordin in conversation with a representative of Jacob P. Adler."

Gordin had indeed decided to write, temporarily it turned out, for Adler. Five days after his landing, on August 27, he spoke about his impressions of Europe at a big reception in his honor held at Kalish's theater. The feud between writer and actress, however, was not over; Kalish had recently carped to producer Harrison Fiske that she was not surprised that rival producers "don't want anything to do with Gordin; they are right, and I hope that we will not be obliged to." Kalish was still working in English with Fiske, appearing in a "poetic tragedy" in October.

Before plunging into work, the playwright found it necessary to retire to the country for a few weeks, to recuperate from his vacation. He also put into motion his application to become an American citizen. He told a friend that his exposure to Europe had aroused his gratefulness for the relative orderliness of America, for her firemen and policemen, regulated banks and bureaucrats. After what he had seen in Lemberg, he praised the Yiddish theaters in New York, their fine buildings and quality productions. For the first time since his arrival in 1891, Jacob Gordin was glad to have settled there. "Goethe, Schiller, Heine, Lessing, Wagner, Kant, Nietzsche . . ." he wrote, on his return, "all of these are not equal to the Declaration of Independence."

I have in front of me his "Certificate of Naturalization," number 58508. "Description of holder," it says.

Age: 54 years. Height: 5 feet, 8½ inches. Color: white. Complexion: fair. Color of eyes: brown. Color of hair: dark brown. Visible distinguishing marks: none. Name, age and place of residence of wife: Annie Gordin age 50 256 Madison St. Brooklyn. Names, ages and places of residence of minor children: Michael Gordin age 19; George Gordin age 16; Leo Gordin

age 12; Jeanette Gordin age 18; Helen Gordin age 10. All reside at 256
Madison St., Brooklyn.

Be it remembered, that at a stated term of the District court of the
United States held at Brooklyn New York on the 3rd day of October in the
year of our Lord nineteen hundred and seven—Jacob Michael Gordin,
who previous to his naturalization was a subject of Russia, at present re-
siding at number 256 Madison Street, Brooklyn, New York, having applied to be admitted a citizen of the United States of America. . . .

Vera was now unhappily married to a Russian opera singer, Alex was
still in Philadelphia, Jim had offended almost everyone by marrying a
Catholic and finding work as a janitor, and Sam, as always, was simply not
mentioned. But Jacob Michael, his wife Annie (who was actually only 48),
and their dependent children Michael, George, Leo, Jeanette, and Helen,
residents of Brooklyn—what could be more American than that? This decisive ceremony was a giant step for a man who had hitherto only considered
himself a "locked out," unhappily transplanted Russian. "Said petitioner
intends to reside permanently in the United States," said the certificate.

Gordin's next work, *Ohn a heym (Without a Home* or *Homeless)*, produced just after his return, was his last fairly successful play, with a seven-
week run. Like *Mirele Efros*, it became a star vehicle for generations of
Yiddish divas; a film version made in Europe still circulates to Yiddish film
festivals. In 1907 it was Sara Adler who fashioned the part of Bathsheba
into one of her most noteworthy roles. In the story of an immigrant woman
whose family life is destroyed by America, who cannot adjust to the new
world and goes quietly, heartrendingly mad, Sara found a part that, like
her husband in *Lear* and *The Stranger*, she would reprise again and again
until the end of her life.

The play hammers the idea of "home." The grandfather, lost in his
scholarly religious books and hopelessly out of touch, demonstrates the
old way of living, but those representing the new American way are worse.
Bathsheba's young son is a liar and a cheat, driven by greed, and her husband is a symbol of all that is venal and soulless about American values. Of
his ambition to become an architect, his wife says, "He wants to build
homes for strangers, but cares nothing about a home for himself." Their
landlady, a wealthy Russian Jew pretending to be German, lives in a hotel
(like Cahan and his wife). Bathsheba says, "You have many houses, but no

home? And you go around the world looking for happiness? Was it not better in the old country? We were poor, we struggled hard—but everyone had a home." The writer, idealizing the old country, has already forgotten the "frighteningly dark and sad pictures" he had just witnessed there.

When the landlady remarks, "Children are a nuisance and a bother. They don't pay," Bathsheba cries, "If I couldn't be a mother any more, I'd be better off dead!" Perhaps this play was Gordin's tribute, at last, to his wife, hospitable, endlessly attentive, motherly to both children and husband. Perhaps as his illness grew more pronounced, he was more grateful for her ministrations and her availability.

Cahan denounced the play, calling it "false, untruthful, longwinded" and, a bit later, "cheap, pasted-together, unsuccessful." In one of the most self-serving, defensive sections of his memoirs, he describes his relationship with Gordin that fall and how it finally turned to poison. "Gordin used to write from time to time in Miller's paper 'Truth' where he often attacked me personally but I never replied," he writes. "[In my] reviews of his plays I would point out his mistakes as helpfully as possible . . . Almost every play had important good points, as well as glaring mistakes. Therefore it usually happened that in evaluating one of his plays, I in fact spoke about his whole literary effort. This type of critique I wrote about the play 'Homeless' in November 1907. This was a weak play, and my review was not favorable. But it was not in any way personal."

In response, Gordin attacked Cahan from the stage and in the *Truth,* where he flung out an article lavishing sarcasm and ironic praise upon his foe. The piece finished, "How can you harm such a person! No, I've decided not to answer Herr Cahan's critique."

In December, just as the United States itself entered a full-blown depression, the situation for my great-grandfather deteriorated on all fronts. He was finding it hard to swallow. Increasingly preoccupied with his health, he resigned from his position as president of the Russian Publishing Company and editor of the newly founded *The Russian Voice in America.* Reports in other newspapers hint at the usual internecine warfare; Gordin is quoted as saying that he likes neither the *Russian Voice*'s editorial policy nor its business manager.

Leon Kobrin's *The Power of Love* with Lipzin and Kessler at the Thalia—Gordin's own Thalia—was a hit. Abraham Goldfaden, too, had a hit with the operetta *Ben-Ami,* starring Thomashefsky. Cahan praised Kobrin's play, and though he thought *Ben-Ami* "can't be counted among [Gold-faden's] best," still, he continued indulgently, "The audience is amused by the songs and dances, and doesn't ask for more."

Gordin's next work for Adler, *Goles galitsien (Galician Exile),* a drama about life in Galicia, lasted not even a week. Cahan dismissed it as "a miserable piece . . . false, untruthful, boring . . . ugly, wild, unsympathetic" and concluded that Gordin hadn't written a serious play in years.

Star-managers and producers were now more reluctant to take on a new Gordin work, which brought with it the burden of controversial issues, large casts, and the wrath of the *Forward* and the *Daily Page.* They were also aware that their audiences were turning from drama to melodrama; *shund* was resurgent. A tearjerker by Lateiner, *The Jewish Heart* starring David Kessler, set a record for the number of consecutive performances, and a new *shund* playwright, Zolatarevsky, hit gold with *The White Slave.* Zolatarevsky went on to become immensely popular with melodramas like *The Blind Mother, Children, Come Home,* and *A Mother's Sacrifice,* works that were the antithesis of everything Gordin had worked for, all his years in the theater.

Before *Ben-Ami,* Goldfaden too had suffered a lengthy dry spell; at the end of his life he was a crushed man, poor and forgotten. On January 9, 1908, he died, and received a wave of accolades that had not been granted him while he lived. "The Father of the Yiddish Stage" was inscribed upon his tombstone, and a crowd of 75,000 mourners gathered for his funeral. These bitter ironies were not lost on Jacob Gordin, who was feeling his own mortality in his throat.

• • •

Now Abraham Cahan, deciding, it seems, to rid himself of his enemy for once and for all, set out to deliver the coup de grace. He overlooked the fact that his adversary was a mortally ill man, daily growing thinner and paler, looking, said one writer, as if an ox was gnawing at his vitals. At the end of January, Cahan wrote an article mocking a benefit Gordin and Miller had recently organized on Gordin's behalf. After two weeks of advertising the event, Cahan exclaimed, they weren't able to draw more than half a house. The audience expected Gordin to make his usual fiery speech of denunciation, but he lost courage and made a few "mild and pitiful" remarks, lasting "only a few nervous minutes. Besides the cheap kibitzing against the Forward, Jacob Gordin, as usual, took the time to advertise his wares and brag about himself like a schoolboy. He said, 'The world looks on my works as treasures. They search for them, they dig up the earth to look for them—even for my smallest sketches. And the Forward says my writing is a bluff.'. . . We will answer this point in a few days," finished Cahan ominously. "The Forward should have done this long ago. We will do our duty."

On February 1, 1908, the editor announced the beginning of a new series in the *Forward*—"Gordin's Place as a Yiddish Playwright—a Few Personal Words." That day he launched a series of blistering critiques of Gordin's work and persona, which appeared at a pace of one or two or even three a week, month after month. His "few personal words" turned into some forty articles. The relentless attacks didn't stop until May 31.

The critic took some time to explain and justify his barrage, beginning with the complaint that Gordin had been attacking him personally "mainly in the last 8 years." However, "I have up to this point not once answered these attacks," he assured his readers. When Gordin speaks on stage, "he behaves in a childish fashion, showing off his arrogance and conceit, with no respect for the audience or himself." The man suffers from "Critic Fever;" he cannot tolerate criticism: "Gordin considers himself a fighter because he has a big mouth. That is his heroism. This tall man with the grey beard, the proud carriage and the coquettish walk is as deathly afraid of the mildest criticism as a baby is afraid of lukewarm water."

Sixteen years ago, Cahan wrote, as editor and critic of the "very influential Worker's Newspaper," he spent all his energy agitating for Gordin's first plays, as a step forward in comparison with earlier plays. In one review, he "pointed out in the friendliest manner certain faults" of one play. Because Gordin immediately attacked him, he stopped reviewing Gordin's work. He reminded his readers that even Louis Miller, who had become Gordin's great ally (but, let's not forget, was once upon a time Cahan's) criticized *God, Man, and Devil* and other Gordin works, yet now "raises Gordin's quack plays to the heavens." Miller does so, according to Cahan, because as the editor of his own paper, he needs Gordin in his war against the *Forward*. "Miller knows how to get along with such a person," he charged. "Compliments, constant praise."

His quarry was hyperbolically compared to the Russian tsar Ivan the Terrible in terrorizing and striking down anyone who disagreed with him. Cahan accused the playwright of turning his enemies into characters in his plays.

> These articles by Gordin can't be read aloud when ladies are present, which shows how much he was out of control when he wrote them. In his attacks on me, one time he let loose on questions of my private life.
>
> I've declared many times that Gordin has accomplished good things for the Yiddish theater. He has moved it from the swamp of *shund* a bit closer to literature, we all agree on that. He has earned these compliments, and uses them with great diligence to sing praise for himself and to advertise himself far and wide.

Now, he announced, he would ignore the ban on criticism of Gordin's work and undertake an overview himself, because "I acknowledge Gordin's place in the history of the Yiddish theater, but the real literary value of his drama is a whole different question." And here is a particularly fanciful part of his diatribe:

> If the readers agree with me or not, that's up to them. I simply assure them that I undertake this task with the highest, most ethical motives, in an earnest endeavor to serve the interests of fair play, without fear or favor. There is much in his work for which I give him credit, and I'll show that as strongly as I will what I believe are his faults. Personal feelings between us will play no role at all. All the calumnies he has poured on me all these years will be erased from my mind the moment I begin this critique of his plays.

Finished with generalities, Cahan proceeded with exhaustive attacks on specific plays, tearing apart plot, characterization, dialogue. Mirele Efros doesn't behave enough like a queen. Sappho should have married Boris in the first act. As an example of Gordin's poor writing, he examined the *Sappho* character Shtempl the fishmonger, who speaks often about fish: Shtempl's expression " 'like a fish in water' is especially ridiculous, that an ignorant fishmonger would throw in quotations about live fish in water. As a fishmonger he would throw in sayings of the fish trade, not live fish as they swim around in lakes and seas. That would be done by a fisherman, not a fishmonger from Odessa."

In his stream of acid, the critic makes perfectly valid points. Gordin was indeed hypersensitive; he did overreact, bluster, take criticism too personally. Cahan is justified in complaining that some of Gordin's characters don't sound like real people, speaking instead in "aphorisms, fancy words, witticisms." Gordin's dialogue often, particularly in the last plays, was didactic and labored. But the editor, alert for the most negative interpretation, attributed the instructive dialogue not to Gordin's too-urgent need to teach his audience but to his egotism. "The only interest of this writer is the applause for his cleverness," he wrote.

Next, the critic went to great pains to quote bad reviews of Gordin plays from newspapers in Eastern Europe and Russia. In his memoirs, he explains why: "When Kaminska brought Gordin's plays to Russia, the Russian press made a joke of them. I printed these critiques in the Forward under the heading, 'What they think about Gordin in Russia.' This was very important to me: in case anyone thought my criticism was based on personal feelings, let them see that in Russia . . . they say the same things I say here." He continues with almost unbearable relish, "This had a profound effect—especially on the local Russian-Jewish intelligentsia."

And then, when he had nearly finished, Cahan unleashed his most wounding volley. For several days, without explanation, he reprinted Gordin's 1899 series of articles on the "Great World Dramas." Then, quoting from *The Five Great Skeptical Dramas in History*, a reference book on a similar topic by an obscure English clergyman named John Owens, he set out to show that Gordin's pieces had been plagiarized from Owens's book. Cahan's attacks are devastating to read, even today. He pounded home his point: that Gordin, contracted to write a series of articles about the theater of the world, chose to analyze exactly the same great plays as Owen did, and some of the ideas in his series had first appeared in the reference book. Gordin was branded, shamed as a plagiarist. The charge has stuck to this day.

Gordin's allies were incensed by the *Forward*'s rampage. In shaming the playwright publicly, Cahan had gone far beyond the old shtetl boundaries of acceptable behavior, even between enemies. "Shame is horrible in the *shtetl*," says *Life Is with People*, a book about shtetl life. "To shame a man is the same as robbing him."

Livid Gordinists attempted to rally for the defense in the *Truth*. One pointed out that it was impossible to verify Cahan's charges because he quoted only in loose translations from Owens, without indicating where the quotes could be found in the 400-page book. Another pointed out that Gordin wrote as "a free-thinker and materialist," drawing hugely different conclusions from the English theologue.

None of the playwright's defenders admitted that certain sections of his piece might indeed be close copies, whether advertently or not; that such things happen easily in the world of literature. Gordin, frantically busy in 1899 as always, may well have taken a shortcut and followed Owen's lead too closely. As I write this, I have in front of me two separate articles in which highly respected historians, Stephen Ambrose and Doris Kearns Goodwin, are accused of and admit to plagiarism. Ambrose blames his errors on his quick pace, Goodwin acknowledges carelessness with footnotes and attribution of quotes; they apologize, and the cases are closed. But these accusations were not common in Gordin's day, particularly when leveled against a man so noted for his upstanding leadership, his righteousness.

Around this time appeared a review of a play by *White Slave* playwright Zolatarevsky, in which the anonymous critic suggests that the playwright's name be erased from the poster and replaced with Pinero and Scribe for the first act; Dumas, Fulda, Clyde Fitch, and Sudermann for the second; and for the third, Mirabeau, Gordin, and Goldfaden. "The last act," wrote the critic, "should be attributed to all the writers above mentioned, who are strangely jumbled together." Luckily for Zolatarevsky, he did not attract the enmity of Abraham Cahan.

Gordin withdrew from battle at first. As the *Forward*'s pieces began to appear, he repaired to the country, from which he wrote to Aneuta about his health, finishing, "I feel well here. Even Cahan's articles don't bother me too much. I'm writing a bit. I just began on Saturday, and already I've started on the second act." In May, as the series steamrollered on, he rallied, publishing a series of defensive articles analyzing Cahan's accusations. He attempted to prove them wrong, showing that the critic had mistranslated quotations from Owen, that in one instance his own conclusion was the opposite of Owens's. A truculent open letter to Cahan began, "I'll tell you the truth—in this bit of work you've done, I don't know what makes me wonder more—your idiotic stupidity, your boorishness or your unspeakable chutzpah." He ends, with bravado, "I'm beginning to feel sorry for you. Poor thing—what did you get yourself into?"

Rebut as he might, he knew that Cahan had triumphed. Gordin's dominant position and prestige, to many Jews in New York and the wider world, were no more. In *The Celia Adler Story,* published in 1959, Adler's daughter confirms this fact. An old woman reminiscing about her life on the Yiddish stage, the actress, who played a number of Gordin roles throughout her career, wrote that theater people were always nervous and upset when Cahan was in the theater; they feared the power of his enormous influence and his sharp tongue.

> Many of you will remember that around 1907–08, Gordin was at the height of his popularity with playgoers and with readers of the Jewish press as well. At that time, Abe Cahan wrote a long series of articles in the Forward with his appraisal of Gordin's talents as a playwright. He tore apart many of his successful plays, and in an unfavorable and unpleasant summary, completely undermined Gordin's position as an important figure in the Jewish theater.
>
> Then, remarkably, after reading these lengthy and negative articles, many of my friends who, like me, had the highest regard for Gordin's work, suddenly, to my great surprise, lost their good opinion of him. They spoke of him and his plays almost with disgust.
>
> Cahan's opinions, for a large part of readers, carried a lot of weight and were almost holy. They thought he was honest and a friend of the masses and of the underdog. With this series of articles he seriously undermined Gordin's popularity.

Like teenagers, Gordin's audience of nervous new citizens had gained confidence enough to grow tired of his heckling; they were only too eager to discredit him, to cast him aside and turn to more indulgent, amusing voices. Cahan did his job well; he was a good writer. I think the cloud of suspicion and dishonor he cast over Gordin's name is the reason my father was forever embarrassed by his grandfather.

My dad, it is true, could not take seriously anything written in Yiddish, with its folksiness and superstition, its ties to the muddy shtetl. He had hated hearing endlessly about the great playwright all through his childhood only to discover that his grandfather was not the greatest of playwrights. But most of all, it was the odiferous whiff of plagiarism, disgrace, and failure, still clinging to Gordin's name decades later, that turned many in the writer's family away.

Another of Gordin's great-granddaughters, when I met her for the first time only a few years ago, shocked me with the vehemence of her dismissal. "Sure, he was loved because he had become an icon," she said, "not for who he really was or his talent. Gordin stole Shakespeare's plays and renamed them and passed them off as his. What's so great about that? He was just a big ego."

. . .

Through the onslaught, Gordin left town when he could, spending much of the spring and summer at a guesthouse in Sea Isle City, New Jersey. "The only trouble is," he wrote to Aneuta, "there are too many of 'ours' here—but I leave them alone." He continued, in Russian as was usual in his familial letters:

> I'm lazy to write in English, I have to think about the spelling. Therefore translate the following for the children: I received Nadia's lovely letter. [My grandmother had given up "Jeanette."] She shouldn't worry—she'll go to Barnard College. [She didn't.] I'll always have money for education. I only wish all eleven wanted to study, there would be no question of money. I hope to be well soon, so there will be money. And even now that I'm sick, I'll always have enough for their education. It is unpleasant that I have to worry about children who aren't worthy of being my children. Read this to George. He doesn't have to go around looking for jobs, if he plans to study . . . Vera, Jacob, Michael and the others have only fooled themselves.
>
> Has the professor [Alex] got the play back? . . . I promised my boys [his grandsons] I'd come back if they'd have a tea-party . . . I'll stay here until I stop enjoying myself.

Nadia joined him in the country to convalesce from an illness. My grandmother, aged nineteen, enjoyed an extended time alone with her father for the first and only time in her life. Gordin wrote cheerily to Aneuta, "So far we're holidaying like God in Odessa . . . Nadia has improved a bit. She takes hot baths every day, but she has to be driven to it. I've also taken a few baths, but yesterday I bathed in the sea for the first time. Now that's a bath, a real bath!"

On August 5, he wrote that he intended to stay in Sea Isle the whole month of August. "Nadia is ready to leave today, but she's afraid to travel alone and has to have a companion," he told his wife, unaware that his daughter was echoing the fears expressed in his own letters from Europe. "So far I've had a few cold baths. As soon as the foot starts to pain, I take a hot bath. . . . I'll send you a cheque for ten dollars," he continued, "and a cheque for the milkman." He finished with a reprimand in his own kind of English. "Helen, you are smarter," he admonished his youngest, in the tongue she spoke much better than he, "and you still remain in the same Klass? How is it?"

The news that Gordin was ill had reached his family in Ukraine, and he received a shy letter from his sister Masha.

> Dear brother Jacob and dear sister Aneuta:
>
> I am very grateful that you do not forget me. When we received your letter, we were very happy. But we're not rejoicing about the state of your health. We now have a Jewish theater troupe in town staging your plays. They played "The Brothers Luria" and "The Wild Man." I saw both of them. They had great success.
>
> I'll write quickly about my life. I live modestly, but thank God, I can't complain about my fate because my family life is very happy. My health is fine. I had one child, and he died, but other than that I have a decent family; thank God I have four more children. [Perhaps one of her five children died, or else this means she has four step-children, but lost the only child of her own; it's unclear.]
>
> Heartfelt regards from my husband, from Polya; she is well too. Dear brother, I am asking you to send us your family pictures—if not the whole family, then at least a portrait of you. Your children must be grown up now. I'm sure they're all well educated. We can only dream about such things! Maybe there'll be a time when you'll finally come back to visit us. We'd be so happy to welcome such dear guests. I wish everybody good health.
>
> Your sister, Masha Asrorin

In a subsequent note from Masha, it is clear that the last time there had been an exchange of letters was fifteen years before, when Leon was a baby.

From the country, Gordin wrote to his friend Gershon Rubin, who had appeared in several of his works and would become one of the great actors of the Yiddish stage, that he had just finished the first draft of his new play

Dementia Americana but that "in general, my thoughts are very far from the Yiddish theater. I don't feel very well; I suffer from rheumatism of the feet. I'm limping like the poor Yiddish drama. It is quiet in this small town. The sea doesn't stop pounding."

It sounds as if, to add to his troubles, Gordin was suffering from gout (which also afflicted my father). Away from home, distressed and in pain, he sent a number of letters that year. He corresponded frequently with a friend and new business associate from his voyage to Eastern Europe: Gershon Bader, a lecturer, dramaturge, and founder of Austria's first Yiddish daily, had become a fan of Gordin's in Lemberg. He was impressed by the way the playwright listened to everyone's ideas, "taking the time to have a drink and a bite with everyone, because he felt he could learn something from everyone." Gordin asked Bader to become his agent and representative in Eastern Europe. The two men wrote often about Bader's lack of success either in protecting Gordin's copyright or in receiving payment for his own work from New York editors, except, implausibly, from the anti-Gordin *Daily Page.*

Bader's letters complain of slow lawyers, unsuccessful court cases, and dissembling theater directors impeding any flow of revenue to the playwright, but mostly he informs Gordin that he hasn't received a penny from New York for his own articles; could his friend there give the editors a nudge? "If you have the opportunity and it is not too unpleasant for you," was one request, "could you speak to Mr. Winchevsky of the *Future* and tell him one could faint away waiting for money or even a letter?" It is clear that although eager and loyal, he is too gentle to hound producers for royalties; he gives in whenever there is an altercation.

In the fall of 1908, as a reporter for the *Daily Page*, Bader attended an important conference on the current and future status of the Yiddish language in Czernowitz (now Chernivtsi, in Ukraine). My great-grandfather's presence at the conference had been solicited repeatedly by the organizer, the Yiddishist Dr. Nathan Birnbaum, who early that year engaged in a friendly correspondence with Gordin while rallying the troops in New York. The playwright invited Birnbaum to spend a few days in the country with him "to rest." Birnbaum, known as a difficult man though obviously not to Gordin, had no time to rest but urged his correspondent to come to "a mass meeting about the Yiddish language" in New York on

March 4, imploring, "We need you there. Without you, the whole thing will have no meaning." Birnbaum himself, paradoxically, spoke such poor Yiddish that he had to deliver his speeches in German.

Gordin went neither to New York nor to Czernowitz. Had his health been better, I wonder, would he have gone, or had Cahan's articles forced him into hiding? Linking his friend's current troubles and the conference, Bader wrote to Gordin on October 20, "It saddens me that you are a bit 'dethroned.' You know that I am one of your staunchest disciples. I had a few altercations on your behalf [in Czernowitz] with Peretz and Sholem Asch." I. L. Peretz was and has continued to be one of the most revered Yiddish writers. Asch was also well-known and important, if more controversial. Neither was a fan of Gordin; Peretz, like Cahan, once said that Gordin's work was midway between *shund* and literature. Yet Asch's story connects in a fascinating way with my great-grandfather's, although the two men never met.

A few years before the Czernowitz conference, Sholem Asch had written the most scandalous play of the time, *God of Vengeance*, in which a brothel keeper tries to buy a torah scroll to purify his home while his cherished daughter liberates herself in a love affair with one of his prostitutes. The play was unapologetic about both prostitution and lesbianism. Adler turned it down in 1906, saying it could not be presented before proper Jewish women, and Peretz urged Asch to burn it. Kessler finally produced and starred in it in October 1907, advertising it as "the greatest Yiddish drama being performed all over the world."

God of Vengeance played for six weeks and was the subject of much debate, setting off, of course, a high-pitched chorus of disapproval from the conservative papers. As in old times, Gordin and Cahan were on the same side, giving qualified support for the play. Cahan found much to admire in the lesbian love scene. Gordin wrote that an intelligent playgoer sees "not the naked bodies of fallen creatures, but only their damaged souls . . . Sholem Asch," he concluded, "gives us the great drama of these small people with the innocence and sincerity of a true poet." He decreed, however, as did Cahan, that the Jewish audience was not yet sophisticated or educated enough to understand the nuances of the play, and so it should not be presented.

Decades after Gordin's death, Asch outraged many by writing a series of novels, one called *Mary* and another *Jesus of Nazareth*, with Christian themes and characters. Perhaps for this reason, or perhaps for some other, the author and his works triggered in Cahan a level of vituperation he had so far only employed against his least favorite playwright. He spent his time obsessively finding ways to assault the novelist, again to huge effect. Hardly writing anything else for two years, he even put out a small book attacking both Asch's person and his work. According to Melech Epstein, Cahan left Asch "a deeply wounded man."

After the novelist's death in 1957, almost none of the Yiddish cultural bodies dared to produce a memorial event for one of the greatest Yiddish writers. The animosity aroused by Cahan still lingered, as powerful a negative force as it had been in Gordin's life. When his influence cast a shadow on Asch's memorial, however, Cahan had been dead himself for five years.

• • •

Jacob Gordin passed the summer of 1908 mostly alone, sequestered in Sea Isle, completing his last play *Dementia Americana*, also called *Di meshugas in amerike*. He was ill and downhearted, sick in body and soul, but nothing stopped him from working. Finishing the first draft at the end of July, he hadn't the energy to write the next until he knew which troupe would buy the work; he would tailor it for that particular company. Adler bought the play originally but after reading it divined that the nasty satire on American greed and consumer impulses would be a disaster. Gordin's play starred a Russian intellectual émigré who is corrupted by the easy money of gambling and real-estate speculation, and whose "get rich quick" schemes leave him with nothing but debt. The trouble with this plot, Adler saw, was that many in his audience had behaved just like the play's flawed hero during a recent New York real-estate boom and bust, and had lost their life savings. They would not appreciate seeing themselves caricatured in such an unflattering light and being reminded of failure and financial disaster.

A lawsuit, too, was pending between the two men; Gordin was suing the actor for back royalties, and a few months hence the Court of Appeal would force Adler to pay the writer $2,000 plus interest. Surely for these reasons only, and not because Gordin was now something of a pariah in the circles where he had formerly reigned as king, Adler decided not to produce the play and sold it to Thomashefsky.

Though accepting the risk of putting on the play, Boris too worried about what his public would make of it. In a move automatic now but not common at the turn of the century, Thomashefsky decided on an out-of-town try-out. He took his troupe to rehearse and open the play in Trenton, New Jersey. Gordin joined them there. One day at lunch all color drained from his face; he was hardly able to breathe, unable to swallow a bite of food. He told Bessie, "It is happening to me too often, lately."

Gordin was unusually nervous before the opening in Trenton. Bessie asked him why, joking that this was not his first play. Stroking his graying beard, Gordin answered quietly, "It isn't my first play but I'm afraid, Bessie, it is my last."

Thomashefsky requested that the playwright not become involved in rehearsal or production decisions, and so rather than fussing backstage before the New York opening, Gordin arrived at the premiere like any other theater-goer, sitting with some of his family in a loge. After the third act, he was called out to enthusiastic applause. He thanked the audience for its support, and Thomashefsky for the performance, hyperbolizing that of all his plays, no other had been "so realistically presented, and so well acted."

Even in his debilitated state, Gordin was able in his speech to praise Thomashefsky and simultaneously make a dig at Adler. I assume that the applauding audience on the first night was made up of Gordin's staunchest allies, because from then on the play struggled, and failed, to survive. It received some good reviews but was viciously derided in the conservative press, and Thomashefsky was pressured by New York real-estate interests to close it. Though the production was costing him several thousand a week, Thomashefsky tried to keep it open to prevent the playwright from being humiliated. "The newspapers helped kill the play," he reflected later, "crying out that it was wrong for a play to prey on the feelings of others, and *Dementia Americana,* which I had produced so beautifully, had to be taken off."

Just after the opening, Boris tells us in his memoirs, Gordin came into Thomashefsky's dressing room shaking from head to foot, his face white. He lay down on the couch, the same one on which Goldfaden had lain before his death, and whispered, "Thomashefsky, I don't feel well. I seem to have fever, I'm hot and then cold. Maybe I'll feel a bit better if I lie here awhile." The actor covered him with a coat.

"Maybe a glass of tea and rum?" he asked. "I'll turn out the light and you can rest here quietly. After the third act I'll come and wake you. I did the same with Goldfaden." Gordin sprang up. "That means I too will die?" he cried. "I don't want to die!"

He did not want to die, but he was preparing nonetheless. Wrapping up his business affairs, he sent to Keni Lipzin and Michael Mintz such contracts as had been drawn up between them, from 1897 to 1906. The sick man who could hardly swallow managed to lecture a few times that fall, addressing the Hebrew Literature Society about modern drama and how it should be played, and even traveling to Philadelphia to speak and to see Sasha. After his lecture there, his *patriyotn* banded together to found the Philadelphia Jacob Gordin Dramatic Society, the latest of many in cities and towns all over the United States and Canada.

In October, Gordin commented in a letter to Bader that he didn't feel too badly. He was able to receive a fellow playwright, young Percy Mac-Kaye who had recently graduated from Harvard and who was a strong believer in noncommercial, subsidized theater. Percy afterwards wrote Gordin, "It was a very great pleasure to me to spend those two evenings with you, and I look forward to many more in the future." But in December, when Gordin was asked again to lecture, he wrote back that he could not because he was very ill and leaving town for a month. Perhaps, he said, he would be able to lecture in February.

Was it any comfort to him, now, that Yiddish theater was at last finding an audience in the old country? In Odessa Gordin's plays and those of his colleagues were being presented by a Yiddish troupe newly founded by playwright Peretz Hirschbein. Esther Kaminska's troupe was roaming throughout Eastern Europe and soon would tour the world, her every season based on what she called "the Gordin repertoire." At one point in their travels, they were asked to perform a benefit for a Russian actor, not in Yiddish but in Russian. When Gordin's *The Slaughter* was chosen as the benefit play, Kaminska's troupe knew it so well that they simply translated the lines from Yiddish to Russian as they went along.

This year the troupe traveled to St. Petersburg, where they had to wait for both a performance and a residence permit before they, as Jews, could stay and work. They premiered with *The Slaughter* and continued with *The Kreutzer Sonata*. After their first presentation of the latter, the audience rushed forward to touch the actors. They swept from the stage eight-year-old Ida, who had played the heroine's son, and passed her from hand to hand to the back of the theater, kissing and embracing her, before handing her the same way back to her mother. The company enjoyed great popular success and was favorably reviewed by Vladimir Jabotinsky, later an important Zionist leader.

After her Russian triumph, Kaminska was invited to America by Kessler. She brought her troupe over the sea for the first time, although because of the usual uncertainty about who owned the rights for Gordin's work and the subsequent dispute, she was unable to present her favorite *Mirele Efros*. She was eager to meet the playwright whom she called "my spiritual father, my Messiah," but he must have been too ill to see her. In 1912 Kaminska returned, invited, according to one story, by Lipzin's husband Michael Mintz in order to discredit the European actress. Esther Kaminska and Keni Lipzin embarked upon the dual of the divas, with rival interpretations of the Gordin heroine who had made them both famous.

As the Old Man withered, around him in the United States Jewish performing and literary arts were prospering. A recent arrival in New York, the English playwright Israel Zangwill, writer of *Children of the Ghetto*, enjoyed a smash hit with his play *The Melting Pot*. The reverse of Gordin's *The Truth*, Zangwill's play portrayed David, a Russian Jew, and Vera, a Russian Christian, finding love on the Lower East Side. It played in Washington with President Roosevelt, this time, in attendance. Kessler and Lateiner steamed on with their sentimental *Jewish Heart*.

Most threateningly to the theater, a hundred movie houses were now operating in New York, many of them on the Lower East Side. The *Forward* reported that the cinemas "open at one in the afternoon, and customers, mostly women and children, gossip, eat fruit and nuts, and have a good time." The *Forward* itself had grown so large and prosperous that it moved into its own ten-story skyscraper at 175 East Broadway, sporting the largest Yiddish neon sign in New York.

In 1908 the whole Jewish world celebrated Sholem Aleichem's twenty-fifth anniversary as a Yiddish writer, and in March of the following year, his fiftieth birthday. Gordin, meanwhile, was the subject of a small article in an American paper:

JACOB GORDIN, ILL, WRITES A PLAY
Friends Anxious about Him, While He Keeps Faith
with the Thalia Theater

Jacob Gordin, the Yiddish playwright, has been ill for more than a week at his home, 256 Madison Street, Brooklyn. He is suffering from a complication of troubles, and his condition has caused some anxiety among his friends and in theatrical circles.

Despite his illness, however, the playwright continued, until a day or two ago, to work hard on his new play scheduled as the Passover production for the Thalia Theater. Hastily as the play was written, the actors of the Thalia, who heard the piece read at Mr. Gordin's residence, are much pleased with it. It is called "God and the King," and the plot is taken from an old English drama.

But the playwright's "complication of troubles" did not abate, and the play did not appear. Instead a *shund* masterwork called *Dos pintele yid (The Jewish Essence)* ran the whole season at the People's, showing the audience what it meant to be a good Jew, and ending with a giant electric Star of David dropping down from the flies. Bertha Kalish, in a gloomy interview in the *Kansas City Journal* in April, complains that there is no future for the Yiddish theater in the United States because immigrants are so fast Americanized and because there are no playwrights, no actors, and no audiences. "There was a time when Yiddish theater flourished," she says. "Jacob Gordin was producing his best plays. But now Mr. Gordin, like many of the best-known Yiddish artists, is old. And the younger generation has not produced any talented artists and writers to take the places of these men." When she spoke, Gordin, though mortally ill, was only fifty-five, and there were plenty of actors, audiences, and new writers of note. Madame Kalish cannot have made herself any friends with this pessimistic forecast.

Gordin's colleagues had not given up hope for his recovery. Jacob Adler wrote that his heart ached for his friend who had been laid low. Gershon Bader wrote from Lemberg that he was worried; also that he still had not received "one cent from the Future and the Truth," and was sending the manuscript of his play *Reb Israel Baal Shem Tov,* for which he hoped Gordin would find a publisher and producer. Gordin managed a few letters back, briefly informing a friend that he was in the country "to repair my constant friend 'health.' "

His last published work is a profoundly sad fable—he can be forgiven for the trace of self-pity there, too—in which the Jewish people are called Jehudith; the theater is Jehudith's neglected, sick child, whom Gordin alone cares for, clothes, praises, and loves. "My gifts were perhaps of no

value," he wrote, "but they were the best I had. I have given better to no
one else."

> And for all that I had done the mother hated me. She hated the gifts I had
> given her child. She hated the good clothes in which I had dressed her,
> and put her back again in dirty old rags. Nevertheless, I continue to love
> the child. And though today Jehudith and I have nothing to give one an-
> other, we remain one body and soul. She concerns herself little with me,
> yet she is my love. I know that when I fall, her friends, bought for a few
> pennies, will dance on my body and she will look on, indifferent. The day
> I die is the day she will forget me.

All pretense was over. He was not going to finish his play, he was not
going to lecture anywhere, he would never go to the country again. Instead, for a few weeks in the spring, Gordin lay in Beth Israel Hospital, but
when it became evident that nothing would help, not even his friends the
doctors who produced five cancer specialists to tend to him, he came
home, where he was given morphine to dull his pain. Louis Lipsky wrote
with more than a little compassion this time: "All his life he fought like a
bear. He prized loyalty and friendship and fought for friends, but when he
saw his friend stick a dagger in his back, he did not care to fight any more.
He gave it up. He made up his mind to die, and . . . not all the East Side
doctors could make it different. There was no use arguing with him."

On the day of his fifty-sixth birthday, May 1, 1909, he posed for a photograph, the only shot of my great-grandfather with several other family
members, although of the eight people clustered around him in this picture, only three are Gordins. Where are the others, as this one and only
family portrait is taken? Most are married or gone, except Leon, who was
eighteen and simply not there, and Sam the ever-invisible.

The playwright, wearing a white, high-necked Russian shirt, sits on
the grass behind the house, his gaunt face lit with the ghost of a smile, his
eyes hollow. The famous black beard is now white and the prosperous
belly is gone—he had lost more than forty pounds. In his right hand he
holds the stub of a cigar. Beside him is the ample form of his wife, thick hair
piled loosely on top of her head, her eyes teary and her face blurred. She
too is in white, as are all the other women: my future grandmother Nettie,
then twenty, hiding her soft little chin with her hand as she often did in

*A family gathering in Brooklyn on May 1, 1909, Gordin's fifty-sixth birthday, six weeks be-
fore his death. To his right is Anna, his wife; directly behind him is his youngest daughter
Helen, and beside her is Nadia, the author's grandmother. The others are family friends.*

photographs; my great-aunt Helen, twelve, protectively grasping her
father's shoulders; and the young Garfin sisters, friends of the family. Two
Russian musicians, the Fonaroffs, loll in the center; they later became my
father's violin teachers.

On the edge of the group is perched a stern little man with round spec-
tacles and a very long nose, a Mr. Gershoyg, whose name appears on a few
unproduced Russian translations of Gordin's work. Gershoyg was a theater lover so devoted to the playwright that he moved in with the family to
spend years as a factotum and collector of royalties. After Gordin's death,
the devastated *patriyot* cried out that the playwright had died because he
was tired of living. "Just when he was feeling at peace with the world,
when his family had food, he had money in his pocket," said Gershoyg,
quoted by Lipsky, "he was stabbed in the back . . . [by] the vile sheet which
printed the articles that killed him."

This May Day, as Gordin sat with friends and family smoking a cigar
on the grass, he was gratified to hear that the annual labor parade downtown had featured a protest against the horrific abuses of child labor.

Through the day, a few messages of support and hopes for recovery arrived at 256 Madison Street. "Best wishes to the master from his disciple," wrote Keni Lipzin. "Congratulations and best wishes from Bogen and his *mishpokhe* [family]," from Boris Bogen, social worker and superintendent of the Baron de Hirsch Agricultural School. The actor Morris Moskowitz sent a telegram, and so did sculptor Jules Butensky.

These final days of Gordin's life, as the illness ate him alive, are chronicled by the most loyal friend of all, Morris Winchevsky. By May, he writes, even Gordin's wife and older children had finally accepted that he was dying, although the man himself was never told the truth. "A day or two before May 27th," writes Winchevsky, "he was occasionally in good spirits and had quiet and hopeful moments." Reading between the lines, we can guess that after May 27 until his death two weeks later, he wasn't, and didn't.

A daily visitor, Winchevsky one day broached the topic of putting out a "Special Edition" of Gordin's plays. Gordin could only respond with his eyes. Winchevsky told the sick man that his expenses would be high until he recovered, and that such a project, besides providing much-needed funds, would ensure a definitive printed version of his best-known plays. Winchevsky convinced his silent friend; "it was the first time in weeks he had shown interest in anything." He told Gordin, "I'll prepare a prospectus for the *Truth* and the *Forward* and even the conservative papers. I'll show it to you as soon as you're up to reading it."

"That was the last discussion I had with him until the end," he tells us.

Throughout the day of June 10, the sick man didn't recognize faces, even those of his devoted doctors, Comrade Dr. Sergei Ingerman and Dr. George Price, who had been the publisher of his first newspaper in New York in 1892. Gordin waved away anyone who came near. At 9:15 P.M., Winchevsky was the only one of Gordin's friends in the house when the day nurse arrived to summon him to the sick room. "He looked much better than I'd expected," he writes. "We'd had bad reports during the day."

Winchevsky took Gordin's hand, expecting "to hear that 'song without words' that his slowly departing great spirit had sung in the last days." To his surprise, the dying man began to speak in a strong voice. So clearly that everyone in the room could hear, Jacob Gordin enunciated his last words. "Winchevsky," he rasped, "finita la comedia."

An hour later, he was barely breathing, and not long after that, unconscious. At 12:15 A.M. on Friday, June 11, after a hemorrhage in his lungs, he died.

"At that moment," wrote Winchevsky, "his great spirit left his body, and the Yiddish theater, and many other cultural and educational institutions, were orphaned."

•　•　•

"La commedia è finita" ("the comedy is over") is the famous last line from Leoncavallo's *Pagliacci,* a tragic opera in which the lead actor of a troupe of players is destroyed by betrayal and jealousy.

The words are also spoken in *The True Power* by Gordin's mouthpiece character Goldenweiser, a humane, sometimes misguided doctor of excessive integrity. In Goldenweiser, Gordin had written the part of a father, like King Lear, who makes one tragic mistake and loses the child he loves more than anything in the world.

EPILOGUE

Gordin's Legacy to the World and to His Family

> When Gordin died, he was mourned by hundreds of thousands of people. Jewish New York has never witnessed such a funeral. Only then could one sense who Gordin was, what he meant, and how much he was admired by the masses.
>
> —Leon Kobrin, *Memoirs*

I HAVE A PHOTOGRAPH OF ANNA, in black, at the unveiling of her husband's headstone in June 1910. Her face wretched under a round black hat, looking far older than fifty-one, she presses one hand to the massive chunk of ragged, rough-hewn granite. Under a laurel wreath are carved Gordin's heavy-lidded portrait, name, and dates: 1853–1909. Beside her in the plot are shrubs and trees, a bench, and a huge open book carved out of granite.

When I went, eight decades later, to visit the site in Brooklyn's Washington Cemetery—Jehuda Westernitza Burial Society, Cemetery 4, post 396, southwest corner—everything had gone but the imposing rock. Though usually a funeral plot was a Jewish immigrant's first important purchase, Gordin had not made that investment; his gravesite is registered under the name of Mintz. Even after his death, Keni Lipzin—Madame Mintz—was looking after him. She herself is buried at his feet. Her husband lies nearby under a smaller marker, as does Sophie Greenspoon, Gordin's eldest daughter the epileptic, who died only nineteen years after her father.

Anna Gordin at the unveiling of her husband's headstone, June 11, 1910.

Many of the tombstones in the old cemetery are crooked or cracked, in disrepair through occasional vandalism or, more frequently, neglect, but the ones in this plot are neat and trim. I introduced myself to my great-grandfather and reached up to place a small stone on his memorial. Then I went to do honor to Aneuta, who according to the records is also buried nearby, under the misspelled name "Anna Gordon." True to form, my great-grandmother was so inconspicuous that I could not find her.

In the June days following Gordin's burial here in 1909, the Yiddish and the English-language press, including the *Forward*, continued their lamentations and eulogies. Because the *Forward* editorials were usually un-signed, there is no knowing now who wrote them. There is good reason to suppose they were not written by Abraham Cahan.

> Yiddish Shakespeare Dead . . . The big Jewish population on the East Side loved him because, better than anyone else, he seemed to understand them.—*New York Daily Mirror*

> He is mourned as scarcely another figure could be on the Jewish East Side.—*New Jersey Sun*

The Greatest of the Yiddish Dramatists . . . a man who commanded the respect of, not alone all of his race, however those might differ from him in opinion, but of all the students of current theater history.—*New York Dramatic Mirror*

Peace to your spirit, great teacher of the long-suffering people.—*Russian Voice in America*

Word quickly reached Russia. An emotional letter, signed by a long list of old friends in Elizavetgrad, paid tribute to "Yakov Mikhailovich, who was always fighting for the high ideals of truth and love." Eva wrote with empathy to her sister-in-law, informing her, "They want to build Yakov a statue in Elizavetgrad." Masha didn't respond until the sixth of September, telling Aneuta that she had only recently found out about Yakov's death. Why did it take three months for her to hear? "You cannot imagine," she wrote, "how stunned I was [to hear of his death]. My heart shed blood, not tears, to have an only brother and to be deprived of him. Keep your chin up, Aneuta," she counsels. "We cannot bring him back."

Both sisters continue with queries about the family, Masha asking again what kind of education the young Gordins were receiving, and Eva hoping "that they're as talented as their father." As always, the sisters beg, hopelessly, for photographs.

Just after Gordin's death, a letter arrived from the Russian Imperial Theatrical Society, telling him that yes, his membership in the Union of Theatrical and Musical Creators would give him copyright protection for his plays in Russia. Also arriving from the motherland was Misha, a young cousin of the Gordin children, though again, not a child of Eva's. In this awkwardly distanced family, even the simplest of reunions, a Russian nephew and his famous relative in America, did not take place. Misha arrived one week too late.

The Jewish Literary Society of St. Petersburg held a special meeting during which Gordin was praised as the "first Jewish playwright, the first realist." The Yiddish critic and philologist Noah Prilutzsky gave the eulogy, concluding that if Goldfaden was the father of the Yiddish theater, Gordin was the father of the Yiddish drama. Prilutzsky later astutely summed up Gordin's contribution by saying, "The Yiddish theater was not able to make the transition between Goldfaden and, let's say, Ibsen; neither the actors nor the public was ready for this evolution. There was a need for a playwright who would be a man of letters on the one hand, and a people's writer on the other."

In the year of Gordin's death, *God, Man, and Devil* was successfully staged in Russian in St. Petersburg and several provincial theaters under the title *Satan*. These productions would have been the height of success for Yakov Mikhailovich. If only the man of letters, the people's writer, had known.

Two weeks after the funeral, the theatrical community of New York produced a theatrical display of grief. A Memorial Programme, a kind of Gordin's greatest hits, was presented on Saturday, June 26, at the Manhattan Opera House, whose director, Oscar Hammerstein, donated the house "absolutely free of any cost" for the night.

Keni Lipzin presented the second act of *Mirele Efros*. The Thomashefskys put on the second act of *Dvoyrele*, also starring Bina Abramowitz, to whom Gordin had shouted, "Stick to the script!" eighteen years before. Sara Adler appeared in the last act of *Without a Home*. Kessler and Mogulescu mounted the second act of *God, Man, and Devil*. And as the grand finale: Adler in the second act of *The Madman*, with the love interest, Lisa, played by his eighteen-year-old daughter Frances. Henry Ginsburg, who had toured Europe with Gordin, appeared as the brother.

The drama of grief played on. According to Celia Adler, Gordin's death "shortened the life of the Yiddish theater and orphaned a large number of Yiddish actors. Jews young and old cried bitter tears, as they would mourn a family member." Theater historian Mukdoni noted, "After Gordin died and I would talk to the actors about him, they would cry like little children who had lost their father, their bread-giver. They didn't believe, didn't want to believe, that anyone could fill his shoes." Bertha Kalish said that every word the playwright spoke was a bit of Torah for her. "A warmth radiated from him," she said. "He was the only person in the theater everyone looked up to."

But in his acerbic way, Louis Lipsky reported what the theatrical community really felt after the playwright's death: Gordin's portrait was hung in every Yiddish theater, his name always mentioned at banquets, but his plays remained unproduced. Producers preferred Zolatarevsky's melodramas because they made money. They liked Hurwitz's "feeble stories for they had tears in them and the public paid dearly for the satisfaction of weeping. They preferred the plays yokels came to see, for there were more yokels in the world than philosophers. [Gordin's] words—those thick juicy words about which they would often brag in his lifetime—gave the actors a headache to memorize, and besides, why should the public think of the playwright when there were actors who were dying for applause and appreciation?"

On Christmas Day 1909, in a series of *Forward* interviews with the star managers of the Yiddish theater, Keni Lipzin was determinedly true to the memory of her master. She blames the unfortunate resurgence of *shund* on the "post-Gordin dramatists," on theater managers who are afraid of literary drama, and, of course, on the press. "I have faith," she concludes devoutly, "and believe the Jewish drama will flourish again in the spirit of Gordin."

Lipzin wasn't wrong in her faith, but neither was she right. There was rarely again such intense dramatic activity and audience involvement as during the Golden Age. Gordin himself was shelved for a decade, except when a grand gesture was needed: in 1912, when the mayor of New York cut the ribbon at the opening of David Kessler's own Second Avenue Theater, the play presented afterwards at the grand premiere was *God, Man, and Devil.* Adler's remount of *Elisha ben Avuya,* as its author had predicted, was a success, perhaps because audiences were glad to hear the hectoring voice of their father figure again, at a safe distance, and also because Adler had added music by Joseph Rumshinsky.

As Winchevsky had promised, Gordin's friends put out two collected works editions of his best plays, sold by subscription. The literary socialist newspaper *The Day* published a book of Gordin's one-act plays with a foreword by Sasha. For a few years, a Jacob Gordin memorial meeting was held at the Cooper Union on the anniversary of his death. A group of young people meeting in a candy store on Columbia (candy stores, the coffeehouses of the day, were often used for meetings) started the Jacob Gordin Dramatic Club to promote the search for better quality theater. Kobrin, Libin, and Pinski, "the post-Gordin dramatists," became much-produced playwrights, and serious literary talents like Peretz Hirschbein flowered in the old country.

But theater "in the spirit of Gordin" didn't truly flourish again in the

United States until 1918, when former Kessler *patriyot* Maurice Schwartz founded the Yiddish Art Theater, which remained active until the 1950s. For his first season, Schwartz chose *Tevye the Dairyman* by Sholem Ale-ichem, who had died two years before, and he chose four plays by Jacob Gordin.

Though in the twenties and thirties Yiddish theater prospered in East-ern Europe and South America, its life force in the United States began to fail. American immigration laws were tightened during the early 1920s, and the number of fresh audience members arriving from the boats dwin-dled drastically. *Mama-loshen* diminished in importance as Jews flooded the night schools to learn English.

Still, for the Yiddish American companies that did still produce, Gordin's work was often the foundation. Between the opening of the De-troit Yiddish Playhouse in 1924 and its closing thirteen years later, twenty-nine of Gordin's "literary" plays were produced there (as opposed to "non-literary" plays, or musicals). The next most produced literary play-wright was Peretz Hirschbein, with seven. Hirschbein's poet wife Esther once said that the refinement in the language of the Yiddish stage brought about by Gordin was as important for the culture of her people as the writ-ing of *The Divine Comedy* was for the Italians. I am happy to add "the Jew-ish Dante" to Gordin's list of famous European predecessors.

Gordin acquired other eminent fans. Emma Goldman, the notorious anarchist, often gave lectures in both Yiddish and English. In Chicago in 1914 she delivered a series of English-language talks with the title "The Modern Drama as a Mirror of Individual, Class, and Social Rebellion against the Tyranny of the Past." She spoke about various European dramatists but also about writers closer to home and to her heart: Yiddish playwrights Sholem Asch, David Pinski, and Jacob Gordin.

A few years before, in Prague in 1911, a brooding civil servant named Franz Kafka was charmed by the Yiddish plays presented by a ragged troupe at the Café Savoy, probably the same troupe Gordin had disdained four years before in Lemberg. Kafka saw at least four plays by Gordin, and, despite some criticism of the concessions the playwright had made to win over his audience, judged him to be the best of the Yiddish playwrights.

After seeing *The Wild Man,* he enthused in his diary about "the obvi-ously great powers of the playwright." He had difficulty, however, believing in "all the whipping, snatching away, beating, slapping on the shoulder, fainting, throat-cutting, limping, dancing in Russian top boots, dancing with raised skirts, rolling on the sofa. . ." In a book entitled *Kafka and the Yiddish Theater,* author Evelyn Beck analyzes characters, lines, and ideas of Gordin's that are echoed in Franz Kafka's works. Other scholars have noted similarities specifically between Gordin's *The Wild Man,* in which a defective son is kept hidden though protected by a sibling, and Kafka's extraordinary *Metamorphosis,* in which a son who turns into a giant cockroach is kept hidden, and tended by a sibling.

Though Kafka didn't go to see Yiddish cinema, he could have; Yiddish movies were being produced and shown all over Eastern Europe. Jewish film directors took their inspiration and their first scripts from the Yiddish theater. One of the first Yiddish movies was adapted from a Gordin play, followed by *Khasia the Orphan,* filmed in Vilna, and then others. J. Hoberman, author of *Bridge of Light,* the definitive book on Yiddish film, writes that half of the two dozen Yiddish plays filmed in Eastern Europe between 1911 and 1916 were either taken from Gordin's oeuvre or "falsely attributed to him."

Indeed, Hoberman continues, "Gordin virtually brackets Yiddish film. Adaptations of his *Homeless* [starring Ida Kaminska] and *God, Man, and Devil* were the last Yiddish features released, respectively, in pre-Holocaust Poland and post–World War II America." One of the happy surprises of my research was picking up Hoberman's just-published book, expecting to find a few vague references of interest, and reading instead his generous and thoughtful evaluation of Gordin's central position not only to the theater but to early Jewish cinema. His thorough compendium misses only a silent version of *The Kreutzer Sonata,* produced by "The William Fox Vaudeville Company," released in March 1915 and featuring Theda Bara (a Jewish actress originally named Theodosia Goodman) as Celia.

I was amazed when I found out that as recently as 1979, the Third New York Yiddish Film Festival, held at the 92nd Street Y, was "dedicated to Jacob Gordin, playwright." Launched with a showing of the film version of *Mirele Efros* shot in the United States in 1939, the festival was introduced by Harold Clurman, famous American critic and producer, who once wrote that the Yiddish theater of the Golden Age was "probably the best in the city." It pains me to acknowledge that had I known, had I been interested, I could have flown to New York to attend and to meet Clurman, who was Stella Adler's ex-husband and knew everything and everybody. I could have seen Ida Kaminska, a celebrity in America after her 1965 Oscar nomination for *The Shop on Main Street*, and her daughter Ruth in *Mirele Efros* in New York in 1967, a production granted a glowing review in the *New York Times*. Kaminska and Clurman both died in 1980, just before I began my work. So many missed opportunities.

Though in the United States the Jewish theater itself diminished in importance, its influence infiltrated and permanently altered the culture of the country in which it first flourished. Paul Muni (whose first stage name was Muni Weisenfreund), Eddie Cantor (Isidore Itzkowitz), Sophie Tucker (Sonia Abuza), and Walter Matthau (Walter Matuschanskayasky), among other notable talents, debuted on the Yiddish stage. And of course to this day, the number of gifted Jewish musicians, performers, and comics on stage and screen, many disguised behind gentile names, is staggering.

The famous Group Theater, cofounded by Harold Clurman with members Stella and Luther Adler, Clifford Odets, and Elia Kazan, transformed American theatrical life with its version of Stanislavsky's Method, which came to define American acting. Clifford Odets's plays *Waiting for Lefty*, *Golden Boy*, and *Awake and Sing!* and Marc Blitzstein's *The Cradle Will Rock* brought the serious Yiddish theater's socialist zeal onto the American stage.

Stella Adler, who grew up on the Yiddish stage, subsequently taught in her own studio where she was the seminal influence on hundreds of young American performers, most famously Marlon Brando, creator of a uniquely American brand of screen naturalism. After the unknown Brando had spent a week in her class, Stella divined that he would become "the best young actor in the American theater." Brando later observed, "If there wasn't a Yiddish theater, there wouldn't have been Stella. If there hadn't been Stella, there wouldn't have been all these actors who studied with her and changed the face of theater—and not only acting, but writing and directing." Once when I was visiting my colleague, Jacob Adler's granddaughter Lulla Rosenfeld, she left to speak on the phone for fifteen minutes. "That was Stella, from California," she told me when she returned. I can hardly bear to imagine what Lulla's Aunt Stella might have told me.

A great deal has been made recently, including a book subtitled "How the Jews Invented Hollywood" and an engaging Canadian documentary, of the fact that almost all the Hollywood studios were founded and run by immigrant Jews. These driven newcomers entered the movie business because it was wide open and required daring, vision, and a work ethic, which they had, rather than capital and connections, which they didn't. Their movies were set in a mythical America they had invented, the America of their fantasies rather than the actual society around them, and yet still echoed their own past. The standard scene in Westerns, in which helpless, isolated settlers are terrorized by bloodthirsty wild Indians, looks a lot like a pogrom.

I have a further theory about the phenomenal early success of greenhorn Jews in the entertainment business. I think these immigrants, desperate to belong in their new world, were more ready to risk everything in show business than they might have been, had Jacob Gordin and his realist colleagues not elevated the status of performing artists and producers. Before them, the theater and its actors were disreputable, sneered at socially although enjoyed at a distance by upright Jews. Gordin, another kind of upright Jew, made the theater, or at least his theater, a far more acceptable place both for those who attended and for those who found employment there. Because of his aura of moral rectitude, the tinsel world of Jewish show business donned for a while a propriety it had never had. Perhaps this newfound status helped to attract talents who might otherwise have stayed in the more respectable domains of retail or fur. I know, in intimating that my great-grandfather helped boost the success and scope of the American entertainment industry, that I'm perhaps taking family pride a bit too far.

There's no doubt that in times of crisis and celebration, producers and audiences continued to turn to the reassuring bulk of Jacob Gordin's collected works. Between 1935 and 1939, in the terrible heart of the Depression, Roosevelt's Federal Theater Project under the Works Progress Administration sponsored various ethnic theaters, including a Yiddish troupe. *The Jewish King Lear* and a play by Hirschbein were presented free in Chicago, New York, and Boston before thousands of unemployed spectators, who must have enjoyed watching a man lose his fortune and gain it all back again. Perhaps it is from this time that the well-known jokes about

Gordin's play popped up. In one, a Jew tells his goyish friend, better he should see *King Lear* "in the original Yiddish." In another version, a British actor sitting in a New York taxi informs the driver that he's in town to play in *King Lear*. "No kidding," muses the driver. "So they're doing it in English now."

After the war, Ida Kaminska founded the Jewish State Theater of Poland, which in 1947—a few years early—celebrated the seventy-fifth birthday of professional Yiddish theater with productions of Goldfaden and Gordin. (The celebrations must also have honored the fact that there were any Jewish artists at all in Poland after the war.) In 1967, a fiftieth anniversary show about Ida Kaminska's career was produced with one act of *Mirele Efros* and several scenes from Brecht's *Mother Courage*. In 1976, to honor the 100th birthday of the Yiddish theater, the Folksbeine bravely toured *God, Man, and Devil* around Israel, where Hebrew is the chosen language of pride and statehood, and Yiddish was then a symbol of weakness and compromise. Over and over, on meaningful occasions, producers have chosen from the Gordin repertoire.

But of all his ongoing appearances, I am proudest by far of this: after his death my great-grandfather continued for three decades to be the most produced playwright of the Eastern European Yiddish theater troupes, until those actors, and their audiences, and the *heymish* language common to them all were all but wiped from the face of the earth.

And even then, even as the Jewish citizens of Warsaw and Vilna were hounded into ghettos to starve or be massacred, they kept their theater alive. Even in the ghettos, professional actors and amateur theater lovers put on complete plays by Kobrin, Goldfaden, and Gordin. Even in the camps, even after the war in the displaced person camps, there were performances of the best plays, recited by memory, to keep the souls of the nearly dead thinking, remembering, alive.

The death of millions of Yiddish-speaking Jews dealt their language and theater a mortal blow from which neither can ever recover. The rich culture and tongue that were the lifeblood of Jews throughout Eastern Europe and Russia have but few adherents left. And yet, while tragically diminished, Yiddish persists as a language, and so does its theater. In America, although the second generation, the children born to immigrants, moved further from the shtetl into the mainstream of American life, their children, the third generation, are starting now to look backwards—securely installed and so safe to indulge in nostalgia for the world of their ancestors.

The invaluable, well-nigh miraculous National Yiddish Book Center has managed to preserve and catalog more than a million Yiddish books, and the third generation of young Jews is producing more, writing novels and nonfiction about the shtetl and making documentaries about pilgrimages to Eastern Europe to look for roots. The survival of the Yiddish language itself is guaranteed in academe. Yiddish departments and language courses are sprouting at universities all over the globe, and bright young academics are making careers in Yiddish studies. Just as Gordin would have scoffed at the notion of a Nobel Prize for literature in Yiddish—won by Isaac Bashevis Singer in 1978—he would have found equally absurd the idea of Yiddish studies at Oxford or Harvard or the Universities of Texas and Pennsylvania, among many others.

Enthusiastic amateur Yiddish theater groups perform around the world, and companies both professional and amateur have settled in major Jewish centers like Montreal and New York. Most recently a number of related Web sites have sprung up, including for a time a Yiddish theater site sponsored by Steven Spielberg. For the first time in its history, the Folksbeine Theater in New York not long ago produced a reading aimed specifically at the Hasidic community, which still uses Yiddish in daily life. The play chosen for this historic attempt to reach out to a new audience was *The Jewish King Lear.*

Jacob Gordin's name appears not only in reference to the Yiddish theater but in the remembrances of Jews who grew up under his shadow on the Lower East Side. Great-Aunt Helen loved to recall the day that the entrepreneur and inventor David Sarnoff, head of RCA, was dedicating a new wing at the Educational Alliance. In his speech, he spoke of his respect for Gordin. "He talked about all the things Papa did for the poor people, he always had time to listen to them, always gave of himself to the young students," Helen told me. "They'd write something and bring it to him, do you think I have talent, Mr. Gordin? He never turned them away. And Sarnoff, who was then a multimillionaire, spoke of Papa with such love, and I sat there, I can't tell you the feeling of gratitude, that I was related to that wonderful person." Philosopher Morris Raphael Cohen spoke of Helen's father with the same kind of admiration in his memoirs, and there are others. An interesting contrast, though, are the pages devoted to Gordin in the famous memoirs of Abraham Cahan.

Cahan outlived almost all his peers by decades. He died in Beth Israel Hospital in August 1951, more than forty-two years after Gordin's death, and exactly one year after I was born in Manhattan. The ancient editor lived briefly at the same time, in the same city, as his old adversary's newest descendant. It is the nonobjective contention of that descendent—me—that Abraham Cahan was a cold, envious man whose brilliant practical side was too easily overwhelmed by his sadistic streak. More level-headed observers have concurred; the redoubtable Irving Howe wrote that Cahan could be "narrow, philistine and spiteful," and memoirist Harry Roskolenko called him "scathing, moralistic, a sort of socialist William Randolph Hearst."

Cahan's 1917 masterpiece *The Rise of David Levinsky*, his best-known book and the first Jewish American novel, reprises one of his and Gordin's favorite themes, the corrupting force of capitalism. It is the well-told saga of an observant Jew who emigrates and becomes a rich American industrialist, losing his lofty soul in the process. I can't help but note, however, that though Cahan tries to include a series of tantalizing love affairs for his hero, not one of them ever amounts to anything, and indeed they don't make sense for the character or the plot. David Levinsky understands nothing of love, and it's my contention that his creator didn't, either. Cahan was not good at love, at least of human beings. There's no doubt that he loved his newspaper, his life's work.

The editor, novelist, and agitator accomplished many valuable things during his ninety-one years, including opening the Lower East Side to uptown and publishing and encouraging important writers like I. L. Peretz and the brothers I. J. and Isaac Bashevis Singer. By 1924, the *Forward* was the most successful non-English-language paper in the United States and had become the most widely read Yiddish newspaper in the world. His newspaper flourishes to this day, publishing weekly now in both Yiddish and English and also, paradoxically, in Russian.

For all his achievements, "the guardian angel of young Jewish writers" was lionized, if not canonized. The year after Gordin's death, Cahan's fiftieth birthday was celebrated in Carnegie Hall, and in 1947 the *Forward*'s fiftieth anniversary festivities took place in the vastness of Madison Square

Gardens. Book after book about the era quote him and his ubiquitous, tendentious, very long memoirs extensively, telling his stories as if they are the historically recorded truth. He has become the oracle of the time, the template of the immigrant Russian Jew.

In the section on the Yiddish theater in his memoirs, Cahan betrays a touch of remorse. He struggles to say positive things about Gordin, but in the next line his bile courses though and he mocks and dismisses the playwright, as if to prove his attacks were objective by including faint praise in addition to outright damnation. "Through Gordin, the actors became artists," he wrote. "His plays are very important for the Jewish theater, but they have no literary value and are not part of world literature." Today, anyone reading about Gordin in various encyclopedias and articles, including those online, will find Cahan quoted virtually word for word. "His works are worthless as literature," says one summation after another.

The strength of Cahan's hatreds has been commented upon by biographers and then passed over in the emphasis on the strength of his personality and phenomenal career. "Cahan the fighter had no rival," writes biographer Melech Epstein. Once in a fight, he recalls, Cahan became completely immersed in it, for weeks, months, even, as he did with Gordin and Asch, for years. "He fought with relish, and seemed to thrive upon it. His admirers point with pride to the fact that he never lost a battle . . . It is not uncharitable," he concludes, "to say that his dislikes were more numerous and active than his likes."

Isn't Epstein working too hard to be "not uncharitable"? Great men, great artists are often immoderate and even unpleasant human beings. Tolstoy was a self-centered, tyrannical pedant hated by some of his children; my great-grandfather was inflexible and pompous, unloved by some of his. But these men, impossible as they were, were trying to do good for others. In my opinion, although Abraham Cahan cared deeply about his people and his paper, he had no higher purpose for his vendettas. Once launched, he simply needed, at any cost, to win, and in his terms, he did. He achieved what he set out to achieve no matter what was lost on the way. I contend that he caused a great deal to be lost.

So did a few of his contemporaries. For years after Gordin's death, Morris Winchevsky, for one, continued to struggle with Abe Cahan on the pages of the *Forward*. At last, according to Melech Epstein, the poet was so "shabbily treated by the editor" that he never wrote for the paper again.

Through the years, the stubborn, good-natured Winchevsky contin-ued to write eulogies and remembrances for his beloved friend the play-wright. In 1924 he was invited back to Russia as a hero of the Communist Party. Though offered a life pension to remain, Winchevsky left without re-gret after some months and returned to New York. He died there in 1932, poor, unable to speak, but still writing and a Yankees fan.

Would my great-grandfather, like his best friend, have awaited an in-vitation from the Communists? I think not. After the overthrow of the tsarist regime, he would have sailed eagerly for Russia. Would he have blinded himself to the horrible excesses that followed the Bolshevik Revo-lution? One of the first official acts of the new government was the aboli-tion of the Pale of Settlement, auguring a happier time for Jews. The years that followed, however, were witness not to Jewish safety and freedom but to the worst pogroms of all. Between 1918 and 1921, 150,000 Jews died in Russia either by slaughter or as a less direct result of the many hundreds of anti-Semitic attacks. If Eva and Masha and their families survived the pogroms, they faced Stalin's gulag and the homicidal madness of his col-lectivization campaign, in which an estimated ten million people died in famines across Ukraine.

Then came the invasion of the Nazis. There's a mass grave in the Jewish cemetery of Melitopol dating from 1941. I wonder if Yakov Mik-hailovich would ever have seen or acknowledged the bitterness of Jewish life in the land he loved too well.

In 1949, as Stalin sought to wipe out Jewish intellectual life in the So-viet Union, the last Yiddish theater in Moscow was closed down. Yet tour-ing Yiddish companies were not stopped. In August 1970, the *New York Times* wrote about a triumphant event: a performance of *The Kreutzer Sonata* before an audience of thousands in a luxurious Moscow theater. So-viet authorities, apparently, had no problem with a play that they felt por-trayed American society negatively.

Decades earlier, before the revolution, there was no question of Gordin's thespian colleagues returning to Russia from the golden land in which they continued, like the hardy beasts they were, to thrive. Thomashefsky opened the most magnificent Yiddish theater ever built, the National Theater on Houston Street, in 1912. He and Bessie eventually sep-arated, pursuing successful careers in different theaters. They both wrote autobiographies that were serialized, one in the *Forward* and the other in the *Truth.* According to their grandson Michael Tilson Thomas, charismatic conductor of the San Francisco Symphony, the rapt audience could read Boris's account of certain events in the morning, then compare it to Bessie's in the afternoon. Boris died in 1939. Bessie lived to be eighty-nine years old, remaining a flamboyant grande dame with dyed hair and cigarette holder, and bequeathing to her talented grandson her musicality, her theatrical spirit, and the top hat and tails she used in one of her acts. She died in 1962.

In 1912 Bertha Kalish turned down a job offer of $1,000 a week to play sketch in a London music hall with an upstart comedian called W. C. Fields. Toward the end of her life, she was considered one of the greatest actresses of her time, the female counterpart to Adler. Before her death in 1939, she performed in a series of farewell performances although she was blind.

The spritely, gifted Mogulesco, called by one critic "the comic genius of his generation," died in 1914. Keni Lipzin ended her days tainted by scandal; in 1912, three years after Gordin's death, her husband committed suicide. She herself died in 1918, and was buried with her Master.

In 1920 came the sudden death of David Kessler. Not long before, Kessler had advertised in the *Forward* his next seven days of performances: a different, massive play every night, five plays by Gordin, plus *Uriel Acosta* and *Othello,* with an eighth play in rehearsal. It is not surprising, given this bone-crushing level of activity, that he collapsed onstage during a performance and died the next day. Ronald Sanders describes him as "an uneducated and largely inarticulate man, whom the Gordinian culture enabled to rise to a state of princeliness in the world of the arts." Broadway producer Jed Harris once said that Kessler was the greatest actor he had ever seen.

Also in 1920 came the stroke that debilitated Adler but did not stop him from performing. The great eagle made his last appearance on Broadway in the early twenties at a benefit performance for himself. Every Broadway star of stage, opera, and the music world came to pay homage to the Yiddish actor, and the show, which included Al Jolson singing "Vesti la Giubba" followed by Giovanni Martinelli leading the audience in "Pack up your troubles in your old kit bag and smile, smile, smile," lasted till five o'clock in the morning. Adler himself performed the first act of Gordin's *Lear.* He died in 1926.

Two years later, all his actor children appeared together in a production of *The Wild Man*. In 1937, one last time, Sara Adler staged, directed,
and starred in *Without a Home*. She recreated one of her greatest roles, in
Gordin's dramatization of Tolstoy's *Resurrection*, at a tribute to herself in
1939. Sara Adler lived to be ninety-five, dying in 1953. All her children continued to work on the American stage, especially Stella, who never forgot
her origins.

In February 1941, one of the last efforts of the Group Theater brought
together Stella and her brother Luther with actress Frances Farmer at the
Second Avenue Theater. Produced by Stella's soon-to-be husband Harold
Clurman and playwrights Clifford Odets and Ossip Dymow, among others, the program of play excerpts was an anniversary tribute to Jacob
Gordin, to mark the fifty years since the first production of a Gordin play.
Sylvia Sidney (real name Sophia Kosow) appeared in a specially written
epilogue entitled "My Tribute to Jacob Gordin." Before the show took place
it was written about in the *New York Herald Tribune*. My father, who at eighteen had not yet volunteered for the war, could have gone to see it.

No one in the Gordin family, as far as I know, attended.

• • •

I have one great happiness in my life, one thing in the whole world—one
child, that's all. You, my child, will live after me. You will have sons and
daughters, clever, educated people. Through them, my soul will live
again.

—Jacob Gordin, *Elisha ben Avuya* (1906)

AND WHAT BECAME of the Gordin family? Sad to say, very few of
Gordin's own children led happy or fulfilled lives. The man who put such
energy and warmth into young members of the Jacob Gordin Literary Associations, who meant so much to David Sarnoff and Morris Raphael
Cohen, was not nurturing and accessible to his own offspring. In ordinary
immigrant families, the young assumed power, becoming the "go-
betweens," interpreting America to their parents. The Gordin children
were powerless and belonged nowhere, not in the old world and not in the
new.

Even the numbers tell a story: the Gordin family has grown steadily
smaller through the generations. Ordinarily from eleven children would
grow a forest of offspring; from Tolstoy's children there are hundreds of

descendents, more than a hundred from his son Lev alone. What's pictured on the Gordin family tree is the opposite, only partly because so many in the family are unknown to me. Of the latest, the great-great generation, besides my own daughter and son I know of only ten others, including a young man who is named Jacob Gordin and whose family I have never met.

All of the patriarch's children lived much longer lives than their father, except the eldest. Sophie, always at risk because of her epilepsy, was only fifty-five when she died of pneumonia. Perhaps because her precarious health caused her to be demanding, she was disliked even by her only daughter. "Our mother was not loving," Anna said. "She was a selfish sort of person, very possessive, and should not have been a parent. She always made us feel that she gave birth to us and that was enough, her dues were paid. For some reason she thought she was a genius; she could play guitar a little and sing with a nice voice."

I asked Anna if Sophie got along with her father. "I don't think my mother got along with her father. I don't think she got along with anybody. The thing that really hurt us," she replied, "was that our mother didn't really care for us." Though Anna and her two brothers William and David all enjoyed long, contented marriages, none of the three had children.

Even more sad and strange is the story of Yelizaveta, the second daughter. Around 1900 Lizzie married David Kobin, a ladies' man and a gambler. All Helen would tell me about the Kobins was that "Lizzie only came to the house when she needed help or money. She had six children and lived by *schnorring* [begging], and her husband was an objectionable scoundrel. The less you say about her the more I like it." Lizzie was a second daughter, born to a sixteen-year-old mother and sandwiched between an older sister with epilepsy and a younger brother with a mental disability. There must have been very little time for her.

In 1985 I received a letter in response to my query in the *New York Times*. My correspondent told me that in 1923, in Brooklyn, an impoverished family with four or five young children moved into the neighborhood and were desperately in need of shelter. "The mother," she wrote, "was the daughter of Jacob Gordin." Lizzie. Because the writer's parents were "devotees of Yiddish Literature and Theater," they made room in their house for the waifs, who had little by way of food and clothing.

The couple were slender, soft spoken, mostly taciturn, and never expressed [the] slightest appreciation. After a while, they absented themselves late afternoons, returned at dawn, and slept all day. No cooking or tidying was even attempted. It was a hot summer, and the little children, unhappy and restless, were out on the street all hours through the night.

The aura of the name of Jacob Gordin overpowered my mother (and some neighbors) for several months, and altho' she ran a business all day, her nights were taken up caring, baby-sitting for the pathetic crew. Finally, she gave up on them, and I was too young to remember how, when, or more sequel to report. I appreciate my wonderful Mother as I recall and write this, and wonder if her appreciation of Jacob Gordin diminished. I think not.

That was all I knew of the fate of Lizzie and her family until by chance, one day in Toronto, I heard that Jacob Gordin's great-granddaughter had attended the opening of *Mirele Efros* in Montreal. I had not; who had? A few phone calls later, I'd located my first cousin once removed, Lizzie's granddaughter Elizabeth, also shortened to Beth. For many years, we had lived a few hundred miles from each other without knowing of our connection. As we chatted on the phone, she filled in many blanks on that branch of the family tree.

Lizzie's six children, not surprisingly, were an eccentric bunch as adults. Beth's mother Lucie was helped financially by her aunt Nettie, my grandmother, as were a number of the Gordins. When asked if she spoke Yiddish, Beth replied that she did not, that her mother knew nothing about being Jewish and spoke no Yiddish. "My grandmother Elizabeth never even acknowledged that she was a Jew," she said.

One day I drove to visit my new cousin at her home in Montreal. Though I admired her pretty face, I didn't recognize the family in it, or in her fair hair. She remarked on my set of "the family brackets," the deep lines from the base of my nose to the corners of my mouth, exactly like my father's. Elizabeth's left-wing father immigrated to Canada to escape the scourge of Joseph McCarthy, as did mine. She too worked in the theater, though in costumes, not on stage. She showed me pictures of Lizzie. "My grandmother was a snob," she said, "cold and closed and judgmental, and so was my mother."

Aneuta was revered by the whole family; her granddaughter Anna called her "an angel from heaven if there ever was one." How did a woman so loving raise so many unloving children? I can only assume that Aneuta, naïve and untutored, was overwhelmed by poverty, endless pregnancies, her husband's disappearance, the stresses of immigration, and a new culture. Her placidity got her through, but it did not extend to her offspring. Only one daughter had a sweet temper like her mother's: Vera, almost everyone's favorite. I adored my little aunt, with whom even in childhood I stood eye to eye. Though her first husband, a Jewish Italian opera singer, deserted her and their young daughter Alexandra, Vera's second marriage was a loving partnership. Alexandra's only son Daniel and I have corresponded on occasion, but we have met only once, in infancy.

Nettie went out of her way to avoid the majority of her siblings, but especially Jim, formerly Yasha. Though the favorite of his brother George, this brother was an embarrassment to the rest of the family because he made a living as a janitor, his wife was Catholic, and one of their three children became a cabdriver. My sharp-tongued Uncle Edgar told of sitting in a cab once, driven by a man "so unpleasant, and yet with something so familiar about his face, that I looked at his license in the front, which said 'James Gordin Jr.' I thought, 'God forbid—my cousin!' When I saw a Madonna on the dashboard, I was relieved; obviously, not one of the tribe. And then I remembered that my uncle Jim had married a Catholic." But this story says more about my intolerant Uncle Edgar, who throughout his life had as little as possible to do with his family, than about his cousin Jim.

Mike became a dentist whose clientele consisted largely of friends and family, including many of the Kaplans. Well-liked by everyone, he was described by Helen, in a lawsuit about his estate, as "a refined and gentle man, ethical, honest to a fault, loved and respected for his high principals and integrity." He had a peaceful but childless marriage with Rema, a teacher who worked with disadvantaged children in the projects.

George—Grisha—spent his life as a happily married accountant in Pennsylvania, the father of Gertrude and twins George and Caryl. Gertrude, who never married, was one of my father's favorite relatives, a staunch liberal, and a popular high school English teacher before her death at sixty-one of cancer. Her obituary portrays her as just like my dad and other Gordins: "She was a truly cultured person, honest and sensitive, sometimes irascible, an educator and seeker who made her presence known." Her grandfather would have liked her. It is one of the paradoxes of Gordin's life that he spent much of it urging women to be fearless, independent, ambitious, full of initiative and action, and yet not one of his five daughters grew up to remotely resemble his stage heroines.

I sharply regret missing Gertrude; she was the family historian, and all she knew died with her. Her brother George Jr. didn't know that his father was born in Russia, had once been Grigoriy, and hadn't met his own father until he was three. George told me, "Dad may have been born in Russia but he wasn't Russian, he was a thoroughly typical American. He loved opera and ballet," George went on, "and had a passion for theater. He had a huge library of plays, read plays and critics and went to the theater constantly."

I smiled as he spoke, because that didn't sound a typical American at all, to me.

The twins both told me that George Sr. didn't respect his father. "He thought Jacob Gordin was arrogant and self-righteous, a big ego with a small talent," said George Jr. "Dad worshipped his mother, and didn't like the way his father treated her."

All that is known of gentle Sam is that he worked as a hospital orderly and lived with Aneuta until she died. Where did he go after his mother's death? No one was left to tell me.

Helen enjoyed a long, not very prosperous marriage to Sam Zielstein, who refused to consider having children, she told me, because he didn't want his darling wife to suffer. She spent her life playing the piano and painting without great talent at either, though she also spent considerable time, she said, "schlepping out to Coney Island to visit Alex in that dump he lived in." Helen maintained a lifelong friendship with "Ellie and Julie in the Benedict family," who I believe were Morris Winchevsky's daughters. When David Kessler's daughter Sylvia made an overture of friendship, however, Helen didn't respond. Conceding only that "it wasn't Sylvia's fault," she never forgot that in November 1907 her father had had to sue Kessler, as well as Adler, for payment of royalties.

Youngest son Leon was the joker of the pack, a character, an amusing, high-spirited luftmentsh who never held a steady job. He was happiest in the American army during and after the war, where he and my father rendezvoused several times in Paris for wine, women, and song. Like my dad, he married a gentile Englishwoman after the war—Betty, a redhead from

Manchester who was working as a dancer in Paris—and they had a penurious, cheerful marriage.

Leon's daughter Joan from a brief first marriage vanished from family view six decades ago. Recently, on a Web site that lists all manner of unrelated Gordins, I was excited to find a picture of a dark, bearded twenty-two-year-old looking a great deal like Jacob Gordin and claiming to be his great-great-grandson. After contacting him, I was able to telephone his grandmother, née Joan Gordin, who was only seventy-two when we spoke. Born in 1933, she told me that in her early years she was close to Vera, Nettie, and Helen. When she was only seven, her father left the marriage to join the army, and her mother set in motion a divorce. After that, "the Gordins pretended they didn't know me. I was very hurt by that," she said. "There was a lot of jealousy in that family."

What did she know about her grandfather? "He was a bit of a playboy," she said to my surprise, though she couldn't say how she knew this. "My grandparents weren't together much—just long enough to make children. He was a ladies' man."

"I have two small books, classics, with my grandfather's handwriting in them. They were gifts to my father," she said. She had no Gordin family photographs, and I sent her copies of mine. Joan died less than a year later, before we a chance to meet. Her grandson told me that it had thrilled her to renew contact, however briefly and at a distance, with the lost family of her early childhood.

Finally, there are the two most interesting Gordin offspring, at least to me: Sasha-Alex, and Nettie-Nadia-Jeanette.

Gordin referred to his son Sasha sarcastically as an indecisive Jewish Hamlet, commenting that the manuscripts the young man always carried with him would come to nothing. In one of those cruel "Devil" moments elucidated by Winchevsky, Gordin joked that Sasha should go to a gentile editor and shoot either the editor or himself, creating such a sensation that people would vie to print his work. His letters to his favored son begin with reproach: "I received your letter; although you were silent a hell of a long time, better late than never," or "We were expecting you on Thursday, the children especially were all ready for you. We were all very disappointed." I wonder which came first, the father's disappointment or the son's evasive silence?

To the rest of the family, Alex was the egotistical, increasingly unpopular "Professor." In the classic pattern, this clever but floundering son of a powerful, accomplished father was unable to find his own path to financial or familial success. After years teaching at the Baron de Hirsch Agricultural School and at the Educational League, he wrote, according to Helen, "one successful moving picture story, *Over the Hill to the Poorhouse*. Fox bought that from him, by Alexander J. Gordin, his one and only success."

There were two early movies by that name, which was also the title of a well-known tear-jerking poem: one in 1908 with Mack Sennett, and another in 1920, made indeed for Fox and starring the evocatively named Johnnie Walker. It was the top movie of that year, grossing three million dollars. The name of the screenwriter is not listed, but surely it cannot be Alexander J. Gordin, who never had any money.

After Gordin's death, besides laboriously translating his father's plays, which he continued to do for decades, and writing one of his own—*Time of Bloodshed*, a historical drama in four acts based on one of his father's unproduced dramas and also never produced—Alex appointed himself the guardian of his father's work, sending out countless plaintive or aggressive letters demanding royalty payments. In 1912, with his mother and Winchevsky, he sued Harrison Fiske and Sam and Lee Shubert over copyright. Three years later, he wrote a lovingly crafted foreword to the newly published edition of his father's one-act plays, in which, railing against the "self-appointed arbiters of morality" or lauding the educational value of amateur theater, he sounds exactly like Gordin himself. But he also writes as an affectionate son: "In almost every line, we feel the author's warmth and see the reflection of his great heart. The smile of his great soul shines forth in the theater, on the set, on the actors . . . Thus he attempted to lead the Jewish people (and mankind) in his quest to improve the world, to dislodge outdated ideas, and to laugh satirically at the dangers of fanaticism. He taught the broadest and deepest principles and ideals of life."

"It is the greatest hope and ambition of this writer to achieve, in his lifetime, a complete publication of Jacob Gordin's work," Alex concluded. But he was not good at business, or skilled at translation. A decade after his father's death his relations with his family, even with his mother, reached rock bottom, where they remained. According to Helen, "Alex drained Mama. More and more money disappeared."

By the early 1920s, he was living in near destitution on Coney Island, playing chess for money. In the Zylberzweig *Encyclopedia*, there are stories about Alex who, it is asserted, held a Ph.D. from Columbia—although he earned several degrees, it is unlikely his education had gone that far—and who despite his poverty was always neatly and elegantly dressed, looking like a banker, a theater director, or "even an artist." The writers marvel that Jacob Gordin's favorite son made such a mean living; he had a chess concession with a few tables outside where customers paid him a quarter for every game they lost. What a formidable intellect he must have had, to make even a meager living playing chess all day.

Though Alex spoke only English, it was clear that he understood Yiddish. He never spoke of his past or his father because of his retiring nature, an observer surmised, or because he didn't want to shame his father's memory. Another tells of a woman sitting nearby, "elderly, pretty, an aristocratic look to her, holding a shopping bag in her hand." Because of the strong resemblance between them, he decided she must be Gordin's mother. The fifty cents the player paid Gordin for two lost games went to the woman, who got up quickly to leave. It was clear she had been waiting for the winnings to give her money for shopping.

It hurts to imagine Aneuta, after a lifetime of backbreaking work, waiting for quarters so she could buy groceries for her nearly indigent son. Anna Lazarevna lived fifteen years after her husband, and did not enjoy a serene old age. The $20,000 left to her did not last. Considerable time was spent trying to shake royalties from those performing her husband's plays. When Alex's insistent letters produced no results, Helen and Leon were sent to the stage doors to ask in person for payment of the royalty, which was a mere $5 per performance. "The women used to pay, Mrs. Kalish and Mrs. Lipzin, but not the men," my great-aunt told me bitterly. "Mama used to call them *svolichi*—bastards. She said life is too short, she had rather be poor, and she gave up. I wish you'd put that in your book."

In 1921, Mike sold 256 Madison "for a song! There were no businessmen in our family!" kvetched Helen. Anna and her still-dependent children Sam, Nettie, Helen (who was engaged to Sam Zielstein), and the divorced Vera with her daughter, moved to an apartment in the Tremont section of the Bronx.

It was there, shortly after the family's arrival, that the possibly one-month-pregnant Nettie Gordin married Mike Kaplan, the ceremony witnessed by lots of Kaplans and a few Gordins. I wonder if I owe my existence to the move. With her little sister Helen engaged and ready to move out, Nettie didn't want to be left behind in a small apartment with her siblings and mother, and so, professing to be eight years younger than she actually was, she finally accepted or forced an offer of marriage.

Aneuta lived in the sixth-floor flat only three years. "At the end things were bad for her," Helen confessed. "Her children never helped her as they should." My great-grandmother died in 1924, at the age of sixty-five. In the last photograph of her, taken the year before her death, she is smiling wearily and holding a pugnacious baby boy: Jacob Gordin Kaplan, my father.

One night just after the war, that boy, now a good-looking ex-Army man of twenty-four, and his younger brother Edgar were strolling late at night down seedy Forty-second Street when they saw, above the sign "Hubert's Flea Circus," another sign: "Gordin's Chess and Checkers Center." Curious—the "i" in the name is rare—the Kaplan brothers climbed the stairs to find a silent dingy room filled with men playing chess at long tables. Under the green-shaded hanging lamps, they saw a stump of a man who looked just like many of their other Gordin relatives: the jowls, the squat figure, the sour disposition.

At the end of the game, Gordin and Edgar introduced themselves, and met their Uncle Alex for the first time. They found out that he had come to their home a few times to "borrow" money from his sister Nettie, but she had never let him in when her sons were there. Twenty-one-year-old Edgar, who kept coming back to the club to play chess, became as close to his uncle as was possible for two cerebral loners. When they met, Alex was sixty-seven, living with a woman in Seagate near Coney Island. He still owned a shelf of his father's writings, which he wouldn't part with for any amount of money.

After running the club for twenty years, he left it in 1954 and died shortly thereafter, bequeathing his entire fortune to his nephew—about $250, Edgar told me, not enough to pay his funeral expenses and debts. What happened to his collection of Gordin's work? I assume that Edgar threw it out.

As his leisure activity, Jacob Gordin, who despised card playing, spent many hours at the chessboard. His grandson Edgar, after many hours at the chessboard, shifted his focus to cards. To his mother's despair, her younger son was expelled from Cornell University, where he had been awarded a postwar math scholarship, because he spent all his time in basement rooms playing bridge. When he died of cancer in 1997, Edgar Kaplan had been for decades one of the most famous and respected bridge players in the world, a brilliant writer and witty, articulate commentator on the game, the source of supreme *naches*—pride—for his parents. They did wish that he and his bridge-playing musician wife Betty, originally Elizabeth, had raised children, instead of Abyssinian cats.

Alex—Sasha—the smart, surly, chess-playing romantic lost in unattainable dreams, the petty yet grandiose and volatile schemer unable to find a practical foothold in the world, was the most Russian of all the Gordins. "Mellowness, complacency, geniality and calmness are qualities practically unknown to the intellectual [Russian] Jew," wrote Hutchins Hapgood wryly, after meeting a few. He is describing what Alex did not possess, nor Alex's father, nor mine, at least until late in his life. Though my dad did at last mellow to a magnanimous warmth, he remained an engine, constantly revving. He was not for one moment, ever, complacent or calm.

His mother, my grandmother Nettie, was preoccupied by her boychiks; a clichéd Jewish mother, she was overprotective, interfering, possessive, manipulative. At eleven, my father proudly informed her that he had just begun his own paper route. She immediately made him quit; no grandson of Jacob Gordin was going to deliver newspapers like any common boy. Why was Nettie so joyless? Like her sister Helen, she painted, not very well, in oils and played the piano; she was a superb cook and a good hostess. But she was discontented and rigid and, like many of her siblings, a terrible snob. Nettie Gordin was royalty. Nothing was good enough for her, and nothing was good enough for her boys.

The resemblance between her father and the son she named for him is uncanny. Jacob Gordin was described in one article as "a passionate man, proud and straight-forward, militant without any definite ideology"; this was my father too. My handsome, thick-necked, cigar-smoking father with his dark eyes and coarse black curls was, like his namesake, a big-hearted leader—a *mentsh*. He too was an aggressive, argumentative, charismatic socialist-without-a-party, a hard-working rabble-rouser for issues of social justice, a formidable teacher who hated to be criticized. The joy and pur-

Nettie Gordin Kaplan in 1925 with her sons Jacob Gordin beside her and Edgar Saul on her lap.

pose of his life was in the passionate never-ending struggle against the forces of darkness, at work, at home, in the community, and the world. He too founded a school, and his—the Halifax Grammar School, a relatively small academic school that has produced five Rhodes scholars—thrives to this day. He wrote, spoke, and organized for his many causes, which included the end to nuclear testing and the Vietnam War.

He also wasted his time with foolish feuds, attracting the enmity of smaller men who hurt him both personally and professionally. Like his famous forebear, he lived his adult life in exile, never quite at ease in his adopted home, and driven by a voracious, almost insatiable appetite for knowledge, experience, contact, and recognition. But he lived a decade longer than his grandfather, years during which he was, at last, fulfilled in his work and content with his family.

Like his grandfather, my didactic father had no idea how to relate to young children; it makes me laugh, now, that his choice of bedtime reading for me, when I was four, was a picture book of *The Iliad and the Odyssey* in French. And he too was a feminist happy to have an attentive wife at home, though his lively and clever helpmate Sylvia, unlike Aneuta, was a full partner in the marriage, sometimes at odds with her volcanic spouse. My beautiful six-foot tall English mother was a code-cracker at Bletchley Park when Dad met her during the war, and she later earned a social work degree from the London School of Economics. But it came to be her life's work to care for her husband and to make a welcoming home for her family. Sporty, musical, and artistic, Mum became a skilled cook who made a fine meaty borscht from her mother-in-law Nettie's recipe, and an especially good chopped liver.

Though Dad adored Jewish food and Yiddish phrases, he remained ambivalent about his Jewishness for much of his life. During my childhood, outside of our annual trips to New York I had little contact with my Jewish half, although the reality of that heritage was brought home when we were forbidden to join the Halifax country club to which all of my WASP friends belonged. ("My children are only half Jewish," snapped my father, paraphrasing Groucho to the membership committee. "Perhaps they could wade in the swimming pool up to their navels.")

After the Six Day War in 1967, a decisive military victory for the Israelis, my father was more openly Jewish, proud that Jews had proven to be not only the greatest of musicians, thinkers, and financiers but cunning, fearless warriors as well. A few years before he died, he fought his last great public battle, taking on James Keegstra, a high school history teacher in a small Alberta town who for decades had taught his students that the Holocaust was an invention of the Jews. My father undertook a campaign not only to expose and condemn Keegstra but in support of the one brave mother who had dared to challenge his teachings; he declared this woman, not even Jewish, to be a heroine. It was the first time he had committed himself, as a Jew, to a specifically Jewish issue. It gave him enormous pleasure.

I wonder, now, if Judaism for my dad was like his mother: cherished and indispensable, but also suffocating and intrusive. Yet as I flipped through reference books at the YIVO one day, I came upon an entry for my father in the 1967 *Who's Who in Canadian Jewry*. Listed there were Dad's

A family gathering in Halifax in 1953; in the back row Mike Kaplan flanked by his sons J. Gordin (left) and Edgar (right), and in front his daughter-in-law Sylvia holding Beth (Elizabeth), and his wife Nettie.

dates, parents, education, army record, academic work, and family. And then I was amazed to read, "Grandson of the late Jacob Mikhailovich Gordin, Jewish playwright and author, whose many works have been enjoyed by Jews throughout the world." My father had obviously brought up his claim to Jewish fame with something that sounds suspiciously like pride.

As he aged, the fury burning in Dad's belly abated; he relaxed, becoming a gratified man, close to his children. Like his grandfather, my father died too young, just as he retired at sixty-five, of cancer. Before he died he had read my thesis, which didn't lessen his disdain for his ancestor. There

THE POLISH CULTURAL INSTITUTE PRESENTS THE

Polish State
Jewish Theatre

ייִדישער מלוכה־טעאַטער פֿון פּוילן

(Artistic Director: Ida Kaminska)

in 3 plays in Yiddish

AT THE WINTER GARDEN THEATRE, LONDON, MARCH 1957

*The program of the Polish State Jewish Theatre, starring Ida Kaminska, attended
by J. Gordin and Sylvia Kaplan in London in 1957. Sylvia, who spoke some German, translated for her husband. Kaminska is shown top and bottom in Jacob
Gordin's Mirele Efros.*

was one word in it of which he especially disapproved. I had written, in
summation, "Jacob Gordin Kaplan is, as Jacob Gordin was, a brilliant,
magnetic, overbearing, vulnerable fighter." My father underlined the
word "vulnerable" and scrawled, beside it, "Objection, your honor!"

But it is true. I know that beneath his abrasive erudition and forceful-
ness, my father was vulnerable, easy to wound. How am I so sure? In my

boyish father, who was sensitive to criticism and easily hurt, I felt the hidden weakness and need for approval in many powerful men. In my great-grandfather I sense a similar kind of hidden vulnerability. I can see it in his letters home from Europe, detailing his fear of solitude; in the letter he wrote to Sasha in May 1905, as the campaign against him started to heat up. "Today I received several letters but it is troublesome to read them. The letters are killing me," he wrote. Later that same year, in a newspaper interview, he admitted, "It is hard for me to speak English. I do not know why. I would not speak willingly for the first ten years of my stay here. I was afraid to utter English words."

I read it in the letter to a supporter in the fall of 1908, as illness and Cahan defeat him. "I'll tell you the truth, it's a big surprise to me to find a friend, " he wrote. "It seems to me I have only enemies." I think the bullish defensiveness and granite confidence of these men hid fear, softness, insecurity. They were vulnerable because they could so easily be unmasked.

And yet they could not have accomplished what they did without their blind raging drive and hugeness of personality. My great-grandfather was at least partially undone by the very things that made him an indispensable leader to his people: his intransigence and single-minded, relentless commitment to his causes, which left him unable to change course or adapt. When I think of this man who gave everything he had, whose integrity was intractable to the point of self-destruction, I also see my father as a young man, a Gordin through and through. The Talmud praises three Jewish virtues: modesty, compassion, and charity. I do believe that by this scale the two Gordin nonbelievers would have managed, in their own way, to win the approval of God. Only in the modesty department might they have been found wanting.

I know these men in my breath and in my bones as I know only two others in the world, my son and daughter. Through his young descendants, Jacob Gordin has achieved one great victory, perhaps the greatest victory of all, over Abraham Cahan: Cahan had no children, whereas Gordin's blood flows on through his great-great-grandchildren. My two are only a quarter Jewish, and yet that fraction seems bigger in them both. Though I don't venture to predict whether the Gordin genes have taken hold, it is undeniable that my dark-eyed daughter, an infant when I began this work, has grown up to be a hospitable, bulldozing, fiercely compassionate reformer, *zaftik* with a head of thick black curls. I see my New York family in her face.

My son is a showman with a graceful sense of humor, whose drama teacher once shrugged, "He's a natural. It's in his blood." When he was thirteen, overhearing a foul anti-Semitic conversation on the subway, he planted himself in front of the offenders and barked, "I am Jewish." He told me, "They didn't know what to say, face to face with a real Jew." My son the real Jew, the 6'8" blue-eyed blonde with the Scottish last name. In part I began this book for these two, that they grow up aware of the wealth of their inherited past, at least on one side of my family: the socially active, dramatic, contentious Jewish blood that has flowed from Russia, through New York City, into their young Canadian veins.

As for myself, I think of one particular moment of illumination during my long journey of discovery. Somewhere in the recesses of my heart, I wondered from the beginning if the path toward my great-grandfather would end in a triumphant claiming of my own Jewish identity. There is a growing body of literature about this subject, in which writers unaware of or unconnected to their Jewishness unearth and celebrate their concealed faith, returning to their roots with joy and relief.

This will not be my story. I wish that I had a spiritual identity to pass on to my children: this is who we are, this is what we believe, this is what we do on Friday, Saturday, Sunday. But I cannot say that I have returned to my roots. Which roots? I carry two passports: Canadian, because that's who I am, and American, because that's who my father was, where my life began, where almost all my family resides. I am a nonreligious person with a profound belief in a personal responsibility and a transcendence that might be called God.

Because my mother is a non-Jew I am not by birth Jewish, either culturally or spiritually, but I am more Jewish than anything else. One of the most pleasing rituals of my life takes place on three *yortsayt* days: to memorialize my father, my uncle Edgar, and my great-grandfather, on the day of their deaths I light the candle and say as much of the Hebrew prayer *Baruch atah* as I know. I do the same with our menorah, at Chanukah. I also help to produce a local annual Christmas pageant, because I love singing carols. I am a Jew, and I am not a Jew.

I have always been an outsider, anxious with any kind of definition or confinement. And yet, despite my wholehearted rejection of belonging, despite my profound love for my father and respect for his values, I have spent my life wishing I could find somewhere to belong and feel at home.

Then I had an encounter in my birthplace, New York.

It is the first summer of the new century. I'm standing in a turquoise room in a Jewish convention center in midtown Manhattan, having flown in for the sixty-fifth anniversary of the Yiddish Artists and Friends Actors Club. I am not only one of the youngest people in the room, I am the tallest woman. No wonder my hostess Shifra Lerer, the lifelong Yiddish actress, thinks I look like a shiksa. I'm used to these moments at Jewish gatherings when I feel too prim and sedate, too big, too young, too goyish. Do I care to fit in here? This florid ingrown world means nothing to me except as research, I think, noting that there are several non-Jews present, including an inebriated young Irishman, who have made the effort to become fluent in Yiddish.

After dinner, Shifra and her colleague Mina Bern, who at the same advanced age is just as springy, perform a skit in Yiddish, two mothers-in-law who despise each other and pretend to be friends. Both the actresses and the dialogue they speak are merry and sharp. If only Gordin could have forgiven *shund* for being fun, filled with simple pleasure like this lighthearted skit, I think. But fun was not in his vocabulary, even on Coney Island. Though he pretended otherwise, it was not in my father's, either. But it is very much present in mine.

Shifra promenades me round the room, suspended from her arm like a charm on one of her many bracelets. She seeks out another elderly woman, a statuesque actress with stiff golden hair who has just performed "Life Is a Cabaret," in Yiddish.

"This is the great-granddaughter of Yankev Gordin," says Shifra.

"Yankev Gordin!" the other cries. She leans in, takes my hand, beams into my eyes. *"Yikhes,* darling. You are blessed with such *yikhes,"* she says.

What a rich word, surely unique in any language, to indicate the gift of family status. My eyes overflow. I feel the past keeping me company, filling my very core. I manage to thank her, and then, "He had it. I don't think I do. Is *yikhes* genetic?"

"Oh yes," she replies. *"Yikhes* means pedigree. It is your heritage, your lineage, your inheritance."

I remember reading an article once on reincarnation. Some native tribes believe that we are our own ancestors. They believe that the dead come back as their own great-grandchildren. "You have the bearing of an actress," says my new friend, still holding my hand.

"You have his eyes, his brow. Such a Jewish face," says someone else.

Standing in the turquoise room, I think, I belong here as much as anywhere, as much as anyone. I belong here.

APPENDIX

SELECTED BIBLIOGRAPHY

ACKNOWLEDGMENTS

INDEX

APPENDIX

PARTIAL LIST OF GORDIN'S PLAYS WITH ORIGINAL TITLES, 1891–1908

MANY OF GORDIN'S PLAYS are listed below, by English title (although most were not translated) and performance date, where that date is known. Only the best known plays were collected and published in Yiddish. A selected list of books in print in Yiddish follows the list of performed works below, and then a list of the few plays translated into English, both published and not.

After the Slaughter [*Nokh der shkhite*] (1903). One act; published in 1917.

America [*Amerike*] (1901).

The Aunt from Warsaw [*Di mume fun varshe*] (unknown). Comedy.

The Bad Shepherds [*Di shlekhte pastekher*] (1899). Adaptation; translated from Octave Mirbeau's *Les mauvais bergers.*

The Bastard [*Der mamzer oder lukretsia bordshia*] (1901). From Hugo's *Lucretia Borgia.*

The Beautiful Miriam [*Di sheyne miryem un di gepeynikte*] (1900). Historical operetta; published in 1908.

Before Sunrise [*Zunenoyfgang*] (1904). From Hauptmann's *Vor Sonnenaufgang.*

The Benefactors from the East Side [*Di vohlteter fun der ist sayd*] (1903).

The Black Jew, or Meir Yosefovich [*Der shvartser yid oder meyer yosefovitsh*] (1895). Adapted from Eliza Orzenszkowa's novel *Meir Ezofowicz.*

The Brothers Luria [*Di litvishe brider lurie, or Di gebrider lurie*] (1894).

Captain Dreyfus [*Kapitan drayfus*] (1898). One act; published in 1917.

Capital, Love and Murder [*Kapital, libe un mord*] (1896).

The Children Go [*Di kinder gehen*] (unknown). Comedy; published in 1909.

Children of the Sun [*Di kinder fun der zun*] (1905). From Gorki.

A Complaint between Man and Wife [*A tayne tsvishn man un froy*] (unknown). Published in 1917.

The Crisis [*Der krizis*] (1898). Two acts; published in 1917.

The Dead Artist [*Der opgeshtorbener kinstler*] (1893). A dramatishe stsene in eyn akt.

Dementia Americana [*Dos meshugas in amerike; Dementia amerikana*] (1908). Folksshtik.

Dvoyrele [*Di dvoyrele meyukheses*] (1897). From Ostrovsky; published in 1907.

Elisha ben Avuya [*Elisha ben avuya*] (1906). Drama; published in 1907.

The Enemy of the People [*Der folks faynt* (1896). From Ibsen.

The Father [*Der foter*] (1904). Adapted from Strindberg's *Father*.

Forward [*Forverts*] (1896). From Stepniak.

Galician Exile [*Goles galitsien*] (1907). Drama.

Galileo, the Martyr of Knowledge [*Galilei martirer fun visnshaft*] (1985).

The Gallery of Types [*Di tipn galerie*] (1901). Series of monologues; published in 1917.

The Genius [*Der goen*] (1900).

God, Man and Devil [*Got, mentsh un tayvl*] (1900). Published in 1903.

The Golden Calf, the Golden God [*Eygl hazohev, der goldener got*] (1895). Drama.

The Great Play [*Di gevaldige pley*] (1904). One-act.

He and She [*Er un zi*] (1901 or 1902). One-act sketch; published in 1917.

The Head of the Community [*Der parnes khodesh*] (1894). Comedy from Gogol's *Inspector General*; published in 1910.

Homeless [*On a heym*] (1907). Drama; published in 1911.

Ida, or The Child on the Devil's Mountain [*Ida, oder Dos kind af dem tayvls-barg*] (1902). Probably the same as 1895 play.

Ida, or The Polish Treasure [*Ida, oder der shats fun poyln*] (1895). Drama in five acts (di geshikhte kumt for afn tayvls barg lebn krakov).

In the Mountains [*Af di berg*] (1907). Drame in 4 aktn, prolog un epilog; published in 1911.

The Insane Actress [*Di vanzinike aktrise*] (1903). One-act; published in 1917.

Is He Guilty? [*Iz er shuldik?*] (unknown). Published in 1917.

The Jewish Ghetto [*Di yidishe gheto*] (1899) Lokale folksshtik; from Zangwill's *Children of the Ghetto.*

The Jewish King Lear [*Der yidisher kenig lier*] (1892).

The Jewish Priest [*Der yidisher galekh*] (1894).

Khatskl Drakhme's Monologue [*Khatskl drakhmes monolog*] (1904). Published in 1917; adapted from Gordin's *God, Man and Devil.*

King and God [*Kenig un got* (unproduced). Satiric drama in five acts; writing at time of death.

The Kolel Rabbi [*Der rov hakoylel* (1894).

The Kreutzer Sonata [*Kroytser sonate* (1902). Published in 1907.

Libussa [*Libusie*] (unknown). From Grillparzer.

The Lost, or Rosa Berndt [*Di farloyrene oder Roza Berndt*] (1904). From Hauptmann.

The Madman [*Der meturef, oder a mentsh fun an anderer velt*] (1905). Published in 1907.

Medea [*Medea*] (1896). From Grillparzer; iberzetsung; published in 1897.

Messiah's Times [*Meshiakhs tsaytn*] (1892). From Goldfaden.

Minna, or Nora from the Jewish Quarter [*Mina oder Nora fun yidishn kvartal*] (1899). In collaboration with Kobrin, from Ibsen.

Mirele Efros, the Jewish Queen Lear [*Di yidishe kenigin lir oder mirele efros*] (1898). Lebnsbild in 4 aktn; published in 1898.

Mohammed's Fight against the Arabian Jews [*Makhmed un di yiden in arabien*] (1894). Hist. oper. 5 aktn, 11 stsenes.

Murder on Madison Avenue [*Der mord in medison evenyu*] (1893).

The Mysteries of London [*Di geheymnise fun london*] (unknown).

Nathan the Wise [*Nosn hakhokhem* or *Di yidn*] (1897). From Lessing.

The New Generation, or A Forced Match [*Der nayer dor oder getsvungener shidekh*] (1904). Play by Friedrich Feldmann, translated by Leon Gotlieb, adapted by Gordin.

Nora, or A Miracle Within a Miracle [*Nora, oder Nes bitokh nes*] (1895). Adapted from Ibsen's *A Doll's House* with Winchevsky.

The Oath, or Ronye the Postman [*Di shvue oder Ronye di potshterke*] (1900). From Hauptmann's *Fuhrmann Henschel;* published in 1911.

The Orphan, or Chasia the Orphan [*Khasye di yesoym*] (1903). Published in 1907.

Over the Abyss [*Afn opgrund*] (unknown). From Gorki.

Own Blood [*Dos eygene blut*] (1902). Adaptation.

Pantole Polge [*Pantole polge*] (1891). Monologue.

Petit Bourgeois, or Summer [*Meshchane*] (1903). Russian; iberzetsung; from Gorki.

The Philistines [*Di plishtim*] (1904). Musical drama.

The Pogrom in Russia [*Der pogrom*] (1892).

The Power of Darkness [*Di makht der finsternish*] (1901). Translated from Tolstoy.

Purity of the Family [*Tares hamishpokhe*] (1904). Lebensbild mit gezang in 5 aktn.

Queen of England [*Kenigin fun England*] (1899).

Reisele, or Zelig Itzik the Musician [*Reyzele oder zelig itsik der klezmer*] (1894). From Schiller's *Kabale und Liebe*.

The Russian-American Association for Broad Aims [*Der rusish amerikanisher fareyn mit breyte idealn*] (1896). One-act satire in Russian; published in 1917.

A Russian Jew in America [*Rusisher yid in amerike*] (1895).

Sappho [*Safo*] (1900). Published in 1907.

She Does Not Want the Match [*Zi vil nit dem shidekh* (unknown). Published in 1917.

Shloymke the Charlatan [*Shloymele sharlatan* or *Der sharlatan*] (1896). Published in 1912; from Ostrovsky.

Siberia [*Sibiria, lebnsbild in 4 aktn un prolog*] (1891).

The Slaughter [*Di shkhite*] (1899). Published in 1908.

Solomon the Wise [*Shloyme chuchem*] (1906). Based on French history.

The Spanish King [*Der shpanisher kenig,* or *Di yidn fun toledo*] (unknown). From Grillparzer.

Spirit of the Ghetto [*Der gayst fun der geto*] (1904). One act; published in 1917.

The Stepmother [*Di shtifmame*] (1903).

The Stilled Song [*Dovidl meshoyrer oder dos ibergerisene lid*] (1898). Musical drama; published in 1899 or 1908.

The Stranger [*Der fremder*] (1906). From Tennyson. Romantic drama; published in 1922.

The Striker before the Court [*Der shtrayker farn gerikht*] (1895). One-act.

A Tragedy through Fun [*A tragedye durkh shpas*] (unknown). Published in 1917.

The Three Princes [*Di dray printsn*] (1896). From Victor Hugo.

Tree of Knowledge [*Der eyts hadas*] (1902). Four acts.

The Triumph of Justice [*Meylets yoysher*] (1892). From Goldfaden.

The True Power [*Di emese kraft*] (1904). Drama; published in 1904.

The Truth [*Di varhayt, Der emes*] (1903). Published in 1908.

Two Worlds, or The Great Socialist, or The Strike in Bialystok [*Der groyser sotsyalist, oder Tsvey veltn oder der shtrayk in bialystok*] (1891). Four acts with a prologue.

The Unknown [*Der unbekanter*] (1904). Four acts and prologue; published in 1905.

Vengeance [*Di nekome oder der first fun shumrum*] (1895). Adapted from Victor Hugo.

The Voice of the Shofar [*Kol shoyfer*] (1896). Based on Hugo and on Verdi's opera *Ernani.*

Why Men Love [*Farvos mener liben*] (unknown). Published in 1917.

The Wild King [*Der vilder kenig*] (1896). Fantastishe oper.

The Wild Man [*Der vilder mentsh*] (1893). Published in 1907.

The Wild Princess, or Medea's Youth [*Di vilde printsesin oder Medeas yugent*] (1897). Published in 1898.

Yokel the Opera Maker [*Yokl der opern makher*] (1894). One-act satire published in 1907.

Jacob Gordin's Published Plays

In Yiddish

Many of Gordin's works are available digitally from the National Yiddish Book Center. Books in print include:

Ale Shriftn fun Yankev Gordin [Collection of Gordin's Writings]. 4 vols. New York: Hebrew Publishing Company, 1910.

Dertseylungen fun Yankev Gordin (stories). New York: International Library Publishing Co., 1909.

Kreytser sonata: a drame in fir aktn fun Yakov Gordin. New York: M. Mayzel, 1907.

Yankev Gordin's Dramen [Plays of Jacob Gordin]. 4 vols., including *Mirele efros, Gott, mensh und teufel, Elisha ben avuya, Der metureff, Safo,* and *Af di berg*. Published by his friends.

Yankev Gordin's eyn-acters [Yankev Gordin's One-Acts]. Foreword by Alexander Gordin. New York: Tog, 1917.

In English

Captain Dreyfus (one-act). Booklet, 1908.

The Debtor (one-act). Trans. Oscar Leonard. *New York Call,* February 6, 1910.

God, Man, and Devil: Yiddish Plays in Translation. Nahma Sandrow, trans. Syracuse: Syracuse University Press, 1999.

The Jewish King Lear, a Comedy in America. Trans. Ruth Gay (translation of *The Jewish King Lear*). New Haven: Yale University Press, 2007.

The Kreutzer Sonata. Adapted from the Yiddish by Langdon Mitchell. New York: Harrison Grey Fiske, 1907.

Besides the above, I have unpublished translations by Alexander Gordin *(The Truth, The Madman, The Wild Man,* and excerpts of *Homeless* and *The True Power)* and by Sarah Torchinsky *(Elisha ben Avuya* and the sketches *She Doesn't Want the Match* and *The Gallery of Types)*. Nathan Gross translated *Mirele Efros. The Debtor,* a one-act, was translated by Oscar Leonard. Lulla Rosenfeld translated an excerpt of *The Stranger* and wrote a synopsis. A brief excerpt of *Sappho* appears in Nahma Sandrow's book *Vagabond Stars*. There are excerpts from unknown translators of *God, Man, and Devil, In the Mountains,* and *The Unknown* at YIVO.

Films Still Circulating

Distributed by the National Center for Jewish Film

God, Man and Devil USA, 1949 directed by Joseph Seiden.

The Yiddish King Lear USA, 1935 directed by Harry Thomashefsky.

Mirele Efros USA, 1939 directed by Josef Berne.

Without a Home Poland, 1939 directed by Alexander Martin.

SELECTED BIBLIOGRAPHY

I AM INDEBTED to the following authors, whose works proved so invaluable they permeate every page of this book: in Yiddish, B. Gorin, Leon Kobrin, Kalmon Marmor, Morris Winchevsky, and Zalmen Zylberzweig; in English, Lulla Rosenfeld, Melech Epstein, Hutchins Hapgood, Irving Howe, and Ronald Sanders.

Yiddish

Adler, Celia. *Celia Adler dertzeylt* [The Celia Adler Story]. New York: Shulsinger Bros., 1959.

Algemeyne Entsiklopedie. Vol. 11. Paris: Dubnov Press, 1940.

Cahan, Abraham. *Bleter fun mayn lebn* [Pages from My Life]. 5 vols. New York: "Forverts" Association, 1926.

Gorin, B. *Di geshikhte fun yidishn teater* [History of the Yiddish Theater]. 2 vols. New York: Max N. Maisel, 1923.

Ignatoff, David. *Af Vayte Vegn* [Pathways Far Away]. 3 vols. New York: Farlag America, 1932.

Kobrin, Leon. *Erinerungen fun a Yiddishn dramaturg* [Reminiscences of a Jewish Playwright]. New York: Committee for Kobrin's Writing, 1925.

Marmor, Kalmon. *Mein Lebns Geshichte* [My Autobiography]. 2 vols. New York: Yiddisher Kultur Farband, 1959.

———. *Yankev Gordin, a Biografie.* New York: Yiddisher Kultur Farband, 1953.

Winchevsky, Morris. *Collected Works.* Ed. Kalmen Marmor. New York: Freiheit, 1927.

———. *A tog mit Yankev Gordin* [A Day with Jacob Gordin]. New York: 1909.

Young, Boaz. *Mayn lebn in teater* [My Life in the Theater]. New York: YKUF, 1950.

Zylberzweig, Zalmen. *Di velt fun Yankev Gordin* [The World of Jacob Gordin]. Tel Aviv: Elisheva, 1964.

————. *Leksikon fun Yiddishn teater* [Lexicon of the Yiddish Theater]. New York: Hebrew Actor's Union, 1931.

English

Adler, Jacob, and Lulla Rosenfeld. *Jacob Adler: A Life on the Stage—A Memoir.* New
York: Applause, 2001.

Adler, Stella. *The Technique of Acting.* New York: Bantam, 1990.

Adler, Stella, and Barry Parris, ed. *Stella Adler on Ibsen, Strindberg, and Chekhov.* New
York: Knopf, 1999.

Aleichem, Sholem. *The Best of Sholem Aleichem.* Ed. Irving Howe and Ruth R. Wisse.
Washington: New Republic Books, 1979.

————. *From the Fair: The Autobiography of Sholem Aleichem.* Trans. Curt Leviant.
New York: Viking Penguin, 1985.

————. *Tevye the Dairyman and the Railroad Stories.* Trans. Hillel Halkin. New York:
Schocken Books, 1987.

————. *Tevye's Daughters.* Trans. Frances Butwin. New York: Crown, 1952.

————. *Wandering Star.* Trans. Frances Butwin. New York: Crown, 1952.

Ansky, S. A. *The Dybbuk.* Trans. S. Morris Engel. Washington, D.C.: Regnery Gate-
way, 1974.

Antin, Mary. *The Promised Land.* New York: Houghton Mifflin, 1912.

Asch, Sholem. *God of Vengeance.* New York: Theater Communications Group, 2004.

Ausubel, Nathan. *Pictorial History of the Jewish People.* New York: Crown, 1961.

Baron, Salo W. *The Russian Jew under the Tsars and Soviets.* New York: Schocken
Books, 1987.

Beck, Evelyn Torton. *Kafka and the Yiddish Theater.* Madison: University of Wiscon-
sin Press, 1971.

Bellow, Adam. *The Educational Alliance: A Centennial Celebration.* New York: Educational Alliance, 1990.

Berkowitz, Joel. *Shakespeare on the American Yiddish Stage.* Iowa City: University of
Iowa Press, 2002.

Birmingham, Stephen. *The Rest of Us: The Rise of America's Eastern European Jews.*
Boston: Little, Brown, 1984.

Blech, Benjamin. *The Complete Idiot's Guide to Learning Yiddish.* Indianapolis: Alpha
Books, 2000.

Blum, Martha. *Children of Paper.* Regina, Sask.: Coteau Books, 2002.

Blumenson, S. L. "The Golden Age of Tomashefsky." *Commentary* (April 1952):
344–51.

Bordman, Gerald. *The Oxford Companion to American Theater.* New York: Oxford University Press, 1984.

Boris, Martin. "An American Kibbutz: From Odessa to Oregon, Utopia in Brief." *Jewish Monthly* (May–June 2000): 10–14.

———. "A Place in the Country." *B'nai B'rith Magazine* (September–October 1998): 10–38.

———. "Biography of Maurice Schwartz." (unpublished).

Burns, Ric, James Sanders, and Lisa Ades. *New York: An Illustrated History.* New York: Knopf, 1999.

Byron, Joseph. *New York Life at the Turn of the Century in Photographs.* New York: Dover, 1985.

Cahan, Abraham. *The Education of Abraham Cahan.* Philadelphia: Jewish Publication Society of America, 1969.

———. *Grandma Never Lived in America: The New Journalism of Abraham Cahan.* Ed. Moses Rischin. Bloomington: Indiana University Press, 1985.

———. *The Imported Bridegroom and Other Stories.* New York: Signet Classics, 1996.

———. *The Rise of David Levinksy.* 1917. New York: Penguin Classics, 1993.

———. *Yekl: A Tale of the New York Ghetto.* New York: D. Appleton and Co., 1896.

Carmichael, Joel. *A Cultural History of Russia.* New York: Weybright and Talley, 1968.

Cassedy, Steven. *The Other Shore: The Russian Jewish Intellectuals Who Came to America.* Princeton: Princeton University Press, 1997.

Cassedy, Steven, trans. and ed. "Realism and Romanticism, by Jacob Gordin." *Building the Future: Jewish Immigrant Intellectuals and the Making of the Tsukunft.* New York: Holmes and Meier, 1999.

Chametzky, Jules. *From the Ghetto: The Fiction of Abraham Cahan.* Amherst: University of Massachusetts Press, 1977.

Charyn, Jerome. *Once upon a Drosky.* New York: McGraw-Hill, 1964.

Chotzinoff, Samuel. *A Lost Paradise: Early Reminiscences.* New York: Knopf, 1955.

Classic Yiddish Stories of S. Y. Abramovitsh, Sholem Aleichem, and I. L. Peretz. Ed. Ken Frieden. Trans. Ken Frieden, Ted Gorelick, and Michael Wex. Syracuse: Syracuse University Press, 2004.

Clurman, Harold. *All People Are Famous (instead of an autobiography).* New York: Harcourt, Brace and Jovanovich, 1974.

———. *The Fervent Years: The Group Theater and the Thirties.* New York: Da Capo, 1983.

Cohen, Morris Raphael. *The Dreamer's Journey: The Autobiography of Morris Raphael Cohen.* Glencoe, Ill.: Free Press, 1949.

Cordesco, Francesco, ed. *Jacob Riis Revisited: Poverty and the Slum in Another Era.* New York: Anchor Books, 1968.

Cowan, Neil M., and Ruth Schwartz Cowan. *Our Parent's Lives: The Americanization of Eastern European Jews.* New York: Basic Books, 1989.

Dawidowicz, Lucy. *The Golden Tradition: Jewish Life and Thought in Eastern Europe.* New York: Schocken Books, 1967.

De Lange, Nicholas. *Atlas of the Jewish World.* Oxford: Phaidon, 1984.

Dimont, Max I. *Jews, God, and History.* New York: New American Library, 1962.

———. *The Jews in America: The Roots, History, and Destiny of American Jews.* New York: Simon and Schuster, 1978.

Eban, Abba. *My People: The Story of the Jews.* New York: Random House, 1968.

Edel, Leon. *Henry James, the Master.* Philadelphia: J. B. Lippincott, 1972.

Eliach, Yaffa. *There Once Was a World: A Nine-Hundred-Year Chronicle of the Shtetl of Eishyshok.* New York: Little, Brown, 1998.

Epstein, Melech. *Profiles of Eleven.* Detroit: Wayne State University Press, 1965.

Fast, Howard. *Max.* Boston: Houghton Mifflin, 1982.

Fink, M. R. "The Dramas of Jacob Gordin." *The Play-book* (approx. 1912): 5–15.

Finkelstein, Morris R. "The American Stage—What It Is—What It Should Be: An Interview with Mr. Jacob Gordin, the Famous Playwright." *Echo* 1, no. 2 (April–May 1902): 1–3.

Gabler, Neal. *An Empire of Their Own: How the Jews Invented Hollywood.* New York: Crown, 1988.

Gay, Ruth. *Unfinished People: Eastern European Jews Encounter America.* New York: W. W. Norton, 1996.

Gitelman, Zvi. *A Century of Ambivalence: The Jews of Russia and the Soviet Union, 1881 to the Present.* 2nd ed. Bloomington: Indiana University Press, 2001.

Gogol, Nikolai. *Mirgorod.* Trans. David Magarshack. New York: Minerva, 1965.

Gold, Michael. *Jews without Money.* New York: Carroll and Graf, 1996.

Goldberg, Isaac. *The Drama of Transition: Native and Exotic Playcraft.* Cincinnati: Stewart Kidd, 1922.

Goldberg, Itche. "The Story of a Play: Jacob Gordin and His Yiddish Classic, *Mirele Efros.*" *Jewish Currents* (January 1967): 7–11.

Goldman, Frederick. "When Lear Spoke Yiddish: 100 Years of Jewish Theater." *New York Times,* September 19, 1982, pp. 22–24.

Goodman, Matthew. "Yesterday with the Jews: Kafka Encounters the Yiddish Theater." *Pakn Treger* (Fall 1999).

Goren, Arthur Aryeh. "Sacred and Secular: The Place of Public Funerals in the Immigrant Life of American Jews." *Jewish History* 8, nos. 1–2 (1994): 269–303.

Hapgood, Hutchins. *The Spirit of the Ghetto.* 1902. New York: Funk and Wagnalls, 1965.

Hauptmann, Gerhart. *Three Plays.* New York: Frederick Ungar, 1977.

Henry, Barbara. "Tolstoy on the Lower East Side: Di Kreytser sonata." *Tolstoy Studies Journal* 17 (2005): 1–19.

Hindus, Milton. *The Old East Side.* Philadelphia: Jewish Publication Society, 1971.

Hoberman, J. *Bridge of Light: Yiddish Film between Two Worlds.* New York: Museum of Modern Art and Schocken Books, 1991.

Homberger, Eric. *The Historical Atlas of New York City: A Visual Celebration of Nearly 400 Years of New York's History.* New York: Henry Holt, 1994.

Howe, Irving. *World of Our Fathers: The Journey of the East European Jews to America and the Life They Found and Made.* New York: Harcourt Brace Jovanovich, 1976.

———. "The Yiddish Theater: A Blaze of Glory and Claptrap." *New York* (February 9, 1976): 31–38.

Howe, Irving, and Eliezer Greenberg, eds. *A Treasury of Yiddish Stories.* New York: Schocken Books, 1973.

———. *Voices from the Yiddish: Essays, Memoirs, Diaries.* New York: Schocken Books, 1975.

Howe, Irving, and Kenneth Libo, eds. *How We Lived: A Documentary History of Immigrant Jews in America, 1880–1930.* New York: New American Library, 1979.

Ibsen, Henrik. *Six Plays by Henrik Ibsen.* Trans. Eva Le Gallienne. New York: Modern Library, 1957.

James, Henry, and Leon Edel. *The American Scene.* Bloomington: Indiana University Press, 1968.

Kadison, Luba, and Joseph Buloff, with Irving Genn. *On Stage, Off Stage: Memories of a Lifetime in the Yiddish Theater.* Cambridge: Harvard College Library, 1992.

Kafka, Franz. *Diaries 1910–1913.* New York: Schocken Books, 1965.

Kalmar, Ivan. *The Trotskys, Freuds, and Woody Allens: Portraits of a Culture.* Toronto: Penguin, 1993.

Kaminska, Ida. *My Life, My Theater.* Trans. Curt Leviant. New York: Macmillan, 1973.

Kamm, Antony, and Norman Jeffares, eds. *A Jewish Childhood.* London: Boxtree, 1988.

Kanfer, Stefan. *A Summer World.* New York: Farrar, Straus, Giroux, 1987.

———. "The Yiddish Theater's Triumph." *City Journal* (Spring 2004).

Kaplan, Justin. *Lincoln Steffens: A Biography.* New York: Simon and Schuster, 1974.

Kleebatt, Norman L., and Susan Chevlowe, eds. *Painting a Place in America.* New York: Jewish Museum, 1991.

Klier, John. "From Elisavetgrad to Broadway: The Strange Odyssey of Iakov Gordin." In *Extending the Borders of Russian History: Essays in Honor of Alfred J. Rieber.* Ed. Marsha Siefert. Budapest and New York: CEU Press, 2003.

Kumove, Shirley. *Words Like Arrows: A Collection of Yiddish Folk Sayings.* Toronto: University of Toronto Press, 1984.

Landis, Joseph C., ed. *The Great Jewish Plays.* New York: Horizon, 1972.

———. *Three Great Jewish Plays.* New York: Applause, 1986.

Lansky, Aaron. *Outwitting History: The Amazing Adventures of a Man Who Rescued a Million Yiddish Books.* Chapel Hill: Algonquin Books of Chapel Hill, 2004.

Lawrence, Jerome. *Actor: The Life and Times of Paul Muni.* New York: Putnam, 1974.

Levin, Nora. *While Messiah Tarried.* New York: Schocken, 1977.

Lifschutz, Ezekiel. "Jacob Gordin's Proposal to Establish an Agricultural Colony." *American Jewish Historical Quarterly* 56, no. 2 (December 1966): 151–62.

Lifson, David S. *The Yiddish Theater in America.* Cranbury, N.J.: A. S. Barnes, 1965.

Lipsky, Louis. *Tales of the Yiddish Rialto: Reminiscences of Playwrights and Players in New York's Jewish Theater in the Early 1900s.* New York: Thomas Yoseloff, 1962.

Liptzin, Sol. *The Flowering of Yiddish Literature.* New York: Thomas Yoseloff, 1963.

———. *A History of Yiddish Literature.* New York: Jonathan David Publishers, 1985.

Lyman, Darryl. *Great Jews on Stage and Screen.* New York: Jonathan David Publishers, 1987.

Lyons, Eugene. *David Sarnoff: A Biography.* New York: Harper and Row, 1967.

Madsen, Catharine. "Out of My Dialect: Lear in Translation." *Pakn Treger* (Winter 2002): 32–35.

Manners, Ande. *Poor Cousins.* New York: Coward, McCann, and Geoghega, 1972.

Medres, Israel. *Montreal of Yesterday: Jewish Life in Montreal 1900–1920.* Trans. Vivian Felsen. Montreal: Vehicule Press, 2000.

Meir, Golda. *My Life.* New York: Putnam, 1975.

Metzker, Isaac, ed. *A Bintel Brief: Sixty Years of Letters from the Lower East Side to the Jewish Daily Forward.* New York: Schocken Books, 1971.

Meyer, Michael. *Ibsen, a Biography.* New York: Doubleday, 1971.

Miller, James. *The Detroit Yiddish Theater, 1920–1937.* Detroit: Wayne State University Press, 1967.

Miron, Dan. *A Traveler Disguised: The Rise of Modern Yiddish Fiction in the Nineteenth Century.* Syracuse: Syracuse University Press, 1996.

Muggamin, Howard. *The Jewish Americans.* New York: Chelsea House Publishers, 1988.

Nattel, Lilian. *The River Midnight*. Toronto: Alfred Knopf, 1999.

Neugroschel, Joachim, ed. *The Shtetl: A Creative Anthology of Jewish Life in Eastern Europe*. Woodstock, N.Y.: Overlook Press, 1989.

Ozick, Cynthia. "Actors." *New Yorker* (October 5, 1998): 80–92.

Picon, Molly. *Molly!: An Autobiography*. New York: Simon and Schuster, 1980.

Potok, Chaim. "A Subtle Effort to Deconstruct the Shtetl." *New York Times*, October 23, 1994, pp. 44–48.

Prager, Leonard. "Of Parents and Children: Jacob Gordin's The Jewish King Lear." *American Quarterly* 18, no. 3 (1966): 508–16.

Reisen, Avraham. *The Heart-Stirring Sermon and Other Stories*. Trans. Curt Leviant. Woodstock, N.Y.: Overlook Press, 1992.

Ribalow, Harold U., ed. *Autobiographies of American Jews*. Philadelphia: Jewish Publication Society, 1965.

Richler, Nancy. *Your Mouth Is Lovely*. Toronto: Harper Flamingo Canada, 2002.

Rischin, Moses. *The Promised City: New York's Jews, 1870–1914*. Cambridge: Harvard University Press, 1962.

Rosenfeld, Lulla Adler. *The Yiddish Theater and Jacob P. Adler*. (Formerly *Bright Star of Exile*.) New York: Shapolsky, 1988.

Rosenfeld, Max, trans. *New Yorkish and Other American Yiddish Stories*. Philadelphia: Sholem Aleichem Press, 1995.

———. *Pushcarts and Dreamers: Stories of Jewish Life in America*. Philadelphia: Sholem Aleichem Press, 1967.

Roskolenko, Harry. *The Time That Was Then: The Lower East Side, 1900–1913—An Intimate Chronicle*. New York: Dial Press, 1971.

Rosten, Leo. *The Joys of Yiddish*. New York: McGraw-Hill Book Co., 1968.

Rubin, Rachel. "His Head in Russia and His Belly in New York: American Writing in Russian, 1880–1924." American Literature Association Annual Meeting, Cambridge, MA, May 2001.

Rubin, Rachel, trans. "Letter from a Jew to Alexander III" by Jacob Gordin. *The Multilingual Anthology of American Literature*. Ed. Marc Shell and Werner Sollors. New York: New York University Press, 2000.

Samuel, Maurice. *The World of Sholem Aleichem*. New York: Atheneum, 1986.

Sanders, Ronald. *The Downtown Jews: Portraits of an Immigrant Generation*. New York: Harper and Row, 1969.

———. *Shores of Refuge: A Hundred Years of Jewish Emigration*. New York: Schocken Books, 1988.

Sanders, Ronald, and Edmund V. Gillon. *The Lower East Side: A Guide to Its Past in Ninety-Nine Photographs*. Mineola, N.Y.: Dover Publications, 1980.

Sandrow, Nahma. *Vagabond Stars: A World History of Yiddish Theater.* New York: Harper and Row, 1977.

Sandrow, Nahma, ed. and trans. *God, Man, and Devil: Yiddish Plays in Translation.* Syracuse: Syracuse University Press, 1999.

Schoener, Allon. *The American Jewish Album: 1654 to the Present.* New York: Rizzoli International, 1985.

———. *Portal to America: The Lower East Side, 1870–1925.* New York: Holt, Rinehart, and Winston, 1967.

Schreier, Barbara A. *Becoming American Women: Clothing and the Jewish Immigrant Experience, 1888–1920.* Chicago: Chicago Historical Society, 1994.

Secunda, Victoria. *Bei Mir Bist Du Schon: The Life of Sholem Secunda.* Weston, Conn.: Magic Circle Press, 1982.

Sharp, Rosalie, Irving Abella, and Edwin Goodman, eds. *Growing Up Jewish: Canadians Tell Their Own Stories.* Toronto: McClelland and Stewart, 1997.

Shepard, Richard F., and Vicki Gold Levi. *Live and Be Well: A Celebration of Yiddish Culture in America from the First Immigrants to the Second World War.* New Brunswick: Rutgers University Press, 2000.

Shulman, Abraham. *The New Country.* New York: Charles Scribner and Sons, 1976.

Silvain, Gerard, Henri Minczeles, and Donna Wiemann. *Yiddishland.* Corte Madera, Calif.: Ginko Press, 1999.

Simons, Howard. *Jewish Times: Voices of the American Jewish Experience.* New York: Doubleday, 1988.

Singer, Isaac Bashevis. "Yiddish Theater Lives, Despite the Past." *New York Times,* January 20, 1985, pp. 1–22.

———. *The Collected Stories.* New York: Farrar, Straus, and Giroux, 1982.

Smale, Alison. "Putting Sholem Aleichem on a Belated Pedestal." *New York Times,* January 5, 2002, p. A4.

Smith, Hedrick. "The Russian Character." *New York Times Magazine,* October 28, 1990, pp. 33–71.

———. *The Russians.* New York: Ballantyne Books, 1976.

Steffens, Lincoln. *The Autobiography of Lincoln Steffens.* New York: Harcourt, Brace, 1931.

Tax, Meredith. *Rivington Street.* New York: Jove, 1983.

Tolstoy, Leo. *The Death of Ivan Ilych and Other Stories.* Trans. Aylmer Maude and J. D. Duff. New York: Signet Classics, 1960.

———. *The Kreutzer Sonata, The Devil, and Other Tales.* Trans. Aylmer Maude. London: Oxford University Press, 1968.

Troyat, Henry. *Gogol: The Biography of a Divided Soul*. New York: Allen and Unwin, 1974.

———. *Tolstoy, the Biography*. Trans. Nancy Amphoux. New York: Harmony Books, 1967.

Tuchman, Barbara W. *Proud Tower: A Portrait of the World before the War—1890–1914*. New York: Macmillan, 1966.

Waife-Goldberg, Marie. *My Father, Sholem Aleichem*. New York: Schocken Books, 1971.

Warnke, Nina. "Immigrant Popular Culture as Contested Sphere: Yiddish Music Halls, the Yiddish Press, and the Processes of Americanization, 1900–1910." *Theater Journal* 48, no. 3 (1996): 321–35.

———. "Of Plays and Politics: Sholem Aleichem's First Visit to America." *YIVO Annual* 20 (1991): 239–76.

Weidman, Jerome. *Fourth Street East*. New York: Pinnacle Books, 1970.

Weinberg, Sydney Stahl. *The World of Our Mothers: The Lives of Jewish Immigrant Women*. Chapel Hill: University of North Carolina Press, 1988.

Weiner, Leo. *The History of Yiddish Literature in the Nineteenth Century*. New York: Charles Scribner's Sons, 1899.

Weinstein, Miriam. *Yiddish: A Nation of Words*. South Royalton, Vt.: Steerforth Press, 2001.

Weizmann, Chaim. *Trial and Error: Weizmann's Autobiography*. Philadelphia: Jewish Publication Society of America, 1949.

Wengeroff, Pauline. *Rememberings: The World of a Russian-Jewish Woman in the Nineteenth Century*. Potomac: University Press of Maryland, 2000.

West, Rebecca. *1900*. New York: Viking, 1982.

Wisse, Ruth R. *A Little Love in Big Manhattan*. Cambridge: Harvard University Press, 1988.

———. "The Smell of the Greasepaint, the Roar of the Torah." *New Republic* (May 1, 2000): 33–39.

Wisse, Ruth R., ed. *A Shtetl and Other Yiddish Novellas*. Detroit: Wayne State University Press, 1986.

Yoffe, Elkhonon. *Tchaikovsky in America*. New York: Oxford University Press, 1986.

Zalewski, Daniel. "From Russia with Tsoris." *Magazine*, June 2, 2002, pp. 54–57.

Zborowski, Mark, and Elizabeth Herzog. *Life Is with People: The Culture of the Shtetl*. New York: Schocken Books, 1952.

Zylbersweig, Zalmen. *Album of the Yiddish Theater*. New York: Trio Press, 1937.

Chief Resources for Research

New York

Ellis Island Museum of Immigration
Jewish Museum
Lincoln Center, Billy Rose Performing Arts Library
Lower East Side Tenement Museum
New York Public Library, Dorot Division
YIVO Institute for Jewish Research

Elsewhere

American Jewish Historical Society, Waltham, Mass.
B'nai B'rith Klutznik Museum, Washington, D.C.
National Center for Jewish Film, Waltham, Mass.
National Yiddish Book Center, Amherst, Mass.

The most useful Internet resources are the mailing list available from Mendele@lists.yale.edu, especially their Yiddish Theater Forum edited by Joel Berkowitz, and http://www.Jewishgen.org and http://www.jewish-theater.com.

ACKNOWLEDGMENTS

I AM ETERNALLY GRATEFUL to Sarah Torchinsky, who gave me the words, and Ben Torchinsky, who helped her. My loving thanks to my father Jacob Gordin Kaplan and my uncle Edgar Kaplan, who gave me the genes; Lulla Rosenfeld, who gave me a push; Bonny Fetterman, who gave me several more pushes; Ruth Gay, who gave me the final shove; Great-Aunt Helen Gordin Zielstein and first cousin once removed Anna Richmond, who talked; my grandparents Nettie Gordin and Mike Kaplan; my mother Sylvia and brother Michael; my New York family and hosts Ted Kaplan and Lola Sherwin; Wayson Choy, Aaron Lansky, Margie Davidson, Ronald Bryden, for editorial support and friendship, inspiration and books; the Yiddish scholars Joel Berkowitz, Nina Warnke, Barbara Henry, Rachel Rubin, Martin Boris, Elly Margolis, Caraid O'Brien, John Klier, Gerry Kane, and David Mazower; Vivian Felson, Miriam Beckerman, Irene Bimman, and Janina Wurbs, who did more translation; Dina Abramowitz, Marek Web, and Yeshaya Metal at the YIVO; Faith Jones at the New York Public Library; my friends Lynn Bevan and Terry Poulton; my agent, Richard Curtis; and my editor, Ken Frieden, who, with his estimable colleagues at Syracuse University Press, brought the book at last to light.

And I am profoundly grateful to all the advisors, readers, and supporters who have kept me going for more than twenty years, including Edgar Dobie, Marilyn Biderman, David Kent, Yiddish Artists and Friends, Shifra Lerer, Bernard Mandelovich, Nathan Gross, Millie Marmur, the Banff Centre for the Arts, Eli Rubinstein, Charis Wahl, Susan Renouf, Ward McBurney, Eilat Gordin, Alberto Ruy Sanchez, Pat Kennedy, Florence Rosberg, Larry Mirkin, Stephen Strauss, Kathleen Gassi, Toronto Friends of Yiddish, particularly Nathan Garnick, Bess Shockett, and Ralph Wintrob, and to George and Caryl Gordin, Beth Shore, Dave Sanders, and all the Gordins I have not yet met.

To Patsy Ludwick and Chris Tyrell, my fellow writers who are always there, if not in person then on the screen.

And most of all, to my beloved children, Anna Elizabeth and Samuel Jacob Edgar, and to their great-great grandfather, who lives on in my blood and theirs.

INDEX

Italic page number denotes illustration.